MAKING SPECIAL EDUCATION INCLUSIVE

From Research to Practice

Falkirk Council

David Fulton Publishers Ltd
The Chiswick Centre, 414 Chiswick High Road, London W4 5TF

www.fultonpublishers.co.uk

First published in Great Britain by David Fulton Publishers 2002

Note: The right of Peter Farrell and Mel Ainscow to be indentified as the editors of this work has been asserted by them in accordance with the Copyright, Designs and Patents Act 1988.

British Library Cataloguing in Publication Data
A catalogue record for this book is available from the British Library.

ISBN 1 85346 854 1

Typeset by Textype Typesetters, Cambridge
Printed in Great Britain by The Cromwell Press Ltd, Trowbridge, Wilts.

Contents

Foreword

The past few years have seen something of a paradigm shift in the way governments, local education authorities, academics, teachers, parents and other professionals have conceptualised notions of inclusive education. This is evident in at least two ways. First, although there are still uncertainties surrounding the definition of inclusion, there is general agreement that the issue is not solely about those pupils who are defined as having special educational needs. Increasingly, it has become more centred around the idea of reducing barriers to participation and learning of all children and young people, recognising that many groups of learners are at risk of marginalisation, exclusion and underachievement. Second, and equally important, the rhetoric surrounding inclusion has changed and it is now rare to hear policy makers question the need to move in a more inclusive direction. At the same time there remains considerable uncertainty as to where this is heading and what it might involve. This sense of uncertainty is particularly evident in the special needs field, where many practitioners feel that their existing practices are no longer valued.

These shifts and uncertainties also have implications for the practice of research. Some researchers in the special needs field argue that the focus of their work must also broaden in order that it can more appropriately address the issues faced by policy makers and practitioners. Conversely, others remain particularly concerned about groups of children with disabilities whose needs, it is argued, may be overlooked within a broader inclusion agenda.

This book arose as a result of a conference that was held in Manchester, in the summer of 2001, to explore these complex issues. Together the chapters set out a range of examples of research that address the issue of inclusion from different perspectives. These examples were provided, in the main, by our colleagues within the Educational Support and Inclusion Group, in the Faculty of Education at the University of Manchester. There are also additional contributions by the Centre for Formative Assessment Studies in the Faculty, and the Special Needs Research

Centre at the University of Newcastle, focusing on certain key issues. The range of work covered illustrates the ways in which research can contribute to developments in the field. It also shows the many different approaches to carrying out research that exist.

Taken as a whole the book provides a range of challenges, both to those readers from mainstream education and, indeed, those in the field of special education. Our hope is that it will both stimulate and inform the debate in ways that can help to move thinking and practice forward.

Peter Farrell and Mel Ainscow
June 2002

Acknowledgements

In compiling this volume we have received invaluable support from Shelley Darlington, Averil Gould, Jackie Chisnall, Lesley Oake and Jane Mortimer, administrative secretaries in the Educational Support and Inclusion Research and Teaching Group within the Faculty of Education, University of Manchester. Not only have they helped in putting together the final touches to the book but the cheerfulness with which they approach their work, their willingness to take on new and challenging tasks and their sense of humour help to make our busy lives run more smoothly.

About the authors

Most of the authors are members of the Educational Support and Inclusion Group in the Faculty of Education, University of Manchester. Three others are researchers in the Centre for Formative Assessment Studies in the Faculty of Education and two work in the Special Needs Research Centre, School of Education, University of Newcastle.

Brief details on each of the contributors are given below.

Educational Support and Inclusion Group, Faculty of Education, University of Manchester

Mel Ainscow, Professor of Education, is co-director of the Educational Support and Inclusion Group. He is currently co-directing the Economic and Social Research Council (ESRC) research network, Understanding and Developing Inclusive Practices in Schools.

Maggie Balshaw is a freelance consultant and independent educational researcher.

Mark Barber is a temporary Lecturer in Learning Disabilities. He has recently completed his PhD into communication and interaction for pupils with profound and multiple learning difficulties.

Iain Carson is Programme Director of the BA in Learning Disability Studies and has a long-standing interest in carrying out emancipatory and participatory research with adults who have learning difficulties.

Pauline Davis is Programme Director of the MEd in Special and Inclusive Education. She has recently completed as ESRC-funded project on inclusive classroom practice for children with visual impairments.

Judith Emanuel, Lecturer in Education, has directed a research project on the impact of three nurture groups in one LEA.

Peter Farrell, Professor of Special Needs and Educational Psychology, is Research Dean and co-director of the Educational Support and Inclusion Group. He has recently directed two research projects on the role of teaching assistants in schools and LEAs.

Jo Frankham is a lecturer in research methods. She has a long-standing research interest in pupils' perceptions of gay and lesbian young people and is also part of the ESRC network on understanding and developing inclusive schools.

Henry Hollanders is Programme Director for the Professional Doctorate in Counselling. He has a deep-rooted interest in integrative approaches to counselling and how these methods can be used in schools.

Vicky Hopwood is a former research assistant in the Faculty of Education who worked with Pauline Davis on the ESRC project on the inclusive education for pupils with visual impairments.

Andy Howes is Research Associate on the ESRC research network, Understanding and Developing Inclusive Practices in Schools. As part of this network he has been involved in carrying out research into the impact of a nurture group in one primary school.

Wendy Lynas, Programme Director of the BA in Human Communication Studies, has a long-standing interest in how to develop effecting inclusive provision in mainstream contexts for pupils with hearing impairments.

Susie Miles is the director of the Enabling Education Network (EENET). This organisation disseminates information about international developments in inclusive education around the world. She is also directing a project funded by the Department for International Development (DIFID) in this area.

Alan Millward is Reader in Special Educational Needs at the School of Education, University of Newcastle, and has a longstanding research interest in policy developments and inclusion. He, and his colleague Alan Dyson, have carried out a number of research projects for the DfES.

Sue Palmer is Programme Director of the MEd in Educational Psychology. She has carried out research projects into children with hearing impairments and literacy difficulties.

Gill Parkinson is Programme Director of the MSc in Profound Learning Difficulties and Multisensory Impairment. She is the co-author of a major new text on helping children with epilepsy and has carried out a programme of research on epilepsy and pupils with language disorders.

Rea Reason, co-director of the Doctorate in Educational Psychology, has carried out a number of research and development projects on children with literacy difficulties and has worked clearly with the directors of the National Literacy Project.

Steve Rooney is an Academic and Professional Tutor on the MSc professional training course for educational pyschologists. He has also developed expertise in working with teachers using approaches derived from Soltuion Focused Brief Therapy.

Anne Rushton is an Academic and Professional Tutor on the MSc professional training course for educational pyschologists. She has a long-standing research interest on the impact of domestic violence on children and families and on professional practice in this field. She is currently working on her doctorate in this area.

Kevin Woods is Programme Director of the MSc professional training course for educational psychologists. For some years he has been carrying out research into pupils with dyslexia and he is currently coordinating a research project that is focusing on ways teachers and psychologists can work together to improve their practice in this area.

The Centre for Formative Asssessment Studies (CFAS), University of Manchester

Bill Boyle is Head of CFAS and has directed a large number of studies on behalf of the Qualifications and Curriculum Authority (QCA) and more recently for the Department for Education and Skills (DfES) on post-16 transition.

Afroditi Kalambouka is a research assistant in CFAS and has worked on the DfES-funded transition project.

Filiz Polat is a reseach associate in CFAS and has managed the DfES-funded project on transition. She has also been the lead researcher on a research project that followed up the progress made by former pupils at a residential school for pupils with emotional and behavioural difficulties.

The Special Needs Research Centre, School of Education, University of Newcastle

Alan Dyson is Director of the centre and, with his colleague **Alan Millward**, has carried out a number of research projects on behalf of the DfES on the development of educational services for children with special educational needs (SEN).

CHAPTER 1

Making special education inclusive: mapping the issues

Peter Farrell and Mel Ainscow

In recent years the issue of inclusion has become more of a feature of discussions about the development of education policy and practice around the world. These developments have in part been informed by ongoing debates in the field of special education that have focused on questions about what forms of provision should be made for children with disabilities and others who experience difficulties. In the United Kingdom the Government's discussion paper 'Excellence for All Children: Meeting Special Educational Needs' (DfEE 1997) and the subsequent 'Programme for Action' (DfEE 1998) referred to the right of all pupils to be educated in a mainstream school, wherever possible. And, more recently, the revised Code of Practice on Special Educational Needs (DfES 2001) and the Special Needs and Disability Act provide yet further impetus towards the idea of a more inclusive education system.

Such movements are strongly endorsed internationally by the Salamanca Statement (UNESCO 1994) and reflect the United Nations' global strategy of 'Education for All'. Both have had a major impact on policy debates in many different countries. Meanwhile there is no shortage of books and articles that have extolled the values of inclusion and which have provided a whole range of accounts of 'good practice' in inclusive education (see, for example, Ainscow 1999; Ballard 1999; Dyson and Millward 2000).

Despite these developments, however, inclusion remains a complex and controversial issue which tends to generate heated debates (e.g. Brantlinger 1997). For example, there is a great deal of uncertainty about the definition of inclusion (Ainscow, Farrell and Tweddle 2000); there are several pressure groups in society that seek to maintain separate provision; and it is difficult to find research evidence that can provide definitive guidance as to where policy and practice should be heading. Meanwhile in the United Kingdom, alongside policies that are promoting notions of inclusion, schools are under even more pressure than ever to raise academic standards. In this climate some schools are expressing increasing reluctance to admit and retain pupils whose presence could have a negative impact on their overall profile of results. In addition, the recent emphasis on beacon and specialist schools, and the evidence of an increase in the use of various forms of selection, suggests that there is a growing movement in education towards differentiated provision – a trend that seems incompatible with an inclusive philosophy.

Set within this potentially confusing context, this book reports on research being carried out by a team of researchers, mainly at the University of Manchester. In particular it explores the contributions that educational research can make in throwing light on the factors that lead to these confusions in order to suggest ways of moving policy and practice forward. It also illustrates the variety of forms that such research can take, recognising that different types of questions require different methodologies.

The aim of this introductory chapter is to map out the key themes that are reflected in the rest of the book. We start by providing a brief historical review of definitions of inclusion and follow this with a critical discussion of the inclusion debate in relation to pupils with disabilities in order to reflect upon the implications for the special education field. We then consider the crucial role of research in helping governments, local authorities and schools to develop and improve their practice. Finally, we conclude by providing a brief overview of the contents of the book and show how each of the chapters has made a unique contribution to the debate by drawing on contrasting research methodologies to illustrate the impact of inclusion in respect to different groups of learners.

Defining inclusion

Within this country, current views of inclusion in respect to pupils with disabilities and others categorised as having special educational needs (SEN) have been influenced by debates on how to provide the most effective education for these groups. Indeed, as many readers will recall, in the 1980s the terms 'integration' or 'mainstreaming' were used to refer to the placement of 'pupils with SEN' in mainstream schools. The Warnock Report suggested there were three main kinds of integration: locational, social and functional (DES 1978). 'Locational integration' was seen as being where pupils with SEN were placed in special classes or units located within a mainstream campus, without there necessarily being contact with their mainstream peers. 'Social integration' was seen to involve pupils interacting for social activities, such as meal times and school visits, but for the rest of the time the categorised pupils were segregated from their mainstream peers. Finally, 'functional integration' was where all pupils, whatever their difficulties or disabilities, were placed in their local mainstream school, in a regular classroom setting alongside their same-age peers.

Developments following the Warnock Report meant that, by the early 1990s, the term 'integration' was used to describe a much wider variety of educational provision than the three types outlined in the report. Hegarty (1991) indicates that this could range from occasional visits by a pupil with a disability from a special to a mainstream school, to full-time placement in such schools.

An obvious problem with defining integration solely in terms of provision (i.e. the setting in which a pupil is placed) is that it tells us nothing about the quality of the education that is received in this provision. Are pupils placed in units attached to a mainstream school, for example, more 'integrated' than if they were taught in a special school? Jupp (1992) argues that such units can be just as segregating. Indeed, even pupils placed in a mainstream class may be isolated from the rest of the class and not truly 'integrated' within the group, particularly if they are supported in one-to-one sessions for the majority of each day. Integrated placements, therefore, may still leave the pupil 'segregated'.

Partly for these reasons, the term 'inclusion' has become a more usual way of describing the extent to which a pupil categorised as having SEN is truly 'integrated'. Used in this way the term refers to the extent to which a school or community welcomes pupils as full members of the group and values them for the contribution they make. This implies that for inclusion to be seen to be 'effective', all pupils must actively belong to, be welcomed by and participate in a mainstream school and community – that is they should be fully included. Their diversity of interests, abilities and attainment should be welcomed and be seen to enrich the life of the school. In this sense, as Ballard (1995) argues, inclusion is about valuing diversity rather than assimilation.

Recently definitions of inclusion have broadened still further (see, for example, Booth and Ainscow 1998). These writers take the view that policies on inclusion should not be restricted to the education of pupils thought to have special needs. Inclusion, they argue, is a process in which schools, communities, local authorities and governments strive to reduce barriers to the participation and learning for all citizens. Looked at in this way inclusive policies and practices should consider ways in which marginalised groups in society, for example people from ethnic minorities and those who are socially and economically disadvantaged, can participate fully in the educational process within mainstream contexts.

This broader view of inclusion is reflected in recent guidance from Ofsted for inspectors and schools (Ofsted 2000). In addressing what is referred to as 'educational inclusion', the document focuses attention on a wide range of vulnerable groups. It states:

An educationally inclusive school is one in which the teaching and learning, achievements, attitudes and well-being of every young person matters. Effective schools are educationally inclusive schools. This shows, not only in their performance, but also in their ethos and their willingness to offer new opportunities to pupils who may have experienced previous difficulties . . . The most effective schools do not take educational inclusion for granted. They constantly monitor and evaluate the progress each pupil makes. They identify any pupils who may be missing out, difficult to engage, or feeling in some way apart from what the school seeks to provide.

Here the sentence 'Effective schools are educationally inclusive schools' is particularly significant. In essence it redefines the way school effectiveness will be determined, drawing attention to the need for inspectors to go beyond an analysis of aggregate performance scores in order to determine the extent to which a school is supporting the learning of all individuals.

The Ofsted guidance is important for two reasons. First of all, it reinforces a much broader view of inclusion, in that the concept is widened to include pupils other than those thought to have SEN. Secondly, it forces schools to focus on the achievements of all of their pupils and, indeed, to pay attention to a wider range of outcomes than those reflected in test or examination results.

Nevertheless, as implied above, deep contradictions in national policy continue, and these mean that schools and LEAs are facing challenging dilemmas. In particular, they find themselves under pressure to raise academic standards at the same time as being asked to develop more inclusive policies and practices.

Implications for the field of special education

As the above discussion illustrates, concepts of integration and, more recently, inclusion have been evolving over the last 20 years or more. However, the issues remain controversial, and among academics, policy makers and practitioners there are still different views about the meaning of the terms and about the feasibility of developing more inclusive practice in schools.

The particular focus of this book is on how the field of special education can be made more inclusive. Consequently we focus more specifically on policies for pupils with disabilities and others who are defined as having special educational needs. This does not mean that we are rejecting the broader view of inclusion referred to above. Rather, we are engaging with the debate about policies for those groups of pupils that have traditionally been the concern of special education in the context of this broader definition.

The field of special education has developed relatively recently and unevenly in different parts of the world. Its development has involved a series of stages during which education systems have explored different ways of responding to children with disabilities and others who experience difficulties in learning. As a result, special education has sometimes been provided as a supplement to general education provision, although in other cases it may be totally separate.

An analysis of the history of special education provision in many Western countries suggests certain patterns (Reynolds and Ainscow 1994). Initial provision frequently took the form of separate special schools set up by religious or philanthropic organisations. This was then, eventually, adopted and extended as part of national education arrangements, often leading to a separate, parallel school system for those pupils seen as being in need of special attention. There is also some evidence of similar trends in developing countries (see, for example, various chapters in Mittler, Brouillete and Harris 1993).

In the early 1990s, however, the appropriateness of having such a separate system was challenged both from a human rights perspective and, indeed, from the point of view of effectiveness. This led to an increased emphasis in many countries, in both the developed and developing countries, on the notion of integration (Ainscow 1991; Hegarty 1990; O'Hanlon 1995; Pijl and Meijer 1991; UNESCO 1995). This emphasis, involving attempts to increase flexibility of response within neighbourhood schools, seems sensible for economically poorer countries given the extent of the need and the limitations of resources (UNESCO 1998). It is also important to recognise that in many developing countries substantial 'casual' integration of children with disabilities in local schools already occurs, particularly in rural districts (Miles 1989).

The existence of well-established separate provision in special schools and classes creates complex policy dilemmas, leading many countries to operate what Pijl and Meijer (1991) refer to as 'two tracks'. In other words, these countries have parallel, but separate segregation and integration policies. A rather obvious problem here, of course, is the costing implications of maintaining such parallel arrangements.

In other countries integration/inclusion still largely represents an aspiration for the future. In Germany, for example, while some pilot initiatives based on the idea of integration are underway, students who are declared eligible for special education must be placed in a special school. While in the Netherlands it is reported that almost 4 per cent of all pupils aged 4–18 attend full-time special schools, although the exact proportion varies with age. So, for example, 7.4 per cent of 11-year-olds are in special schools (Reezigt and Pijl 1998). More recent national policy developments are attempting to change this emphasis. Similar developments in other countries, such as Austria, England and New Zealand, have led to major discussions of what might be the future roles of special education facilities and support services within a system driven by a greater emphasis on integration.

Some countries (for example, Australia, Canada, Denmark, Italy, Norway, Portugal and Spain) have shown considerable progress in implementing the integration principle universally. Here the local community school is often seen as the normal setting for pupils with disabilities, although even in these contexts the situation often exhibits variation from place to place (Booth and Ainscow 1998;

Mordal and Stromstad 1998; Pijl and Meijer 1991).

Dissatisfaction with progress towards integration and inclusion has caused demands for more radical changes in many countries (e.g. Ainscow 1991; Ballard 1999; Skrtic 1991; Slee 1996). One of the concerns of those who adopt this view is with the way in which pupils come to be designated as having special needs. They see this as a social process that needs to be continually challenged. More specifically they argue that the continued use of what is sometimes referred to as a 'medical model' of assessment, within which educational difficulties are explained solely in terms of child deficits, prevents progress in the field, not least in that it distracts attention from questions about why schools fail to teach so many children successfully. Such arguments lead to proposals for a reconceptualisation of the special needs task. This suggests that progress will be much more likely when it is recognised that difficulties experienced by pupils come about as a result of the ways in which schools are currently organised and the forms of teaching that are provided. In other words, as Skrtic (1991) puts it, pupils with special needs are 'artifacts of the traditional curriculum'. Consequently, it is argued, the way forward must be to reform schools and improve pedagogy in ways that will lead them to respond positively to pupil diversity, seeing individual differences not as problems to be fixed but as opportunities for enriching learning. Within such a conceptualisation, a consideration of difficulties experienced by pupils and, indeed, teachers, can provide an agenda for reforms and insights as to how these might be brought about. However, it has been argued that this kind of approach is probably only possible in contexts where there exists a respect for individuality, and a culture of collaboration that encourages and supports problem solving (Ainscow 1991; Skrtic 1991).

All of this has helped to encourage an interest in the issues discussed in this book, those of *inclusive education*. This adds yet further complications and disputes to those that already exist. Driven, in part at least, by ideological considerations, the idea of inclusive education challenges much of existing thinking in the special needs field while, at the same time, offering a critique of the practices of general education. Put simply, many of those who are supporting the idea are raising the question, why is it that schools throughout the world fail to teach so many pupils successfully?

As explained earlier, this inclusive orientation is a strong feature of the Salamanca Statement on Principles, Policy and Practice in Special Needs Education, agreed by representatives of 92 governments and 25 international organisations in June 1994 (UNESCO 1994). Moves towards inclusion are also endorsed by the UN Convention on the Rights of the Child. Specifically the adoption of the Convention by the UN General Assembly and its subsequent ratification by 187 countries imposes a requirement for radical changes to traditional approaches to provision made for children with disabilities.

The Convention contains a number of articles that require governments to undertake a systematic analysis of their laws, policies and practices in order to assess the extent to which they currently comply with the obligations they impose with respect to such children.

Article 28 of the Convention asserts the basic right of every child to education and requires that this should be provided on the basis of equality of opportunity. In other words the Convention allows no discrimination in relation to access to education on grounds of disability. Furthermore the continued justification of the types of segregated provision made in many countries needs to be tested against the child's rights not to be discriminated against, not least in that Articles 28 and 29, together with Articles 2, 3 and 23, seem to imply that all children have a right to inclusive education, irrespective of disability.

Other sections of the Convention reveal interesting contradictions. Article 23, for example, states that 'children should be helped to become as independent as possible and to be able to take a full and active part in everyday life'. Nowhere does it mention specifically that these pupils should be taught in mainstream educational settings and, indeed, it might be argued that the aims of the Article are quite compatible with the notion that pupils with special needs may receive excellent education in special schools. Certainly it can be argued that the key point about Article 23 of the UN Convention is the importance of ensuring that pupils with disabilities become as independent as possible so that they can take a full and active part in everyday life when they leave school. Many will argue that high-quality inclusive education is the only way to make this happen. On the other hand, supporters of special schools and other forms of special provision claim that a concentration of resources and expertise is needed in order to achieve this aim.

In the UK the Centre for Studies on Inclusive Education (CSIE) also take a human rights view of inclusion/integration. Some years ago they advocated this view forcibly in their Integration Charter:

> We see the ending of segregation in education as a human rights issue which belongs within equal opportunities policies. Segregation in education because of disability or learning difficulty is a contravention of human rights as is segregation because of race and gender. The difference is that while sexism and racism are widely recognised as discrimination . . . discrimination on the grounds of disability or learning difficulty is not. (CSIE 1989)

Advancing towards the implementation of this new orientation is far from easy, however, and evidence of progress is limited in most countries. Moreover, it must not be assumed that there is full acceptance of the inclusive philosophy (e.g. Fuchs and Fuchs 1994; Brantlinger 1997). There are, for example, those who argue that small specialist units located in the standard school environment can provide the specialist knowledge, equipment and support for which the mainstream classroom and teacher can never provide a full substitute. On this view, such units may be the only way to provide feasible and effective access to education for certain groups of children.

In summary, then, as we consider ways in which the field of special education can become inclusive, it is necessary to recognise that the field itself is riddled with uncertainties, disputes and contradictions. However, what can be said is that throughout the world attempts are being made to provide more effective educational responses to such children, and that encouraged by the lead given by the Salamanca Statement, the overall trend is towards making these responses, as far as possible, within the context of general educational provision. As a consequence this is leading to a reconsideration of the future roles and purposes of specialists and facilities in the special needs field.

Inclusion and research

As we have seen, the debates about inclusive education are complex and, at times, confusing. Logic would suggest that greater clarity within the field would lead to better progress in respect to policy and practice. It is here, we argue, that research has a major contribution to make. It is through high-quality research that we gain deeper understanding of current arrangements, including the confusions and contradictions that exist. It is also the means by which we can capture and analyse the best practices that exist.

However, it is also true that major debates exist as to the forms of research that are most appropriate. Once again these debates reflect different perspectives as to purpose and method (Hegarty and Evans 1985; Clough and Barton 1995; Brantlinger 1997). Some researchers see inclusion as essentially an empirical issue (see, for example,Harrower 1999). Their overall purpose is to develop explanations, focusing on issues such as does inclusion work and, if so, under what conditions (e.g. Fuchs and Fuchs 1996; Kaufman and Hallahan 1995). Those who take this perspective tend towards the use of experimental methods that compare different approaches, or large-scale surveys that help us to measure views and opinions across populations. (See Farrell 2000 for a review of some key studies.) However, other researchers are more concerned with developing deeper explanations of the complex social factors that bear on issues of inclusion and exclusion. Consequently, they attempt to get close to particular contexts, often favouring case study accounts of schools or classrooms (e.g. Allan 1999; Dyson and Millward 2000; Thomas, Walker and Webb 1998). They also tend to be particularly interested in using interviews to understand the ways in which stakeholders, such as teachers, pupils and parents, construct their experiences in schools. Meanwhile, there are other researchers who adopt what might be seen as a more committed position, stating their beliefs and assumptions at the outset, and using forms of action research to explore ways of moving policy and practice forward (e.g. Ainscow 1999). In a similar vein, Sebba and Sachdev (1997) provide a research review that addresses the question, 'What works in inclusive education?'

The position we adopt in this book is to assume that all these different forms of research have some potential to contribute to understandings that can help the field to move forward, providing, of course, that it is research that has been undertaken in a systematic and self-critical manner.

Overview of the chapters

Our brief overview of the nature of research in the field of inclusion indicates that a variety of approaches can be adopted, each of which has the potential to make a contribution to enriching our understanding of the complex processes involved in developing effective inclusive policies and practices. In the context of these different approaches, reflecting as they do different perspectives on what inclusion is about, there remain major policy questions as to the role that the field of special education should take. Many of these diverse approaches are reflected by the authors who have contributed chapters to this book, most of whom are members of the Educational Support and Inclusion research group here at the University of Manchester.

Each author has his or her own research agenda and methodology, and these are revealed in their text in a way that is intended to inform the debate. In this sense, the book is illustrative of the range of perspectives that exist. Despite these differences, the chapters do interconnect, not least in that each author was asked to bear in mind a common set of questions. These are:

- What are the implications of the research for the development of inclusive policy and practice?
- What are the barriers to development and how can they be overcome?
- What can research contribute to such developments?
- What does this mean for the future of special education as a field?

The book is divided into five interconnected sections, each of which addresses a particular theme. These are:

1. Current developments in inclusion.
2. Reducing barriers to participation and learning for children who may experience social and emotional difficulties.
3. Improving literacy through inclusive practices.
4. Responding to pupils seen as having additional needs.
5. Inclusion beyond the school context.

Section 1 considers some current developments at the national and international levels.

At the national level our colleague from Newcastle, Alan Dyson and Alan Millward, refer to the impact of the recently published revised Code of Practice on Special Educational Needs. They have been centrally involved in research that influenced the changes that have been introduced and is, therefore, in a unique position to comment on the possible implications. There are then two chapters that focus on how schools and LEAs can work together to become more inclusive. The first of these, Chapter 3 by Mel Ainscow, looks at the use of what he describes as collaborative inquiry to take policy and practice forward at the school level. His work is illustrative of a participatory approach to research that explores new roles for academics. The second, Chapter 4 by Peter Farrell and Maggie Balshaw, describes research that examines the increasingly important contributions being made by teaching assistants. Moving to an international perspective, Susie Miles describes recent research on ways in which parents and practitioners in different countries have been working together to move practice forward in order to develop more enabling forms of education.

Section 2 of the book examines ways of responding to children who may experience social and emotional difficulties. At a general level Henry Hollanders discusses new approaches to pastoral care in schools, while Jo Frankham considers the more specific and often overlooked issue of the education of young people who are gay. The next two chapters review the impact of ways of supporting pupils facing emotional and behavioural problems. Steve Rooney draws on his research on the use of Solution Focused Brief Therapy by teachers in mainstream schools, while Andy Howes and his colleagues consider the contributions that nurture groups can make in providing support for younger children. Finally in this section, Anne Rushton discusses the implication for schools of research findings on the impact of domestic violence on children.

Section 3 reviews research on improving achievement in literacy through inclusive practices. Rea Reason and Sue Palmer discuss the impact of ChIPPs (Checking Individual Progress in Phonics), a tool for the development of an effective programme to teach young children with literacy difficulties. A key aim of this approach is to help teachers and assistants to develop classroom practices such that all pupils can be fully involved in literacy activities. Kevin Woods discusses research on how teachers construct the term 'dyslexia' and considers the implications for developing more inclusive policies and practices.

The four chapters in Section 4 discuss research on specific groups of children whose impairments mean that within the education system they are often seen as having additional needs. Two of these address issues related to pupils with sensory impairments. Wendy Lynas reports research on how teachers of the deaf support inclusion in mainstream settings, while Pauline Davis and Vicky Hopwood discuss the findings of their study of classroom practice that can support participation of pupils with visual impairments. Gill Parkinson considers the role of interdisciplinary work in supporting pupils with epilepsy in mainstream classrooms. Finally in this section, Mark Barber focuses on the education of pupils with profound and multiple learning difficulties, and draws on the findings from his research to discuss the meaning of inclusion for this vulnerable group of learners.

The fifth and final section of the book considers research on the challenging issues facing young people as they leave school and enter the adult world. Filiz Polat and her colleagues report on a major longitudinal study in order to discuss ways in which schools can plan for transition. Iain Carson draws on the voice of an adult with learning disabilities to gauge his perceptions of the extent to which he feels included into society.

References

Ainscow, M. (ed.) (1991) *Effective Schools for All*. London: David Fulton Publishers.

Ainscow, M. (1999) *Understanding the Development of Inclusive Schools*. London: Falmer Press.

Ainscow, M., Farrell, P. and Tweddle, D. A. (2000) 'Developing policies for inclusive education: a study of the role of local education authorities'. *International Journal of Inclusive Education* 4(3), 211–29.

Allan, J. (1999) *Actively Seeking Inclusion*. London: Falmer Press.

Ballard, K. (1995) 'Inclusion, paradigms, power and participation' in C. Clark, A. Dyson and A. Millward (eds), *Towards Inclusive Schools?* London: David Fulton Publishers.

Ballard, K. (1997) 'Researching disability and inclusive education: participation, construction and interpretation', *International Journal of Inclusive Education* 1(3), 243–56.

Ballard, K. (ed.) (1999) *Inclusive Education: International Voices on Disability and Justice*. London: Falmer Press.

Booth, T. and Ainscow, M. (eds) (1998) *From Them to Us: An International Study of Inclusion in Education*. London: Routledge.

Brantlinger, E. (1997) 'Using ideology: cases of nonrecognition of the politics of research and practice in special education', *Review of Educational Research* 67(4), 425–59.

Centre for Studies on Inclusive Education (CSIE) (1989) *The Integration Charter*. Bristol: CSIE.

Clough, P. and Barton, L. (eds) (1995) *Making Difficulties: Research and the Construction of Special Educational Needs*. London: Paul Chapman.

Department for Educational and Employment (DfEE) (1997) *Excellence for All Children: Meeting Special Educational Needs*. London: Department for Education and Employment.

Department for Educational and Employment (DfEE) (1998) *Meeting Special Educational Needs: A Programme of Action*. London: DfEE.

Department for Education and Skills (DfES) (2001) *Special Educational Needs Code of Practice*. London: DfES.

Department of Education and Science (DES) (1978) *Special Educational Needs (The Warnock Report)*. London: HMSO.

Dyson, A. and Millward, A. (2000) *Schools and Special Needs*. London: Paul Chapman.

Farrell, P. (2000) 'The impact of research on developments in inclusive education',

International Journal of Inclusive Education, 4(2), 153–62.

Fuchs, D. and Fuchs, L. S. (1996) 'Inclusive schools movement and the radicalisation of special education reform', *Exceptional Children* 60(4), 294–309.

Harrower, J. K. (1999) 'Educational inclusion of children with severe disabilities', *Journal of Positive Behavioural Interventions* 1(4), 215–30.

Hegarty, S. (1990) *The Education of Children and Young People with Disabilities: Principles and Practice*. Paris: UNESCO.

Hegarty, S. (1991) 'Towards an agenda for research in special education', *European Journal of Special Needs Education* 6(2), 87–99.

Hegarty, S. and Evans, P. (1985) *Research and Evaluation Methods in Special Education*. Windsor: NFER-Nelson.

Jupp, K. (1992) *Everyone Belongs*. London: Souvenir Press.

Kaufman J. M. and Hallahan, D. P. (eds) (1995) *The Illusion of Full Inclusion: A Comprehensive Critique of a Current Special Education Bandwagon*. Austin: Pro-Ed.

Miles, M. (1989) 'The role of special education in information-based rehabilitation', *International Journal of Special Education* 4(2), 111–18.

Mittler, P., Brouillete, R. and Harris, D. (eds) (1993) *World Yearbook of Education: Special Needs Education*. London: Kogan Page.

Mordal, K. N. and Stromstad, M. (1998) 'Norway: Adapted education for some?' in T. Booth, and M. Ainscow (eds), *From Them to Us: An International Study of Inclusion in Education*. London: Routledge.

Office for Standards in Education (Ofsted) (2000) *Educational Inclusion: Guidance for Inspectors and Schools*. London: Ofsted.

O'Hanlon, C. (ed.) (1995) *Inclusive Education in Europe*. London: David Fulton Publishers.

Pijl, S. J. and Meijer, C. J. W. (1991) 'Does integration count for much? An analysis of the practices of integration in eight countries', *European Journal of Special Needs Education*. 3(2), 63–73.

Reezigt, G. J. and Pijl, S. P. (1998) 'The Netherlands: a springboard for other initiatives', in T. Booth and M. Ainscow (eds) *From Them to Us: An International Study of Inclusion in Education*. London: Routledge.

Reynolds, M. C. and Ainscow, M. (1994) 'Education of children and youth with special needs: an international perspective', in T. Husen and T. N. Postlethwaite (eds), *The International Encyclopedia of Education*, 2nd edn. Oxford: Pergamon.

Sebba, J. and Sachdev, D. (1997) *What Works in Inclusive Education?* Ilford: Barnardo's.

Skrtic, T. M. (1991) 'Students with special educational needs: Artifacts of the traditional curriculum', in M. Ainscow (ed.), *Effective Schools for All*. London: David Fulton Publishers.

Slee, R. (1996) 'Inclusive schooling in Australia? Not yet', *Cambridge Journal of Education* 26(1), 19–32.

Thomas, G., Walker, D. and Webb, J. (1998) *The Making of the Inclusive School*. London: Routledge.

United Nations (1993) *Convention on Children's Rights*. New York: United Nations.

United Nations Educational, Scientifc and Cultural Organisation (UNESCO) (1994) *The Salamanca Statement and Framework for Action on Special Needs Education*. Paris: UNESCO.

United Nations Educational, Scientifc and Cultural Organisation (UNESCO) (1995) *Review of the Present Position in Special Education*. Paris: UNESCO.

United Nations Educational, Scientifc and Cultural Organisation (UNESCO) (1998) *From Special Needs Education to Education for All: Discussion Paper for the International Consultative Forum on Education for All*. Paris: UNESCO.

Section 1

CHAPTER 2

Looking them in the eyes: is rational provision for students 'with special educational needs' really possible?

Alan Dyson and Alan Millward

Introduction

> Children have *special educational needs* if they have a *learning difficulty* which calls for *special educational provision* to be made for them . . . *Special educational provision* means: . . . educational provision which is additional to, or otherwise different from, the educational provision made generally for children of their age in schools maintained by the LEA, other than special schools, in the area.
> (1996 Education Act, section 312, as cited in the *Special Educational Needs Code of Practice*, DfES 2001b: 6)

The 1996 Act's definition of special educational needs (dating back, of course, to the recommendations of the Warnock Report, DES 1978, and beyond) rests on two assumptions that are shared by education systems across the world, which now seem so self-evident that we tend to take them for granted. The first is that there are some children who 'need' provision that is special in the sense of being 'additional to or different from' that made for other children. The second, which follows from the 'additional' or 'different' nature of special provision, is that such provision will commonly require additional resourcing and hence additional funding. In recent years, of course, there has been considerable debate about whether a separate special education system or a more unified 'inclusive' system is the best way of making provision responsive to individual differences. Nonetheless, all systems, however 'inclusive', tend to accept that children differ from each other in ways that are important for their learning, that these differences should be reflected in the provision made for them and that variations in provision will sometimes demand equivalent variations in resourcing.

It follows that education systems have to make decisions about matching provision and resources to needs. These decisions are made centrally, by national or local government officials or at school level by teachers in management positions, or at classroom level by teachers directing their time and energy towards particular students. Given that this is the case, we have suggested elsewhere (Crowther, Dyson and Millward 1998) that these decisions ought to be tested against two principles – rationality and equity. Decisions ought to be rational in that they are made for good reasons which can be explained and defended in educational terms; and they ought to be equitable in that they result in just treatment for individual children, for instance, by matching the form of provision and level of resources to some notion of the differing levels and forms of 'needs'.

In England (and, to varying degrees, in the rest of the UK), we have had since 1944 two formal systems for decision making of this kind. The 1944 Education Act consolidated a *categorical* system of special education, based on the assumption that skilled professionals – notably doctors and psychologists – could 'ascertain' (in the language of the time) children's difficulties in terms of a series of 'categories of handicap'. On the basis of this ascertainment, children could then be placed in institutions where specialist provision for that sort of difficulty was available. In practice, this tended (though not invariably) to entail placement in special schools – for the 'educationally subnormal', the 'maladjusted', those with 'physical handicaps' and so on.

In the years leading up to the Warnock Report (DES 1978), this system increasingly came to seem less rational and equitable (Stakes and Hornby 1997): children's difficulties did not fit neatly into the categories; arbitrary decisions had to be made to include or exclude 'borderline' children within the categories; formally recognised types of provision tended to be in separate institutions; and 'excluded' children received no formal protection for whatever provision they might or might not receive. Warnock's response was to call for a different system of decision making – a call that was heeded in the 1981 Education Act and that has formed the basis of the statutory special education system ever since. Instead of allocating children to categories, their 'special educational needs' were to be assessed on an *individual* basis, taking into account not only the sometimes complex pattern of individual difficulties but, to some extent at least, the particular educational context within which those difficulties arose. Following this assessment, provision could be made to meet the needs of particular individuals in particular settings. This might still involve placement in specialist institutions, but might equally involve the formulation of individualised 'packages' of provision in ordinary schools, each one resourced differently from the next.

This more individualised system was potentially more sensitive both to individual differences and to contextual factors. However, this sensitivity came at a cost. The categorical system offered the prospect (whatever the reality) that children with similar difficulties in different parts of the country would be assessed and allocated to categories against similar diagnostic criteria and would then be placed in broadly similar types of specialist institution. The new system offered no such guarantees. The more individualised assessment and provision was, the more difficult it became to compare case with case. In practice, provision resulted from a complex interplay of different types of professional advice – educational psychologists, teachers, doctors and others – different (and often conflicting) interests – those of the parents, of the school and of the LEA – all set within the context of a highly variable local pattern of provision and local expectations of what mainstream schools would and should provide.

What finally set light to this tinder box was the far-reaching package of reforms introduced in the late 1980s and early 1990s, notably the 1988 Education Reform Act. Although few of these reforms had much explicitly to say about special needs education, their impact was significant. As has often been argued (see, for instance, Bines 1995; Bowers 1995; Gold, Bowe and Ball 1993; Riddell and Brown 1994; Rouse and Florian 1997), these reforms created a situation in which many mainstream schools sought either to rid themselves of students who presented difficulties or to educate them only if extra resources were available. The statutory assessment procedures introduced by the 1981 Act gave LEAs a set of procedures which they could, in principle, use to control the rising tide of referrals. However, nowhere had Government set down any criteria determining which children, with which sorts and levels of needs should receive which sorts of provision. In the face of mounting pressure from schools, parents and lobby groups, LEAs could only advance the outcomes of individualised (and hence, non-comparable) assessments together with eminently contestible local custom and practice. Not surprisingly, rates of statementing began to rise alarmingly (DfEE 1997), with the imminent threat that LEAs' special needs responsibilities would wreck their budgets (Coopers and Lybrand 1996). At the same time, a series of official reports expressed deep concern about both the quality and the efficiency of special needs education as it had developed under the somewhat laissez-faire arrangements of the post-1981 period (DES 1989a, 1989b; HMI 1990a, 1990b; Audit Commission and HMI 1992a, 1992b). It is in this context that the first SEN Code of Practice (DFE 1994) was introduced.

At the time, the Code was given a cautiously positive welcome right across the special needs community (see, for instance, Dyer 1995; Dyson, Lin and Millward 1996; Garner 1996; Lewis, Neill and Campbell 1996; Russell 1994). Despite its somewhat bureaucratic appearance, it did at least raise the profile of special needs education in mainstream schools, systematise procedures, and offer some additional guarantees to students and their parents. However, the Code can also be understood as an attempt to regain control over the growth in spending on special needs education. The five-stage assessment procedure, in particular, put pressure on schools to meet children's 'special needs' out of their delegated budgets *before* requesting further resources from the LEA.

In effect, the stages constituted an extension of the 'Warnock' statutory assessment procedures to children in mainstream schools with much lower levels of need. The essential format was the same – an individualised assessment, drawing on a range of perspectives (class teacher, Special Educational Needs Coordinator (SENCO), support service member and so on), informing and involving parents and leading on to similarly individualised provision. The principle of matching provision to need at school level was clear enough. However, the very fact that these procedures had so much in common with their statutory counterparts raised the possibility that they might be no more effective in controlling demand, let alone in ensuring equity of provision.

This possibility became even more significant when, in 1997, the incoming 'New' Labour Government committed itself to the development of a more 'inclusive' education system (DfEE 1997; 1998). Since this move involved mainstream schools in accepting greater responsibility for a wider range of students, it inevitably entailed some clarification of the respective contributions to provision made by schools and LEAs. As part of a wider review of the working of the SEN Code of Practice, therefore, the Government resolved to issue guidance as to the criteria that might be used in deciding how to relate children's 'needs' to the forms of action that might be taken and the levels of provision that might be made by schools and LEAs. That guidance was ultimately issued alongside the draft revised Code as the *Thresholds* document (DfEE 2000), and some of the essentials of this work were subsequently incorporated into the SEN Code of Practice 2001 (DfES 2001b) and the non-statutory *SEN Toolkit* (DfES 2001a). The study that is reported in the remainder of this chapter is intended to provide an evidential basis for this guidance.

The Code of Practice Guidance Project

In preparation for the new Code, the Special Needs Research Centre at the University of Newcastle was commissioned by the (then) Department for Education and Employment (DfEE) to investigate, among other things, the sorts of criteria currently being used to place students on the stages of the 1994 Code by schools and LEAs. The study comprised the following phases:

Phase 1: A national questionnaire survey of LEAs to elicit information on the nature and extent of guidance available to schools (118 LEAs responded, some 74 per cent of the total).

Phase 2: Interviews with key informants (deputy directors, assistant education officers, heads of services) in a sample of eight LEAs to elicit the detail regarding the operation of the Code in a sample of LEAs identified from Phase 1.

Phase 3: Case studies in 37 'effective practice' schools identified by the sample LEAs from Phase 2 to establish how the mechanics of the school-based stages operated (principally through extended interviews with the schools' SENCOs).

Phase 4: A series of nine workshops for professionals and parents held in regional centres together with other development activities to field test emerging ideas and models of what might constitute appropriate guidance.

Phase 5: Consultation on the draft guidance with a reference group representing a wide range of experience in the field of special educational needs (including SENCOs, LEA officers, LEA service members, Her Majesty's Inspectorate (HMI) and DfEE officials).

Although the project was ultimately aimed at producing guidance, it also generated important data on the way in which the 1994 Code was being operated by schools and LEAs and, particularly, the basis on which decisions were being made about how to meet students' special educational needs. The following sections summarise the findings of the full report (Dyson and Millward, in press) that bear most directly on our themes:

LEA criteria

Almost all LEAs had produced guidance of some sort relating to the operation of the Code's stage procedures and some had produced detailed and explicit criteria, particularly for the Stage 4 threshold. There were broad similarities in these criteria across LEAs; not surprisingly, 'lack of progress' in some form or other figured prominently almost everywhere. Beyond this, however, the differences between LEA criteria were striking. Some were highly detailed, others were somewhat general. Some extended to all stages, others focused on Stage 4. Some were generic criteria, applying to all forms of special educational need; others were specific to different types of need.

More importantly, LEAs set different terms and conditions to govern which students should be placed at which stages. For instance, many LEAs saw low attainment as a crucial indicator and many of these specified a cut-off point at the second centile; others, however, used different cut-offs and there was in any case considerable variation as to the measures of attainment that were preferred (such as national assessment scores or one or other standardised test); others again used more ipsative indicators such as failure to meet Individual Education Plan (IEP) targets over a given period of time.

These differences became even more marked in criteria for different types of 'special need'. For instance, some LEAs saw discrepancies in performance as a key indicator of specific learning difficulties, but others did not – and even those that did specified different degrees of discrepancy. Criteria for emotional and behavioural difficulties were particularly fuzzy and varied, with the failure of previous provision to make a difference to the child's difficulties commonly cited, or teacher judgement called into play. Even in the case of sensory impairment where some measure of that impairment is possible, those measures tended not to be used, or to be seen only as providing contextual evidence.

There is frequently a complex mixture of criteria relating to students' characteristics, to procedures which schools are required to have followed appropriately and to some judgement about the sort of provision that might be expected to be available in mainstream schools. Such criteria make perfect sense in terms of the individualised and contextual model of assessment and provision proposed by Warnock – particularly when the need for LEAs to control a flood of requests for assessments is taken into account. However, it is evident that they also leave enormous scope for different conclusions to be reached by different professionals in different cases. Quite aside from the question of how individual criteria are weighted in reaching a decision, the response of the LEA might be based on procedural rather than purely educational grounds.

Moreover, even where LEA personnel judged that a particular case met such complex criteria, this tended not automatically to trigger additional provision. This was most obvious at the Stages 4 and 5 thresholds. On the face of it, LEAs operated a set of 'statementing criteria' which governed who would receive a statement and the additional provision that would be released. In fact, the process was more complex than this. Meeting the Stage 4 criteria meant that the LEA would *consider* a statutory assessment; the outcomes of that assessment were then *considered* to determine whether the student would receive a statement. Of course, as LEA officers assured us, these considerations were informed by the Stage 4 criteria. However, those criteria did not in themselves offer a formal guarantee of provision and students were, in practice, refused statements and/or refused additional provision despite apparently meeting them.

Our interviews with LEA officers revealed a strong and – we had every reason to believe – genuine commitment to using the Code for the benefit of students with special educational needs. However, officers were also clear that they could not separate this commitment from highly pragmatic concerns, notably the need to manage budgets that were under constant pressure. The Code was, in the words of one officer, 'a mechanism for controlling access to resources'. The view from many of the schools we visited and parents we talked to was that this was the principal function of the Code as interpreted by LEAs and that the rational and equitable meeting of children's needs came a very distant second.

School decision making

Our interviews with SENCOs revealed every bit as wide a variation in decision making and provision as our work with LEAs. SENCOs, like their counterparts in LEAs, saw the Code as ambiguous. On the one hand, it was a relatively user-friendly means of enhancing provision for students with SEN:

The child is first and then we fit the Code round the child.

Or again:

It makes staff face up to SEN in terms of determining responsibilities.

On the other hand, it was viewed instrumentally as a necessary barrier to overcome in accessing additional resources for the school:

The Code is stuck to as it's the only way to get any resources.

Or:

If we could get all of the SEN pupils statemented, then we would.

These latter comments, of course, explain why LEAs felt it necessary to make the Code's procedures as 'watertight', from their point of view, as possible.

In terms of criteria for placing students at the various stages of the Code, the situation was at one and the same time simple and complex. It was simple in that overwhelmingly schools used just two criteria – some notion of teacher concern and some notion of lack of progress. Many of them made use of 'objective' criteria, such as national assessment or test scores. However, such evidence was typically weighed alongside a wide range of other evidence, such as the strength of concern expressed by class teachers and by parents or the students' response to the interventions that the school had tried. By and large, schools did not set 'cut-off' points at particular levels of attainment nor attempt to construct measures of progress – at least not unless they were effectively required to do so by the criteria operated by their LEAs.

This meant that SENCOs could act flexibly in making decisions about individual students, responding to the particularities of their situations. However, it also meant that the decision-making process was complex and anything but transparent. SENCOs would weigh the evidence before them in the light of these two broad criteria of teacher concern and lack of progress – which themselves elided to become 'teacher concern *about* lack of progress' – and would then reach some sort of judgement. However, they found it extremely difficult to explicate for us precisely what level of concern about what aspects of student performance would trigger action, or precisely what rate of progress would count as 'lack' of progress.

Moreover, the provision that resulted from SENCOs' decisions was a somewhat strange mixture of a response to individual needs and circumstances and a routinised school response to 'students like this', for example help from a learning support assistant (LSA) and some withdrawal work.

The picture was particularly complex at Stages 3 and above. First, schools tended not to have separate criteria for each successive stage. Decisions were still based on 'teacher concern' and 'lack of progress' and therefore partly dependent on the level of concern and degree of progress, but also on evidence that earlier attempts to meet the students' needs had failed. Moreover, an LEA's policy and practice had a more direct bearing on school-level decisions at these stages. Clearly, the decision to undertake a statutory assessment and (in some cases) the production of a statement delivering additional resources depended on the ability of the school to convince the LEA that its case was strong enough.

More surprisingly, a similar process operated at Stage 3. Although, by and large, SENCOs worked closely with LEA services, the fact remained that the latter operated their own criteria. Indeed, it was common for different LEA services (the learning support and educational psychology services, for instance) to operate criteria that were not comparable in any sense that we could detect and even for individual service members to be responsible for their own decisions about which students they would and would not accept. Moreover, even where services did have explicit criteria, these were frequently to do with matching demand to available service time rather than to guaranteeing that students with particular levels of need would receive appropriate provision. The consequence of all this was that most schools could identify students who met their own criteria for further provision but who failed to meet the criteria operated by the LEA and its services.

The limitations of the Code

There is no doubt that the Code has had a major impact on special educational needs provision since its introduction in 1994. One interviewee put it to us that it had 'brought order where there was chaos' and to a large extent he was right. For the first time, schools had guidance on how to go about making decisions about provision for students with SEN and LEAs had a mechanism they could use to ensure that schools did indeed use their 'best efforts' for such students. We certainly found that schools and LEAs were basing their own procedures very firmly on those recommended by the Code and to this extent at least, it seems likely that the situation we found was more favourable than that obtained prior to 1994.

However, it is also evident that the 1994 Code has some significant weaknesses, at least if it is viewed as a means of guaranteeing rational and equitable responses to students' needs. First, the Code actually guarantees nothing. In practice, both schools and LEAs have considerable scope for the exercise of 'judgement' which may be guided, but is not governed, by explicit criteria. Second, decisions are not made purely on the basis of students' needs and different stakeholders apply different criteria to cases. Third, despite the emphasis on individualised assessment, the provision that is made under the aegis of the Code is often routinised. By this we mean that schools and LEAs have, in practice, a limited range of provision that they can deploy.

The perverse consequence of these problems with the Code is that schools and LEAs can follow its procedures to the letter and yet come to quite different conclusions about how similar types and levels of need should be met. Since it is unlikely that every variant of provision is equally effective in meeting those needs, it follows that some children are likely to receive an ineffective variant which their school or LEA happens to prefer or which is dictated by local circumstances.

Small wonder that one SENCO, having surveyed the views of his colleagues, has recently reached the following conclusion:

> In theory [the Code] is clear, logical and effective. In practice, it creates a massive bureaucratic machine that is so unwieldy that it defeats its highly commendable purposes. My research indicates that, in many instances, the Code hinders rather than promotes learning.
>
> (Lingard 2001: 190)

In blunt terms, the Code may well have 'brought order out of chaos'. It has, however, also brought a different kind of chaos of its own.

Towards an alternative system?

It is our contention that the problems embodied in the Code are structural rather than superficial. The recent revision of the Code (DfES 2001b) has doubtless brought about a series of minor, but nonetheless important, improvements. However, it leaves the basic assumptions and processes of the 1994 Code – which themselves date back to Warnock and beyond – substantially unchanged. If we are to tackle the underlying problems of the Code, it is, we suggest, essential to question the orthodoxy of those fundamental assumptions and, particularly, the assumption that special needs provision must be based on a high level of individualisation. Undoubtedly, there are some children 'with special educational needs' whose pattern of difficulties and characteristics is complex and atypical. It may well be that assessment and provision on an individual basis is the only viable approach in such cases. However, it is also arguable that what the Warnock Report and the 1994 Code did was to generalise from this rather small population to another much larger population ('Warnock's 18 per cent') whose situation is quite different.

The majority of so-called special educational needs actually manifest themselves in a limited number of forms – mild or moderate general learning difficulties (usually in literacy), specific learning difficulties (again in literacy) and behavioural difficulties (Croll and Moses 2000; Dyson and Millward, in press). Not only are these forms of difficulty familiar in every school and LEA, but they are also reasonably well understood by both researchers and practitioners and, more important, there is a well-established repertoire of strategies for addressing them.

Indeed, there is some evidence that, as advocates of the 'whole-school approach' (Dessent 1987) were wont to suggest, that repertoire comprises no more than variations on 'good' mainstream teaching (Norwich and Lewis 2001).

With this in mind, it might make sense to recast our notion of individualisation, at least for the majority of children 'with special educational needs'. Of course, *all* children are individuals and ought to have educational experiences that are in some sense tailored to their particular characteristics. However, there is no reason why, for most children 'with special needs', such individualisation has to take the form of complex assessment processes leading to unique packages of provision. Instead, it might, as for most other children, take the form of classroom-level modifications of established approaches – the sort of 'improvisation' that, Ainscow argues, characterises good teaching (Ainscow 1995; 1997; 1999). This would then mean that the energies of the special needs system could be directed not into finding case-by-case approaches to particular configurations of learning characteristics, but into identifying and developing broad strategies for responding to commonly occurring difficulties.

This in turn implies that the task of the central Government need not be confined to issuing procedural guidance. Instead, Government should be in the business of ensuring that the best possible strategies are routinely available in schools by commissioning research and research reviews (involving practitioners, of course, as co-generators of pedagogical knowledge), by issuing substantive guidance, by managing training and by ensuring that resourcing sustains the infrastructure to support these strategies rather than 'packages' for individual students (see Meijer 1999). It would, of course, be unrealistic to expect that such a system could be entirely problem-free. However, it would hold out the prospect both of a greater comparability – and hence equity – of provision for similar needs across schools and LEAs, and of greater rationality in the sense of provision based clearly on an educational response to those needs. Above all, such a system would, we suggest, be much more likely to result in more effective provision – effective, that is, in helping children to learn – than the current localised, individualised and adhocratic hotchpotch.

A few years ago, when the Code was first introduced and, certainly, at the time of the Warnock Report (DES 1978), such a view would, no doubt, have seemed ridiculous. Given the tradition of local decision making and the known limitations of a categorical approach to special educational needs, the individualised model did indeed represent the best available alternative. Since then, however, much has changed. In particular, curriculum, pedagogy and school organisation and leadership have become significantly more centrally directed and – in some respects at least – more evidence-informed. In the light of developments such as the National Curriculum, the Ofsted frameworks, the National Literacy and Numeracy Strategies and the targeted approaches of Excellence in Cities, Sure Start and a host of other initiatives, the post-Warnock approach to special needs education is beginning to look like distinctly old technology. Now may be just the time for a new approach.

References

Ainscow, M. (1995) 'Education for all: making it happen', *Support for Learning* **10**(4), 147–55.

Ainscow, M. (1997) 'Towards inclusive schooling', *British Journal of Special Education* **24**(1), 3–6.

Ainscow, M. (1999) *Understanding the Development of Inclusive Schools*. London: Falmer Press.

Audit Commission and Her Majesty's Inspectorate (HMI) (1992a) *Getting In on the Act: Provision for Pupils with Special Educational Needs: The National Picture*. London: HMSO.

Audit Commission and Her Majesty's Inspectorate (HMI) (1992b) *Getting the Act Together: Provision for Pupils with Special Educational Needs: A Management Handbook for Schools and Local Education Authorities*. London: HMSO.

Bines, H. (1995) 'Special educational needs in the market place', *Journal of Education Policy* **10**(2), 157–72.

Bowers, T. (1995) 'Touched by the invisible hand?' *Support for Learning* **10**(3), 113–18.

Coopers and Lybrand (1996) *The SEN Initiative: Managing Budgets for Pupils with Special Educational Needs*. London: Coopers & Lybrand for The SEN Initiative.

Croll, P. and Moses, D. (2000) *Special Needs in the Primary School: One in Five?* London: Cassell.

Crowther, D., Dyson, A. and Millward, A. (1998) *Costs and Outcomes for Pupils with Moderate Learning Difficulties in Special and Mainstream Schools* (RR89). London: DfEE.

Department for Education (DFE) (1994) *Code of Practice on the Identification and Assessment of Special Educational Needs*. London: DFE.

Department for Education and Employment (DfEE) (1997) *Excellence for All Children: Meeting Special Educational Needs*. London: DfEE.

Department for Education and Employment (DfEE) (1998) *Meeting Special Educational Needs: A Programme of Action*. London: DfEE.

Department for Education and Employment (DfEE) (2000) *SEN Code of Practice on the Identification and Assessment of Pupils with Special Educational Needs and SEN Thresholds: Good practice guidance on identification and provision for pupils with special educational needs (drafts for consultation)*. London: DfEE.

Department for Education and Skills (DfES) (2001a) *SEN Toolkit*. London: DfES.

Department for Education and Skills (DfES) (2001b) *Special Educational Needs Code of Practice*. London: DfES.

Department of Education and Science (DES) (1978) *Special Educational Needs: Report of the Committee of Enquiry into the Education of Handicapped Children and Young People (The Warnock Report)*. London: HMSO.

Department of Education and Science (DES) (1989a) *A Report by HM Inspectors on Special Education within the Technical and Vocational Education Initiative*. London: DES.

Department of Education and Science (DES) (1989b) *A Survey of Pupils with Special Educational Needs in Ordinary Schools: A Report by HM Inspectorate*. London: DES.

Dessent, T. (1987) *Making the Ordinary School Special.* London: Falmer Press.

Dyer, C. (1995) 'The Code of Practice through LEA eyes', *British Journal of Special Education* 22(2), 48–51.

Dyson, A., Lin, M. and Millward, A. (1996) *The Role of Special Educational Needs Coordinators in Schools.* Special Needs Research Centre, University of Newcastle for DfEE.

Dyson, A. and Millward, A. (in press) *Decision-Making and Provision within the Framework of the SEN Code of Practice.* London: DfEE.

Garner, P. (1996) 'Go forth and coordinate! What special needs coordinators think about the Code of Practice', *School Organisation* 16(2), 179–86.

Gold, A., Bowe, R. and Ball, S. (1993) 'Special educational needs in a new context: micropolitics, money and "education for all" ', in R. Slee (ed.), *Is There a Desk With My Name On It? The Politics of Integration.* London: Falmer Press.

Her Majesty's Inspectorate (HMI) (1990a) *Special Needs Issues: A Survey by HMI.* London: HMSO.

Her Majesty's Inspectorate (HMI) (1990b) *Standards in Education, 1988–89: The Annual Report of HM Senior Chief Inspector of Schools.* London: DES.

Lewis, A., Neill, S. R. S. J. and Campbell, R. J. (1996) *The Implementation of the Code of Practice in Primary and Secondary Schools: A National Survey of Perceptions of Special Educational Needs Co-ordinators.* University of Warwick for the National Union of Teachers.

Lingard, T. (2001) 'Does the *Code of Practice* help secondary school SENCOs to improve learning?' *British Journal of Special Education* 28(4), 187–90.

Meijer, C. J. W. (ed.) (1999) *Financing of Special Needs Education: A Seventeen-Country Study of the Relationship between Financing of Special Needs Education and Inclusion.* Middlefart, Denmark: European Agency for Development in Special Needs Education.

Norwich, B. and Lewis, A. (2001) 'Mapping a pedagogy for special educational needs', *British Educational Research Journal* 27(3), 313–30.

Riddell, S. and Brown, S. (eds) (1994) *Special Educational Needs Policy in the 1990s: Warnock in the Market Place.* London: Routledge.

Rouse, M. and Florian, L. (1997) 'Inclusive education in the market-place', *International Journal of Inclusive Education* 1(4), 323–36.

Russell, P. (1994) 'The Code of Practice: new partnerships for children with special educational needs', *British Journal of Special Education* 21(2), 48–52.

Stakes, R. and Hornby, G. (1997) *Change in Special Education: What Brings It About?* London: Cassell.

CHAPTER 3

Using research to encourage the development of inclusive practices

Mel Ainscow

The field that has been known as special education or, more recently, special needs education, is involved in a period of considerable uncertainty. In particular, the emphasis on inclusive education that is now evident in many countries challenges special needs practitioners to reconsider their own thinking and practice. This context of uncertainty provides the special education field with new opportunities for continuing its historical purpose of representing the interests of those learners who become marginalised within existing educational arrangements. At the same time, many of the assumptions that have guided special education practice are, in my view, no longer relevant to the task (Ainscow 1999).

A brief look at history reminds us that in the nineteenth century special educators in this country argued for and helped develop provision for children and young people who were excluded from educational plans. Only much later did this provision become adopted by national governments and local authorities. It is also worth remembering that it was only as recently as 1971 that one group of learners, those categorised as 'having severe learning difficulties', was deemed to be even worthy of education.

Similarly, provision for children experiencing difficulties within mainstream schools grew as a result of a gradual recognition that some pupils were marginalised within and, in some instances, excluded from existing arrangements for providing education. As this provision developed during the latter part of the twentieth century, there was also increased emphasis on notions of integration, as special educators explored ways of supporting previously segregated groups in order that they could find a place in mainstream schools.

It can be argued, therefore, that the current emphasis on inclusive education is but a further step along this historical road. It is, however, a major step, in that the aim is to transform the mainstream in ways that will increase its capacity for responding to all learners. And, of course, such a project requires the participation of many stakeholders in ways that challenge much of the status quo.

My own work attempts to contribute *directly* to thinking and practice in relation to such developments, at the classroom, school and systems levels. For many years I have worked closely with educational practitioners, in this country and overseas, as they have attempted to move towards more inclusive ways of working (Ainscow 1999). Acting as a critical friend, I see my task as helping them to learn from their experiences and, in so doing, to point to patterns and examples of practice that might be instructive to others who are addressing similar agendas. In this sense my aim is not to propose recipes that can be applied universally but rather to suggest ingredients that might be worthy of further consideration within particular contexts.

In this chapter I illustrate the nature and potential of this approach, focusing on research that is concerned with the development of inclusive practices in schools. An important issue within this work focuses on the identification of factors that help to generate a momentum for change. In other words, what are the 'levers', or incentives, that are most effective in changing existing practice?

Collaborative inquiry

My research has involved a search for forms of inquiry that have the flexibility to deal with the uniqueness of particular educational occurrences and contexts; that allow social organisations, such as schools and classrooms, to be understood from the perspectives of different participants, not least children themselves; and that encourage stakeholders to investigate their own situations and practices with a view to bringing about improvements (e.g. Ainscow, Hargreaves and Hopkins 1995; Ainscow, Barrs and Martin 1998; Ainscow 1999). It has involved the development of a form of action research, an approach to inquiry that in its original form sought to use the experimental approach of social science with programmes of social action in response to social problems (Lewin 1946). More recently action research has come to refer to a process of inquiry undertaken by practitioners in their own workplaces. Here the aim is to improve practice and understanding through a combination of systematic reflection and strategic innovation (Kemmis and McTaggart 1982).

Action research is sometimes dismissed as not being 'proper' research by researchers working within more traditional research paradigms. Others, while acknowledging it as a worthwhile activity for practitioners, are anxious that claims for the validity of findings should not be made beyond the particular contexts in which the investigation is carried out (e.g. Hammersley 1992). Proponents of action research, on the other hand, have responded to these criticisms by rejecting the conceptions of rigour imposed by traditional social science, and by mounting their own counter-criticism of the methodology and assumptions about knowledge upon which these conceptions of rigour are dependent (e.g. Winter 1989).

They claim, for example, that the notions of rigour to which both positivist and interpretative researchers aspire are oppressive, restrictive and prescriptive, designed to perpetuate the hierarchical divisions between the producers and users of research (Iano 1986).

In devising a suitable methodology I have been aware of others who have attempted to follow a similar path. For example, Poplin and Weeres (1992) report a study called 'Voices From the Inside', carried out by students, teachers, administrators and parents in four schools. Here the aim was 'to create strategies that allowed everyone at the school site to speak and insured that everyone be heard'. Thus the research allowed all participants to be both the researchers and, at the same time, the subjects of the research. Since the study began with the assumption that academics had already 'misnamed the problems of schooling', the roles of outsiders had to be rethought so that those on the inside could come to know and articulate the problems they experience. The use of this process was reported to have led to many changes in the schools, although it was also found to be extremely time-consuming.

In developing my own approach I have been keen to pursue a similar, participatory orientation, along the lines of what has been defined as 'collaborative inquiry' (Reason and Rowan 1981; Reason 1988). Such approaches emphasise the value of group processes and the use of varied methods of recording. Here my own thinking has been influenced by experience of using collaborative inquiry methods in English schools (e.g. Ainscow, Hopkins, Southworth and West 1994; Ainscow *et al.* 1995; Ainscow *et al.* 1998), and approaches developed for use in countries of the South, such as 'participatory rural appraisal' (PRA), as developed by Chambers (1992) and refined by Stubbs (1995) and Ainscow (1999) for use in educational contexts.

From these earlier experiences I have found it useful to take account of four principles as I seek to involve colleagues in the research process. These are that it should:

- be of direct help to people in the contexts involved;
- demonstrate rigour and trustworthiness such that the findings are worthy of wider attention;
- contribute to the development of policies and practices elsewhere;
- inform the thinking of the 'outsider' research team.

As a result of earlier experiences of using this orientation I have become clearer about both the advantages and, of course, the difficulties involved in carrying out such a study.

In terms of advantages, from the point of view of the research contexts, there was strong evidence that those involved often found the process to be both informative and stimulating. Specifically they found that the need to engage with multiple interpretations of events forced them to think much more deeply about their own perceptions. Furthermore, exploring ways of valuing points of view that they might more usually ignore, or even oppose, also seemed to stimulate them to consider previously ignored possibilities for the development of thinking and practice. At the same time they found the process to be affirming, giving them an opportunity to celebrate many achievements in their working contexts.

Turning to difficulties, these earlier experiences highlight some of the problems that can occur when practitioners take on the task of carrying out what might be referred to as 'insider' research. We found, for example, that despite a commitment to reporting a wide range of opinions, some accounts revealed little evidence of alternative voices, thus giving the impression of what seemed to be most unlikely levels of consensus. Sometimes there was very little evidence presented from children and parents, gaps that seem particularly regrettable when I read the findings of the Poplin and Weeres study, reported earlier. Finally there remain some concerns about confidentiality. Specifically, as the accounts are read by more people in a particular context, can we be sure that the views of certain individuals will remain anonymous?

Overall, then, the methodology described here can be characterised as essentially a social process. It requires a newly formed group of stakeholders within a particular context to engage in a search for a common agenda to guide their enquiries and, at much the same time, a series of struggles to establish ways of working that enable them to collect and find meaning in different types of information. They also have to find ways of reporting their conclusions. All of this has to be carried out in a way that will be of direct benefit to those in the contexts under consideration. In so doing the members of the group are exposed to manifestations of one another's perspectives and assumptions. At its best all of this provides wonderful opportunities for developing new understandings. However, such possibilities can only be utilised if potential social, cultural, linguistic and micro-political barriers are overcome.

It seems to me that such an orientation helps to overcome the traditional gap between research and practice. As Robinson (1998) argues, it has generally been assumed that this gap has resulted from inadequate dissemination strategies. The implication being that educational research *does* speak to issues of practice, if only the right people would listen. She suggests an alternative explanation, pointing out that research findings may well continue to be ignored, regardless of how well they are communicated, because they bypass the ways in which practitioners formulate the problems they face and the constraints within which they have to work. As I have noted, participatory research is fraught with difficulties. On the other hand, the potential benefits are enormous, not least in that the understandings gained can have an immediate impact on the development of thinking and practice.

In what follows I use examples of collaborative inquiry from our Manchester research programme in order to illustrate the nature of the process and the types of outcomes that are generated. As I have suggested, these studies do not set out to develop understandings that can tell practitioners what to do. Rather they provide frameworks that practitioners can use to reflect on their own contexts and their own ways of working in order to formulate relevant ways of moving their practices forward.

Developing more inclusive schools

In recent years my colleagues and I have been involved in a series of collaborative research activities in relation to the development of more inclusive schools (e.g. Ainscow *et al.* 1994; Hopkins, Ainscow and West 1994; Ainscow 1999; Ainscow, Booth and Dyson 2001). In essence this work seeks to address the question, how do we create educational contexts that 'reach out to all learners'?

This research indicates that schools that do make progress in this respect do so by developing conditions within which every member of the school community is encouraged to be a learner. All of this helps to throw further light on what is meant by inclusion in education. It suggests that it involves the creation of a school culture that encourages a preoccupation with the development of ways of working that attempt to reduce barriers to learner participation. In this sense, moves towards greater inclusion can be seen as a significant contribution to overall school improvement.

Our analysis of what is involved in the development of inclusive schools has pointed to the connections between *policies, practices and cultures*. It has also shown that such developments involve an essentially social process within which those within a school learn how to live with differences and, indeed, learn from differences. This orientation underpins the 'Index for Inclusion', a school development instrument that was developed as a result of a collaborative inquiry project (Booth and Ainscow 2000). This project was carried out on behalf of the Centre for Studies on Inclusive Education, over a three-year period. It involved a team of teachers, parents, governors, researchers and a representative of disability groups, with wide experience of attempts to develop more inclusive ways of working. They carried out two phases of action research, in partnership with a total of 22 schools, in six different LEAs.

The Index involves schools in a process of inclusive school development, drawing on the views of staff, governors, pupils, parents/carers and other community members. It is concerned with improving educational attainments through inclusive practices and thus provides an attempt to redress a balance in those schools that have concentrated on raising attainment at the expense of the development of a supportive school community for staff and pupils.

The process of working with the Index is itself designed to contribute to the inclusive development of schools. It encourages staff to share and build on their existing knowledge about what impedes learning and participation. It assists them in a detailed examination of the possibilities for increasing learning and participation in all aspects of their school for all their pupils. This is not seen as an additional initiative for schools but rather as a systematic way of engaging in school development planning, setting priorities for change, implementing developments and reviewing progress.

It is important to understand that the view of inclusion presented in the Index is a broad one, which goes well beyond many of the formulations that have been previously used. It is concerned with minimising barriers to learning and participation, whoever experiences them and wherever they are located within the cultures, policies and practices of a school. It involves an emphasis on mobilising under-used resources within staff, pupils, governors, parents and other members of the school's communities. In this context diversity is seen as a rich resource for supporting the development of teaching and learning.

The Index materials guide the exploration of the school along three interconnected dimensions:

- 'creating inclusive cultures'
- 'producing inclusive policies'
- 'evolving inclusive practices'.

They cover all aspects of school life, from collaboration and values, to induction and learning support policies, to classroom practices and resource planning. The dimensions have been chosen to direct thinking about school change and represent relatively distinct areas of school activity. In the past, too little attention has been given to the potential of school cultures to support or undermine developments in teaching and learning. It is through inclusive school cultures that those changes in policies and practices, achieved by a school community, can be sustained and passed on to new staff and students (Ainscow 1999). However, our experience indicates that sustainable development depends on change occurring in all the dimensions.

The materials contain a branching tree structure allowing progressively more detailed examination of all aspects of the school. The three dimensions are expressed in terms of 45 indicators and the meaning of each of these is clarified by a series of questions. The indicators are statements of inclusive aspiration against which existing arrangements in a school can be compared in order to set priorities for development. The detailed questions ensure that the materials can challenge the thinking in any school, whatever its current state of development. Together, the dimensions, indicators and questions provide a progressively more detailed map to guide the exploration of the current position of a school and to plot future possibilities.

Using the index

Considerable work has already gone on in relation to the use of the Index for school development purposes, including current projects that are going on in countries as diverse as Australia, Brazil, India, Norway, Portugal, Romania and South Africa. Nevertheless, there is still much more that needs to be done in order that we can develop deeper understandings as to how this complex and challenging document can be used effectively within different contexts.

Some examples provide illustrations of how the Index is being used in relation to particular circumstances. They illustrate how those within schools are choosing to select relevant areas of the Index and adjust the materials, including its wording, in order to make them appropriate. So, for example, the coordinating group in one English primary school carried out a survey of the views of pupils, staff and parents, using the indicators as the basis of rating scales. From the analysis of their data it was decided to concentrate on the development of aspects of classroom practice, focusing specifically on the following indicators:

- Lessons are responsive to pupil diversity.
- Lessons are made accessible to all pupils.
- Children are actively involved in their own learning.
- Children's differences are used as a resource for teaching and learning.

Over the period of a school year efforts were made to use these indicators during lesson planning. Eventually it was decided that something more specific was needed in order to stimulate developments in practice. The school was able to mobilise some extra resources so that pairs of teachers could be freed to work in one another's classrooms. Using the four indicators as the basis of a mutual observation schedule, the teachers made a record of what they saw as 'golden moments'. These were examples of classroom interactions that illustrated how the indicators could be turned into action.

Eventually, after every teacher in the school had been involved in these observation activities, a staff meeting was held during which each pair of colleagues talked about their experiences. A document was produced as a result of these discussions which summarised what had been learnt. It focused on issues such as the use of questions and how to respond to disruptive behaviour. In commenting on the document, however, the head teacher explained that it was a poor record of what had been discussed during the meeting. She commented, 'You would have to have been there to appreciate the richness of the professional learning that was going on.' It seems that through shared experiences within classrooms the teachers were stimulated to reflect on one another's styles of teaching. The story suggests that groups of teachers can use elements of the Index to focus investigations into their practice in ways that enable discussions to focus on important details that are often overlooked.

In a large urban secondary school in Portugal a team of eight teachers, including the principal, also carried out surveys of staff, students and parents. As a result of analysing their findings they recommended to their colleagues that efforts needed to be made to address what they saw as three interconnected priority areas in order to make their school more inclusive. These areas were summarised as follows:

Priority 1: During lessons students are encouraged to work together.
1.1 Do lesson activities require students to collaborate?
1.2 Do teachers ask students to discuss the content of lessons?
1.3 Do teachers help students to learn the skills of working together?

Priority 2: Students support one another.
2.1 Do students talk to each other about their learning tasks?
2.2 Do students feel that their classmates help them?
2.3 Are any students ignored by other members of their class?

Priority 3: Staff development policies support teachers in responding to student diversity.
3.1 Are there meetings where teachers can share their ideas?
3.2 Do teachers have opportunities to observe one another's practices?
3.3 Do teachers feel that they are supported in dealing with difficulties?

Over a period of a year the whole school used these indicators and questions as a framework for moving practice forward. They also provided a means of collecting more detailed evidence through mutual classroom observations, including group analysis of video recordings.

Possibly the most powerful strategy they used involved a series of group interviews with groups of students. These were carried out by an advisory team from outside the school. The school coordinating team spent a whole day analysing transcripts from these interviews. They went to use extracts as the basis of staff development activities in the school. Some extracts were also used on posters that were displayed in the staff room. These invited teachers to write their reactions to comments made by the students.

An adapted version of the Index is being used in Romania, in the context of a Unicef-funded project, 'The Development of Inclusive School Environments in the Community'. Here considerable use has been made of visual recording systems in order to encourage participatory inquiry processes in reviewing processes and outcomes of action research in the schools. These approaches have worked well in terms of helping colleagues within networks of schools to share their experiences and perceptions, and to summarise their learning.

Each school has focused on a small number of indicators chosen by their coordinating groups (e.g. 'Students are valued equally'; 'The school has an efficient policy for decreasing student absences'). They have been encouraged to collect and analyse various forms of evidence in relation to these indicators. For example, the idea of 'mindmaps' was used to help school groups to carry out an audit of evidence in order to review progress. The technique was demonstrated on the board and groups were asked to be creative in finding visual ways of illustrating their ideas. Each indicator was written in a circle on a poster. These were spaced apart. Groups then noted any evidence they had that suggested progress towards this indicator. No guidance was given as to what was meant by 'evidence' so as to encourage creative thinking. It was suggested that the relative 'strength' of evidence should be indicated in some way and that efforts should be made to illustrate how particular evidence might relate to more than one indicator. The posters were displayed on the wall and colleagues were asked to go and look at the work of other schools. Here it was emphasised that schools might borrow ideas from one another. Finally, school groups discussed the following questions:

- 'What other evidence do we need to evaluate our work?'
- 'Do we need to change our indicators for the next phase of action research?'

The Romanian schools also used 'timelines' in order to construct both group and individual records of processes used in their schools (Ainscow *et al.* 1995). During the first stage, groups designed a 12-month timeline on a large sheet of paper, noting key events in their schools. This was introduced using an example drawn on the board. Once the overall timeline was designed, each group member was asked to draw a summary version of their own on a small piece of paper. Then pairs of participants were formed from different schools. Before the individuals talked to each other they were asked to record their personal 'highs and lows' along their school timeline. Again, this was illustrated with an example on the board. No talking was allowed while individuals completed this step. Then each person talked to their partner about their personal experience and feelings during the year. It was stressed that active listening was required, only interrupting if it was necessary to seek clarification. Each person had five minutes to explain their timeline. The next stage involved school groups in entering their 'highs and lows' lines on the school poster version of the timeline. Here attention was placed on the need to recognise that school learning involved personal learning. It was also noted that differences can be a useful resource for facilitating deeper understanding of change processes. The final stage in the activity involved the school groups in summarising the outcomes of these processes by completing two sentences, as follows: 'We make progress when. . .', and 'Things are difficult when. . .' During a plenary session each school group read out their two completed sentences.

Learning from difference

In using these types of approaches in schools we have noted that they can lead to a degree of collusion among those involved, such that unwelcome ideas or evidence may be overlooked. Consequently, within our research network 'Understanding and Developing Inclusive Practices in Schools', we have been working with partner schools in order to explore ways of introducing a more critical dimension to the process (Ainscow *et al.* 2001). In particular we have been considering what types of 'levers' can be used to encourage those within a school to question their practices and, indeed, the assumptions behind these practices. So far a number of approaches are proving to be promising. These are:

- mutual observation of classroom practices, followed by structured discussion of what happened;
- group discussion of a video recording of one colleague teaching;
- discussion of statistical evidence regarding test results, attendance registers or exclusion records;
- data from interviews with pupils;
- staff development exercises based on case study material or interview data.

Through these approaches we are seeking to encourage discussions within the schools that are both supportive and yet challenging. In particular, we are trying to 'make the familiar unfamiliar' in order to stimulate self-questioning, creativity and action.

So, for example, in a number of the schools our discussions have challenged existing assumptions as to the nature of educational difficulties experienced by students. Specifically, we have been questioning the assumption that some students' characteristics are such that they require a different form of teaching from that offered to the majority of students. Such an orientation leads to a concern with finding the 'right' response, i.e. different teaching methods or materials for pupils who do not respond to existing arrangements. Implicit in this formulation is a view that schools are rational organisations offering an appropriate range of opportunities; that those students who experience difficulties do so because of their limitations or disadvantages; and that they, therefore, are in need of some form of special intervention (Skrtic 1991). Our concern is that through such assumptions, leading to a search for effective responses to those children perceived as being 'different', vast opportunities for developments in practice may be overlooked.

In introducing a critical perspective to the process of action research we recognise that schools, like other social institutions, are influenced by perceptions of socio-economic status, race, language and gender. This being the case, we feel that it is essential to question how such perceptions influence classroom interactions. In this way we set out to reveal and challenge deeply entrenched deficit views of 'difference', which define certain types of students as 'lacking something' (Trent, Artiles and Englert 1998). Specifically we believe that it is necessary to be vigilant in scrutinising how deficit assumptions may be influencing perceptions of certain students.

As Bartolome (1994) explains, teaching methods are neither devised nor implemented in a vacuum. Design, selection and use of particular teaching approaches and strategies arise from perceptions about learning and learners. In this respect even the most pedagogically advanced methods are likely to be ineffective in the hands of those who implicitly or explicitly subscribe to a belief system that regards some students, at best, as disadvantaged and in need of fixing, or, worse, as deficient and, therefore, beyond fixing.

We should add that all of this is challenging to the thinking of everybody within the Network, not least those of us from universities. Our assumptions are also challenged; we too have to find ways of dealing with and, hopefully, learning from one another's perspectives. We are also finding that we have a lot more learning to do in order to develop our skills in challenging our teacher colleagues in a supportive way.

Final thoughts

No doubt some who read this chapter will be disappointed that despite all the years of efforts, involving so many people, few definitive conclusions are reached. Surely, they might argue, educational research has a responsibility to provide practitioners with direct answers to the problems they face in their day-to-day work. My own view is that it is through such assumptions and expectations that possibilities for using research more effectively are masked. What I have tried to illustrate in this chapter is that by working together practitioners and researchers can use their different skills and perspectives in order to collect and engage with evidence in ways that can have a direct and immediate impact on thinking and practice in the field. Furthermore, I argue that such an approach is particularly important in relation to the development of inclusive practices. As we have seen, this is essentially about those within a given context learning how to work together in order to identify and address barriers to participation and learning experienced by members of their communities. Logic suggests that this requires the use of collaborative inquiry.

So then, returning to the question that I raised at the start of this chapter, what are the implications for those of us who have made our careers in the field of special education? Do we have a role in the development of inclusive practice and, if so, what might it be? I believe that we do have an important contribution to make and it is one that requires us to become more centrally involved in the development of the education system. This is what I meant when I referred to the 'major step' towards the idea of inclusive practice.

Within this formulation the field of special education has a particular tradition which is of importance. If I think of the best special education contexts I have known, including some excellent special schools that I have and do work with, they always seem to involve a particular way of working. In essence this means the creation of a problem-solving culture within which those involved learn how to use one another's experiences and resources in order to invent better ways of overcoming barriers to learning. My view is that this is the most important gift that the special education community can offer to the movement towards more inclusive forms of education.

Note: Part of the research reported in this chapter is funded by Award L139 25 1001 and, as such, is part of the Teaching and Learning Research Programme of the Economic and Social Research Council. Further information about the research can be found at: http://man.ac.uk/include

References

Ainscow, M. (1999) *Understanding the Development of Inclusive Schools.* London: Falmer Press.

Ainscow, M., Barrs, D. and Martin, J. (1998) 'Taking school improvement into the classroom'. Paper presented at the International Conference on School Effectiveness and Improvement, Manchester, UK, January 1998.

Ainscow, M., Booth, T. and Dyson, A. (2001) 'Understanding and developing inclusive practices in schools'. Paper presented at the American Educational Research Association Conference, Seattle, USA, April.

Ainscow, M., Hargreaves, D. H. and Hopkins, D. (1995) 'Mapping the process of change in schools: the development of six new research techniques', *Evaluation and Research in Education* 9(2), 75–89.

Ainscow, M., Hopkins, D., Southworth, G. and West, M. (1994) *Creating the Conditions for School Improvement.* London: David Fulton Publishers.

Bartolome, L. I. (1994) 'Beyond the methods fetish: towards a humanizing pedagogy', *Harvard Education Review* 64(2), 173–94.

Booth, T. and Ainscow, M. (2000) *The Index for Inclusion.* Bristol: Centre for Studies on Inclusive Education.

Chambers, R. (1992) *Rural Appraisal: Rapid, Relaxed and Participatory.* Brighton: Institute of Development Studies.

Hammersley, M. (1992) *What's Wrong with Ethnography?* London: Routledge.

Hopkins, D., Ainscow, M. and West, M. (1994) *School Improvement in an Era of Change.* London: Cassell.

Iano, R. P. (1986) 'The study and development of teaching: With implications for the advancement of special education', *Remedial and Special Education* 7(5), 50–61.

Kemmis, S. and McTaggart (1982) *The Action Research Planner.* Victoria: Deakin University Press.

Lewin, K. (1946) 'Action research and minority problems', *Journal of Social Issues* 2, 34–6.

Poplin, M. and Weeres, J. (1992) *Voices from the Inside: A Report on Schooling from Inside the Classroom.* Claremont, CA: Institute for Education in Transformation.

Reason, P. (1988) *Human Inquiry in Action: Developments in New Paradigm Research.* London: Sage.

Reason, P. and Rowan, J. (1981) *Human Inquiry: A Sourcebook for New Paradigm Research.* Chichester: Wiley.

Robinson, V. M. J. (1998) 'Methodology and the research-practice gap', *Educational Researcher* 27, 17–26.

Skrtic, T. M. (1991) 'Students with special educational needs: Artifacts of the traditional curriculum', in M. Ainscow (ed.), *Effective Schools for All.* London: David Fulton Publishers.

Stubbs, S. (1995) 'The Lesotho National Integrated Education Programme: A Case Study of Implementation'. MEd Thesis, University of Cambridge.

Trent, S. C., Artiles, A. J. and Englert, C. S. (1998) 'From deficit thinking to social constructivism: a review of theory, research and practice in special education', *Review of Research in Education* 23, 277–307.

Winter, R. (1989) *Learning from Experience: Principles and Practice in Action Research.* London: Falmer Press.

CHAPTER 4

Can teaching assistants make special education inclusive?

Peter Farrell and Maggie Balshaw

Introduction – The growth in the number of teaching assistants

In recent years there has been a dramatic increase in the number of teaching assistants (TAs) working in mainstream schools, mainly with pupils who have special educational needs, both in the UK and overseas. TAs are seen as being a relatively cheap resource who can help to make inclusion a reality for pupils who previously may have been excluded from the mainstream school system. The implications of this for the development of effective practice are referred to in the Green Paper *Excellence for All Children: Meeting Special Educational Needs* (DfEE 1997) and in the follow-up document *Meeting Special Educational Needs: A Programme of Action* (DfEE 1998a). Furthermore the Green Paper *Teachers Meeting the Challenge of Change* (DfEE 1998b) signals the projected increase in the numbers of classroom assistants who will provide general support in mainstream schools that is not restricted solely to pupils with special educational needs. The Centre for Studies on Inclusive Education (CSIE) (2000) now estimate that there are as many as 80,000 TAs working in mainstream schools. Recently the Government has announced that further funding will be made available until 2002 and possibly beyond to employ an additional 20,000 TAs making the total number to be in excess of 100,000 and this figure excludes those who work in special schools. Indeed it is now not uncommon for there to be as many or more assistants as there are qualified teachers in many primary schools.

The increasingly important role of assistants is reflected in the growing number of publications in this area. Three studies, one commissioned by Unison (Lee and Mawson 1998), one by the National Union of Teachers (NUT 1998) and the other by the Teacher Training Agency (TTA) (Smith, Kenner and Barton-Hide 1999), have focused on the work of classroom assistants in general, without specifically focusing on those working with pupils with SEN, although these made up half the sample in the Unison study. The studies are complemented by the large number of books and articles that track the changing and developing role of assistants over the last fifteen years (see, for example, Balshaw 1991, 1999; Fox 1993, 1998; Lorenz 1998; Rose 2000; CSIE 2000; Mencap 1999). In addition recent books on special needs and inclusion devote substantial sections to this area of work (see, for example, Thomas, Walker and Webb 1998; Tilstone, Florian and Rose 1998).

Other recent government initiatives have also helped to move practice forward in this area. For example, there are the two sets of induction training materials for newly appointed TAs in primary and secondary schools (DfEE 2000b; DfES 2001). These are available in every LEA and are being used extensively. In addition the Government has supported the work of the Local Government National Training Organisation (LGNTO) which has recently devised a set of occupational standards for TAs (LGNTO 2001).

Although TAs are increasingly being employed to support the education of all children, their work in mainstream schools parallels the growth in the numbers of pupils with statements of SEN being placed in these settings. As the number of special schools continues to fall it is likely that TAs will continue to have a key role to play in helping to make special education inclusive for pupils with a range of disabilities.

The aim of this chapter is to draw on the findings from two complementary studies that have addressed issues concerned with the work of TAs and effective education for pupils with SEN (Farrell, Balshaw and Polat 1999; Balshaw and Farrell 2002). We begin, however, by providing an account of one teacher's experience of working with a TA and the questions she raised. This is followed with a brief outline of the methodology for both our research projects. The sections that follow consider specific aspects of our findings in relation to the importance of teamwork, career development and training, and effective classroom support.

How can TAs support inclusive practice for pupils with SEN? Some key questions

Some of the issues in providing effective support for pupils with SEN can be illustrated with an account of a conversation that took place at the home of one of the authors (Farrell) around two years ago. Some friends had come round for dinner among whom was a newly qualified history teacher (Sue) who was in her second year of teaching. She taught in an 11 to 18 comprehensive school that was developing a reputation at being 'good' with children who had special educational needs (SEN). During the evening Sue recounted an event that had happened the previous week. She was about to begin a new topic for her Year 9 class – The Causes of the First World War. The class of 28 pupils was of mixed ability and had the reputation for being lively, not always easy to control but basically keen on learning provided lessons were planned carefully and taught in a stimulating and imaginative way. Sue told us that on the day she was to introduce the topic to the class she noticed that there was a new pupil in the group who was accompanied by a TA neither of whom she had met before. It turned out that the new pupil had learning difficulties – for example, she could not write her name without help and was only at the beginning stages of learning to read. She was also very restless in class and had great difficulties in concentrating. A special needs statement had been issued and as a result she had been allocated TA support in some of her lessons.

Sue had many questions to ask about this sequence of events. These included the following:

1. Why was she not informed about the arrival of the new child beforehand?
2. Why had she not been introduced to the TA and given an opportunity to discuss the aims and purposes of the lesson?
3. Planning the lesson for 28 pupils of mixed ability was hard enough. How could she find time to plan within a differentiated lesson for a new child who could not read or write?
4. Who should take responsibility for supporting the new pupil? Was that her role or the TA's?
5. Was the TA accountable to her or to someone else, e.g. the SENCO?
6. What might be the best way of supporting the girl in the classroom? Should she receive one-to-one instruction with the TA for the whole lesson, or should she join a group with the TA supporting in the background, or should Sue teach her directly for part of the lesson?

Sue had positive views about inclusion and was keen to do all she could to make the history lessons meaningful and interesting for the new pupil and to involve her in the class as much as possible. However, the questions Sue raised reflect some of the key issues that have to be addressed by LEAs, schools, teachers and TAs, when planning programmes of work for pupils with special needs in mainstream settings. For example, who should offer support: teachers, TAs, speech therapists or a combination of these and other professionals? Who should take responsibility for managing and mentoring support staff? What training should support staff receive? What *is* effective classroom support?

The following studies have attempted to address these questions and to find examples of good practice that can provide indications of how TAs and other staff in schools can work together to develop effective inclusive practice for all pupils with SEN in mainstream schools.

An outline of the DfEE study and the follow-up action research project

The DfEE study, carried out in 1998/99, had two broad aims:

1. To carry out a series of visits to different schools and support services where learning support assistants (LSAs) worked and which exhibited good and innovative practice. (Note: at the time we used the term 'LSA'.)
2. To conduct a nationwide survey of training providers – mainly colleges of further education (FE) and LEAs.

Our overall findings led us to conclude that effective practice in the work of LSAs involve contributions that:

- foster the *participation* of pupils in the social and academic processes of a school;
- seek to enable pupils to become more *independent* learners;
- help to *raise standards* for all pupils.

From this general statement we developed a more detailed set of indicators of effective practice in the work of TAs. These were intended to be used as a tool for staff in schools and support services to stimulate developments in the work of assistants. However, in order to assess the value of these indicators to schools and LEAs we carried out a follow-up action research project in three LEAs. The aim was to pilot indicators through working directly with staff in schools and support services. In this way we could see at first hand how effective this strategy could be in bringing about improvements in the work of TAs.

In setting up the pilot action research project we were keen to work with a variety of LEAs and schools. This enabled us to explore the impact of the action research approach in different settings and to help us obtain a picture of whether the indicators could be applied in settings that were geographically, demographically and organisationally different.

We chose to work with schools and support services in three LEAs: Cheshire, Harrow and Salford. Within each LEA there were four 'sites' that reflected different phases and ages of pupils, some of which had additional provision, for example, for pupils with hearing impairment, and some were LEA support services. The criteria in the choice of representatives from each of these sites was that one should be a senior member of the teaching staff, preferably from the senior management team, and that there should be one or more assistant.

The first phase of the action research plan consisted of the following steps:

1. an initial workshop in each of the three LEAs for the participants from each of the four schools and services. This was also attended by a senior officer from the LEA. At the end of the workshop staff from each school/service developed an

outline plan of how they intended to use the indicators to develop the work of TAs in their own setting;
2. ongoing development work in the schools/services, i.e. staff put their plan into action;
3. a visit from one of the authors (Balshaw) to each of the schools/services;
4. the presentation of a draft report to an evaluation conference.

This evaluation conference was attended by staff from the DfES who, at the time, were in the process of writing the *Good Practice Guide (GPG)* on working with teaching assistants (DfEE 2000a), with the help of one of the authors of this chapter (Balshaw). This Guide contains a similar set of indicators of effective practice to those that were published in the original DfEE study. Furthermore the work that had taken place as part of the action research informed the development of the *GPG*.

The findings from the action research project are written up in detail elsewhere as is the DfEE study that preceded it (Farrell *et al.* 1999; Balshaw and Farrell 2002). In this chapter we will draw on some of the key outcomes from both studies, all of which relate to the questions that Sue raised earlier in this chapter.

The importance of teamwork

In her history lesson Sue had not met the TA before and hence there was a total absence of teamwork and planning – hardly the ideal preparation for a lesson. This experience, though by no means typical, relates to a key permeating within our studies. Like other writers (for example, Thomas 1992) we have found that good practice in the work of TAs depends to a great extent on there being effective teamwork between all staff in the school. But this is by no means easy to achieve and there are many potential threats to effective teamwork that are inherent in the nature of the TA's work and in the contexts in which they are employed. One of these threats centres on the potential number of people who may form the team. There are many people with an interest in teaching the pupil, each of whom has a different amount of direct contact with him or her, has a job of different status and salary, and has different degrees of responsibility for the child's progress. For example, the TA, who may be allocated to the child but who is the least well paid and most poorly qualified, has to work as a team with the class teacher. The TA may be partly accountable to this class teacher and possibly to the SENCO or visiting support teacher. At least one member of this team is accountable to the parents, but who should this be, and do the parents know whom they should consult about their child's progress? Should they consult with the TA directly, the class teacher or other support/advisory teacher? In terms of the child's programme of work, it is important for all members of the team including, where possible, the child and the parents to be in agreement with the approach that is adopted. However, the larger the team the greater the risk that a consensus will not be formed. But without a consensus the programme may fail. Finally, as with all teams who work in the helping professions, the person with the most responsibility and the job with the highest status generally has the most influence in the decision making about planning and provision for a child with SEN. However, it is frequently the case that this person knows the child least well and has to rely on the accounts of others. The person who knows the child best in the classroom may be the TA, who may well have the most to offer when planning the future for the child but whose views can sometimes be overlooked by others.

This analysis highlights the potential pitfalls to effective teamwork when supporting pupils with SEN in mainstream schools. The more complex the network of relationships between staff involved in supporting a pupil with SEN, the greater the likelihood of communication breakdown, misunderstandings between staff and resentment. However, in our research we have come across several examples where teams have overcome these potential obstacles and have worked well together for the benefit of all. These examples, given below, show how it is possible to develop effective teamwork that results in improved practice in this area.

A TA in a secondary school kept a detailed diary of her work when attached to the geography department. In this she included her initial thoughts, the activities she carried out, her planning with the geography department, meetings she attended and her own thoughts as the work developed and she reflected on its impact. This record has been shared and discussed with the learning support team as part of their ongoing research and as they plan further faculty attachments in the new academic year. A key element that is described is the planning and teamwork between the teacher and the assistant about particular lessons and activities and the evaluation of this.

In another school the TAs and the head teacher felt that developing partnership in planning approaches to teaching the curriculum would lead to more flexibility of deployment and clarification of the developing role within the classroom. It was hoped that from using joint staff development opportunities more effective forms of planning would follow.

Effective teamwork between teachers and TAs in one secondary school was noted in its Ofsted report. In particular the report stressed how this teamwork led to positive experiences for all children as well as those with significant special needs. In developing this effective teamwork the school has therefore become more inclusive.

All of these examples, and many others that we found, illustrate that it is possible for TAs and teachers to develop effective teamwork. This ensures a coordinated approach to education in which all involved are clear about how TAs and teachers are expected to work together throughout the school. However, teamwork does not just happen. All schools and services we visited had spent a long time developing mechanisms to enhance teamwork. Overall our research indicates that the following are the key interconnected ingredients for effective teamwork between TAs and teachers.

1. There should be at least one senior member of the teaching staff who is committed to involving TAs in the life of the school and to ensuring that they work effectively as a team with teachers.
2. Time for planning between the TAs and teachers should be timetabled within the school day. This helps to ensure that both TAs and teachers are prepared for lessons and have discussed their respective role within them.
3. The school should organise opportunities for TAs and teachers to attend joint staff development sessions together.
4. The school should develop effective mechanisms for formal and informal communication among and between teachers and TAs.
5. There should be mutual respect for the role and expertise of both groups in the school.
6. The school should develop a culture of continual review and development of their work in which all staff are encouraged to reflect on their practice and to share ideas for developments with their colleagues.

Salary, career development and training for teaching assistants

A major concern expressed by all those interviewed in the original DfEE study was the whole issue of TAs' contracts and pay. Levels of pay, typically around a third of a teacher's salary, were seen as being far too low when set against the work that TAs undertake and the responsibilities they are given. All TAs resented this. As one ruefully remarked 'you couldn't live on this salary'. 'I would get more working at a supermarket checkout,' said another. They all felt that pay differentials between themselves and teachers (often as much as £14,000 per year) were far too large and that the differences in their role were not so great as to justify this huge imbalance. Teachers and senior managers also believed that these pay differentials were totally unjustified given the work that TAs were expected to do.

Although the problem of TAs' levels of pay has been recognised by the Government, currently there are no plans to set up a national body that can negotiate pay levels for all TAs across the country. Therefore salary levels are negotiated locally and this can result in there being differences between, and sometimes within, different LEAs.

In addition to salary problems, many TAs are employed on temporary contracts that are linked to a pupil with SEN whom they support. If the pupil leaves the school the contract could be terminated. In both our studies we have found that this can cause a great deal of anxiety among the TAs, who understandably would prefer permanent contracts. Although the situation is improving, it is still the case that the majority of TAs' hours of work coincides with the time the pupils are in school. As a result, if TAs arrive early or stay late, they receive no extra pay. Despite this major disincentive to work a few extra hours that could be used for meetings, training, planning or preparation, many TAs we have met are prepared to do so even though they receive no extra remuneration.

Problems with contracts and pay are exacerbated by the fact that there is also little or no career structure for TAs in the schools and services with whom we have worked. All those we interviewed saw this as a major problem. There were, however, four examples in mainstream secondary schools where the post of senior TA had been formed and in most cases these staff were paid slightly more than their colleagues were. These posts were created because the TAs in question had worked for several years in the school and were recognised for their outstanding contribution. Generally these senior TAs were well respected and they took on additional management responsibilities in relation to their junior colleagues. For example, in one school the senior TA, in addition to managing the team of two TAs, was responsible for liaison with parents and outside agencies, the TA and feeder schools. In another, where there was a senior and deputy senior TA, they took on the training and induction of TAs and managed the timetable, and they were given non-contact time for this work. In a third school an experienced TA helped to coordinate a reading programme which involved direct contact with parents and she had timetabled time for this.

A further issue of concern is the level, amount and quality of training that is provided for TAs. It is not uncommon, for example, for a TA to be appointed to support a child with autism in a mainstream school who has never met an autistic child before, who has had no prior training and who may have no further education beyond GCSE/O levels. Currently, only a tiny minority of TAs have received any accredited training that is related to their work prior to entering the profession. One TA we met felt very strongly about this and considered that a basic entry qualification was needed otherwise 'anyone can enter the profession'. She believed that currently the profession is devalued, as the job is perceived as being one that anybody could do.

An increasing number of schools and local authorities have recognised this problem and now offer a series of short inservice training courses. Others have begun to plan more extensive accredited courses. All TAs we interviewed welcomed the opportunity to attend training programmes not least because the invitation alone was a recognition of their status in the school. In addition several felt that training was essential in order to help them to meet the needs of the vulnerable pupils they were supporting.

In the past two years there have been several initiatives at a national level that have attempted to address this problem. Chief among these is the new induction training programme developed by the DfES referred to above. In addition there is a whole range of accredited courses run mainly by colleges of FE but also by universities and LEAs. Finally, the Local Government National Training Organisation (LGNTO 2001) has supported the development of national occupational standards for TAs. These indicate the competencies (in NVQ terms) that TAs should possess at two levels, those of a recent entrant into the profession and those of a more experienced assistant.

In future, there may well be a nationally agreed set of qualifications for TAs that will be based around the NVQ framework and that will be complimented by a full range of short courses covering a range of areas from induction to more specialised training in a specific area. These developments should help managers and senior staff in schools and LEAs to work with their TAs in planning a coordinated and ongoing programme of training aimed at meeting the needs of the TAs themselves, teachers and other relevant staff.

What is effective classroom support in relation to the work of teaching assistants?

The way support is provided to pupils with SEN in a mainstream school is central to the debate about developing effective inclusive practices. If pupils with SEN are supported on a full-time basis by TAs who only work individually with them throughout the day, it is difficult to argue that this is an inclusive way of working. This is sometimes referred to as the 'Velcro' model of support with the child and TA stuck together. This practice may prevent the child from making contact with his/her peer group and hence he/she becomes segregated within the school and the presence of the TA serves to accentuate this position. However, many pupils with SEN have specific problems in learning and need one-to-one attention for parts of the day otherwise they will not learn. It is therefore vitally important for programmes of work to combine individualised instruction, either in class or on a withdrawal basis, with supported group work in mainstream classes that encourages the pupils to be included within their peer group. This balance of work is not easy to achieve and inevitably some compromises have to be made. TAs and teachers therefore need to be sensitive to the needs and wishes of all students and to review the situation frequently.

In our research we have found that the style of support offered by TAs in mainstream classes was remarkably similar across all mainstream schools visited. In general they had rejected the Velcro model. Although they kept regular contact with pupils, they supported but did not sit with them throughout a lesson unless they were working on a completely different curriculum area from that of their peer group. Both pupils and TAs preferred to work in this way. Many pupils clearly did not want their problems to be highlighted in front of the rest of the class through the TA spending too much time with them.

A further issue related to the styles of classroom support concerns the role of the class teachers in working directly with pupils with SEN. There were teachers interviewed in our original study who took the view that the TA was employed to work with the SEN child and that their role was to work with the other children. On other occasions, however, we have observed teachers and TAs sharing some of the work both with children with SEN and with the remainder of the class. For example, the teacher might work individually with a child with SEN or with a small group, leaving the TA to support the rest of the class. Our data suggested that teachers, TAs and pupils preferred this more flexible way of working and considered that it was an essential step towards developing more inclusive practices. Interestingly, in an extensive review of literature on inclusion, Harrower (1999) cites several studies that support this overall view.

Concluding reflections

This chapter has referred to some of the key areas that our two research projects have addressed in particular: the importance of teamwork; pay, career development and training; and effective classroom support. Further details about our research can be found in Farrell *et al.* (1999) and Balshaw and Farrell (2002). One striking feature that has permeated all our interactions with TAs has been their unbounded enthusiasm for their work. Despite many of the problems that they face we have found TAs to be an extremely committed and dedicated group of professionals who are keen to learn and to make a contribution towards helping schools to become more inclusive. Indeed our evidence strongly suggests that they have made a huge difference in this area and have helped teachers and LEA staff to appreciate the contribution that mainstream schools can make towards providing effective education for all pupils, including those with SEN. Having been somewhat sceptical and possibly a little threatened a few years ago, teachers now appreciate the value of TA support, and phrases such as 'I do not know what I would do without them' are not uncommon.

However, we must not be complacent. Our research has highlighted many areas where improvements still need to be made. In addition a recent American study (Gerber, Finn, Achilles and Boyd-Zaharias 2001) suggests that Teachers' Aids (as they are referred to in the United States) do not make much difference in raising pupils' attainment. However, although published recently, the data on which the research is based was collected prior to 1990. As there has been a huge development in TA roles and responsibilities over the last decade, it is likely that a different set of findings would result were the study to be repeated now.

If we return to the questions raised by Sue earlier in this chapter, we would not claim that our research has provided definitive answers. However, we consider that our findings do suggest some strategies that she and her colleagues could adopt to improve their practice in the work of TAs in the school.

One final thought: it is indeed ironic that TAs, almost certainly the poorest paid and least well trained of all professionals working with children with SEN, should be given such a key role in supporting the inclusion of a potentially vulnerable group of young people who, because of the nature of their difficulties, may be the hardest to teach. Given this situation, it is all the more remarkable that TAs have made such a huge contribution towards making special education inclusive.

References

Balshaw, M. (1991) *Help in the Classroom*. London: David Fulton Publishers.

Balshaw, M. (1999) *Help in the Classroom* (2nd edn). London: David Fulton Publishers.

Balshaw, M. and Farrell, P. (2002) *Teaching Assistants: Practical Strategies for Effective Classroom Support*. London: David Fulton Publishers.

Centre for Studies on Inclusive Education (CSIE) (2000) *Learning Supporters and Inclusion*. Bristol: CSIE.

Department for Education and Employment (DfEE) (1997) *Excellence for All Children: Meeting Special Educational Needs*. London: DfEE.

Department for Education and Employment (DfEE) (1998a). *Meeting Special Educational Needs: A Programme of Action*. London. DfEE.

Department for Education and Employment (DfEE) (1998b) *Teachers: Meeting the Challenge of Change*. London: DfEE.

Department for Education and Employment (DfEE) (2000a) *Working with Teaching Assistants: A Good Practice Guide*. London: DfEE.

Department for Education and Employment (DfEE) (2000b) *Induction Training for Teaching Assistants (Primary)*. London: DfEE.

Department for Education and Science (DfES) (2001) *Induction Training for Teaching Assistants (Secondary)*. London: DfES.

Farrell, P., Balshaw, M. and Polat, F. (1999) *The Management, Role and Training of Learning Support Assistants*. London: DfEE.

Fox, G. (1993) *A Handbook for Special Needs Assistants*. London: David Fulton Publishers.

Fox, G. (1998) *A Handbook for Learning Support Assistants*. London: David Fulton Publishers.

Gerber, S. B., Finn. J. D., Achilles, C. M. and Boyd-Zaharias, J. (2001) 'Teacher aides and students' academic achievement', *Educational Evaluation and Policy Analysis* 23(2), 123–43.

Harrower, J. K. (1999) 'Educational Inclusion of Children with Severe Disabilities', *Journal of Positive Behavioural Interventions* 1(4), 215–30.

Jerwood, L. (1999) 'Using special needs assistants effectively', *British Journal of Special Education* 26(3), 127–9.

Lee, B. and Mawson, C. (1998) *Survey of Classroom Assistants*. Slough: NFER.

Local Government National Training Organisation (LGNTO) (2001) *National Occupational Standards for Teaching Assistants*.

Lorenz, S. (1998) *Effective In-class Support.* London: David Fulton Publishers.

Mencap (1999) *On a Wing and a Prayer: Inclusion and Children with Severe Learning Difficulties.* London: Mencap.

National Union of Teachers (NUT) (1998) *Associate Staff Support for Teachers.* London: NUT.

Rose, R. (2000) 'Using classroom support in the primary school', *British Journal of Special Education* 27(4), 191–6.

Smith, K., Kenner, C. and Barton-Hide, M. (1999) *Career Ladder for Classroom Assistants.* Hampshire: University of Southampton and Hampshire County Council.

Thomas, G. (1992) *Effective Classroom Teamwork – Support or Intrusion?* London: Routledge.

Thomas, G., Walker, D. and Webb, J. (1998) *The Making of an Inclusive School.* London: Routledge.

Tilstone, C., Florian, L. and Rose, R. (eds) (1998) *Promoting Inclusive Practice.* London: Routledge.

CHAPTER 5

Learning about inclusive education: the role of EENET in promoting international dialogue

Susie Miles

Introduction

The Jomtien Declaration on Education for All, 1990, the Salamanca Statement and Framework for Action (UNESCO 1994) and the Dakar Framework for Action, 2000, have played a critical role in highlighting the issue of exclusion from education. The harsh reality is, however, that 113 million children still receive no form of basic education (Savolainen, Kokkola and Alasuutari 2000). Within this group girls and boys who have impairments continue to be disproportionately excluded from any form of education in countries of the South.[1]

The Enabling Education Network (EENET) was set up in 1997 to support and promote the inclusion of marginalised groups in education worldwide through the sharing of easy-to-read information. It is based in the Educational Support and Inclusion Group within the Faculty of Education, University of Manchester. Its activities are guided by an international steering group, which is made up of parents, disabled people, donor and technical agencies and the University of Manchester.

EENET shares and celebrates examples of instructive practice, where educational exclusion is being challenged, often in small-scale community-based projects. This chapter will provide an account of EENET's activities and describe some of the ways in which the barriers to participation in education have been overcome. The examples are taken from countries facing extreme economic hardship, where class sizes are very large and material resources scarce, yet where teachers and parents are committed to a human rights and social justice approach to educational inclusion.

---

1 The terms 'North' and 'South' are used in this chapter to denote the economic differences between countries. The South includes countries in Africa, Asia and South America. It also includes countries in political transition, such as in the former Soviet Union.

The Salamanca Statement

Any discussion about inclusive education needs to be set in the context of the United Nations (UN) organisation's strategy of 'Education for All'. Within this strategy the influence of the Salamanca Conference, which addressed the future of special needs education, is particularly important:

> More than 300 participants, representing 92 governments and 25 international organizations, met in Salamanca to further the objective of Education for All by considering the fundamental policy shifts required to promote the approach of inclusive education, namely enabling schools to serve all children, particularly those with special educational needs.
>
> (Preface to the Salamanca Statement, UNESCO 1994: iii)

The Salamanca Statement re-affirms the right to education of every individual, as enshrined in the 1948 Universal Declaration of Human Rights, and renews the pledge made by the world community at the Jomtien Conference on Education for All, held in 1990, to ensure that right for all, regardless of individual differences. It also mentions the 1993 UN Standard Rules on the Equalization of Opportunities for Persons with Disabilities which states that the education of disabled children should be an integral part of the education system. The Framework states that:

> Every child has a fundamental right to education, and must be given the opportunity to achieve and maintain an acceptable level of learning.
>
> (Article 2)

And that:

> Educational policies at all levels ... should stipulate that children with disabilities should attend their neighbourhood school, that is the school that would be attended if the child did not have a disability.
>
> (Article 18)

The Framework makes it clear what is meant by 'all children':

> Schools should accommodate *all children* regardless of their physical, intellectual, social and emotional, linguistic or other conditions. This should include disabled and gifted children, street and working children, children from remote and nomadic populations, children from linguistic, ethnic or religious minorities and children from other disadvantaged or marginalized areas or groups.

The Salamanca definition of inclusion was ground-breaking in that it moved beyond a concern with disability, to include all potentially marginalised groups. It goes on to emphasise the wider impact of inclusive education:

Regular schools with this inclusive orientation are the most effective means of combating discriminatory attitudes, creating welcoming communities, building an inclusive society and achieving education for all; moreover, they provide an effective education to the majority of children and improve the efficiency and ultimately the cost-effectiveness of the entire education system.

(Article 2)

Definitions of inclusion

EENET has been instrumental in promoting further discussion of the definition of the terms used in promoting inclusive practices. Greater clarity was encouraged as a result of a formulation that was agreed at a seminar on inclusive education, which took place in Agra, India, co-organised by the International Disability and Development Consortium and EENET (EENET 1998). The Agra definition has since been adopted, almost word-for-word, into the South African White Paper on Education in March 2000.

Inclusive education:

- acknowledges that all children can learn;
- acknowledges and respects differences in children: age, gender, ethnicity, language, disability, HIV and TB status, etc.;
- enables education structures, systems and methodologies to meet the needs of all children;
- is part of a wider strategy to promote an inclusive society;
- is a dynamic process which is constantly evolving;
- need not be restricted by large class sizes or a shortage of material resources.

(EENET 1998)

Beyond Salamanca to the Dakar Framework

At Salamanca, UNESCO was called upon to ensure that 'special needs forms part of every discussion dealing with Education for All (EFA)'. Yet EFA and inclusive education existed in parallel. It was therefore perhaps not too surprising that the discussions held at the world education forum in Dakar, Senegal, in 2000 did not provide a clear vision of future developments, and the concept of inclusive education for all received little attention. The 'Notes on the Dakar Framework for Action' (1999), however, go into some detail about those learners who are vulnerable to marginalisation and exclusion:

The key challenge is to ensure that the broad vision of Education for All as an inclusive concept is reflected in national government and funding agency policies. Education for All . . . must take account of the need of the poor and the most disadvantaged, including working children, remote rural dwellers and nomads, and ethnic and linguistic minorities, children, young people and adults affected by conflict, HIV/AIDS, hunger and poor health; and those with special learning needs . . .   (Para. 19)

The Salamanca and Dakar Frameworks provide a toolkit for UNESCO's work in responding to the challenges of education for all (Vayrynen 2000). It follows, therefore, that inclusive education should be the main strategy for addressing marginalization and exclusion.

The role of information in promoting inclusion

EENET is a post-Salamanca initiative which aims to meet the information needs of practitioners who have limited access to basic information and material resources.

The word 'inclusion' was deliberately omitted from EENET's title. Enabling, we hope, is a broader concept, and may have a longer life than the term 'inclusion'. By avoiding inclusion in the title, we also hoped to encourage a more comprehensive vision and understanding of inclusive education, beyond that associated with disability and so-called 'special needs'. At the same time, of course, 'enabling' provides an important contrast to 'disabling'. It also reminds us that disabling educational environments affect all children, not only those who are identified as having impairments.

A dictionary definition of 'enable' is as follows:

to authorise, *empower*, supply with the means to do.

Whereas to 'disable' is:

to incapacitate from doing, deprive of *power*.

Enablement and empowerment are therefore closely linked. Education should be empowering to all children, but sadly, too often, it is the opposite. This being the case, EENET is both promoting enabling, rather than disabling, education and enabling inclusive education to develop by providing easy-to-read and relevant information. It starts from the assumption that information is power. Therefore access to information is empowering.

Our experience is that the careful use of language is crucial when communicating with culturally diverse countries. Choosing the most appropriate words to describe people who have impairments, and being sensitive about the way we portray countries with few material resources, are similar and related challenges.

Since information is power, it is essential that words are chosen carefully, and with respect. *Respect for difference and diversity is at the heart of inclusive education.*

EENET's underlying values and principles emerged from many hours of discussion among interested colleagues:

EENET:

- believes in the equal rights and dignity of all children;
- prioritises the needs of countries that have limited access to basic information and resources;
- recognises that education is much broader than schooling;
- acknowledges diversity across cultures and believes that inclusive education should respond to this diversity;
- seeks to develop partnerships in all parts of the world.

In conducting its work EENET:

- adheres to the principles of the Salamanca Statement;
- believes that access to education is a fundamental right;
- recognises the intrinsic value of indigenous forms of education.

EENET is committed to:

- encouraging the effective participation of key stakeholders in inclusive education;
- engaging with the difficulties caused by the global imbalance of power;
- encouraging a critical and discerning response to all information and materials circulated.

EENET's strategies

1. Accessibility and participation

Education practitioners in countries of the South have largely been excluded from international conferences and the international literature. Most of the literature paints a negative picture of education systems struggling to cope with poorly trained teachers, inadequate budgets, large class sizes and more recently the HIV/AIDS crisis. This has been called the 'negative deficit model' of developing countries (Stubbs 1995).

EENET aims to promote a positive image of countries of the South. Innovative programmes in the South have a great deal to teach the economically wealthy countries of the North, where increasingly services are faced with diminishing resources. Their strength is that they have tremendous experience of overcoming apparently insurmountable resource barriers. Yet the flow of information tends to be from North to South and inappropriate practices continue to be uncritically exported.

If this imbalance in the flow of information is to be corrected, it is essential to make education conferences and publishers more accessible to Southern contributors. In 2000 EENET organised a pre-congress workshop on presentation skills for participants from the South, prior to the International Special Education Congress (ISEC). This served two purposes: it provided a focus for Southern participants, who may have otherwise felt alienated from the unfamiliar environment; and it helped to validate the experience from the South. One of these participants was invited to participate in concluding the conference in front of an audience of over 1,000. It is unlikely that this would have happened without the extra effort made to make the conference accessible.

2. *Sharing inspiring stories*

Creating conversations across cultures and sharing stories are a key aspect of EENET's participatory network. Reflecting on the experience of other practitioners can help to 'make the familiar unfamiliar'. This has not been an easy task, as many readers use English as a second or third language, and many Southern countries have a strong oral tradition.

The following email message was sent from a refugee camp in Kenya. It illustrates the enormous contribution that practitioners working in very difficult circumstances can make to this global story-telling:

Sudanese, Ethiopian and Somali deaf students are learning together in an integrated classroom. The Somali teacher is about 24 years old and has 22 students ranging from 8 to 38 years old. He introduces the lesson in sign language: 'Good morning! We are here to learn together because we are one.' Occasionally there is inter-clan fighting, yet the learners ignore the clan boundaries and walk to school to learn. In Kakuma refugee camp inclusion is a key factor. It does not really matter how old I am, or what class I am in. What counts is 'let me taste a little of it'. Education is the only worthy weapon of reducing social conflict. It is an economic tool to fight poverty. EENET should be seen as an information-giving tool, as well as a tool for social cohesion.

The following examples may seem exotic, and perhaps too unfamiliar, but the lessons learnt can shed light on the 'familiar'. Parent empowerment in Lesotho has helped fill an enormous gap, where there was a shortage of expertise in inclusive practices. The introduction of democratic practices in classrooms in Zambia, where rote learning was the norm, has transformed the teaching and learning experience for all children and, incidentally, benefited those with learning difficulties. These stories are inspiring and need to be disseminated and celebrated.

Parent activists in Lesotho

A progressive policy on the integration of disabled children into primary schools was developed in 1987 in Lesotho, based on a report by a North American consultant. This was before all the major international conferences on education and child rights. The national disabled people's organisation used this policy to lobby for access to education for disabled children.

Lesotho is a small country of two million people, surrounded completely by South Africa, and economically dependent upon its giant neighbour. The disabled people's organisations in both countries likened their struggle for equality of opportunity with the anti-apartheid liberation struggle. The focus on rights, rather than charity, was an extremely important influence on the development of an inclusive education system in Lesotho.

A national pilot inclusive education programme began in 1991 and its main strategies were as follows:

- awareness-raising at all levels: administrators, teachers, parents, disabled people's organisations, the community, Ministry of Health personnel, and the setting up of a cross-sectoral committee comprising all the key players;
- the formation of a national parents' association;
- an initial three-week inservice training course in the school holidays for *all* teachers from the ten pilot schools, 77 teachers altogether;
- follow-up training, both centrally and in schools;
- production of curriculum materials for teacher training giving basic information about disabled children;
- minimal use of additional resources in order to promote sustainability.

The training provided teachers with the skills to assess and to teach children with all types of impairment. The teachers reported that they had 'become better teachers' as a result. Class sizes in Lesotho are large, with ratios of up to one teacher to 100 children, but teachers still found ways of implementing inclusive education. They did this using the following strategies:

- peer support – seating disabled children next to pupils who could help them;
- seating – sitting children near the front of the class;
- adapting the curriculum;
- group work;
- encouraging sibling support at home;
- promoting positive attitudes.

The national parents' organisation, which has branches all over the country, decided not to wait for the results of the pilot programme, but to take action themselves to promote the development of more inclusive practices. They visited schools to inform teachers in their areas about their children's right to be included, using the Salamanca Statement and the Convention on the Rights of the Child as their lobbying tools.

The parents were trained to communicate more effectively with teachers and other professionals. They are now confident that their experience of being parents of disabled children is extremely valuable. They did not receive special training to be the parents of disabled children, and they do not think that teachers would benefit from special training. They prefer a problem-based approach to training and together with Ministry staff they are able to advise teachers in the school setting. None of the teachers has 'special' expertise in a particular impairment or an increased salary. All the teachers are responsible for ensuring that disabled children are included. The teachers in the pilot schools, together with the parents, have become a major resource for promoting inclusion throughout Lesotho. The parents also provide advice to the teacher trainers, who run the pre-service courses, give talks to the students and accompany them on home visits.

The example of Lesotho is unusual because the Ministry of Education actively encouraged the formation of a parents' organisation precisely because it believed that teachers cannot, and should not, implement inclusive education without family involvement (Khatleli, Mariga, Phachaka and Stubbs 1995). In most other countries parents have had to fight to have their voices heard and have influenced the development of inclusion through their role as lobbyists, rather than as partners.

Inclusion through democracy and human rights: a community-based approach, Zambia

The quality of education has deteriorated in Zambia, despite the introduction of more child-focused educational policies, and society as a whole is concerned about this trend (Mumba 1996). Teacher training colleges emphasise the importance of the relationship between teachers and pupils, but innovative ideas discussed during training are rarely put into practice. Most experienced teachers, who work in isolation from their fellow teachers, continue to teach in the same way they did when they first qualified decades before. Undemocratic and authoritarian teaching practices prevent innovation and African culture reinforces authoritarian relationships between adults and children.

Teachers in Kabale primary school, in Mpika, 600 kilometres from the capital, have radically changed their style of teaching. This has paved the way incidentally for the inclusion of children with learning difficulties. The school is a resource centre for the Child-to-Child programme. Staff are encouraged by the school administration to promote children's participation in their own learning and the equal participation of pupils, parents and teachers in education.

The strategies that have been used to democratise classroom practice are as follows (Mumba 2001):

- introducing children to their rights and responsibilities;
- co-operative group learning and problem solving;
- pupils are encouraged to question traditional sources of knowledge;
- evaluation of the learning process by both pupils and teachers;
- pupils are involved in decision making;
- a strong emphasis on gender equality;
- parents participate in their children's learning.

The combination of these approaches has encouraged ownership of the school by the community – an essential part of the inclusive process as inclusive classrooms are unlikely to work in isolation from the community.

The Mpika Inclusive Education Project was started in 1999 to document the use of the Child-to-Child approach by schools and communities to promote inclusive education. One of the challenges at Kabale school is to integrate the children in the newly created unit for children with learning disabilities into the life of the school. One of the strategies is the twinning of disabled and non-disabled children using Child-to-Child principles.

Gradually the barriers between the unit and the rest of the school have been broken down and the 'specialist' staff now work as resource teachers in the school as a whole. The unit has been transformed into a resource centre which is used by all the teachers. The ideas developed at Kabale have been shared with 17 schools in the surrounding district and regular meetings are held between the teachers to share experiences.

EENET's activities

Currently EENET is engaged in a series of activities related to its overall purpose. These are:

1. Web site   www.eenet.org.uk

'Inclusive Technology Ltd, which markets educational software for special education, provides EENET with technical support in maintaining a large web site free of charge. The site includes: training packages for teachers, parents and children; bibliographies of documents produced by Save the Children (UK), UNESCO, EENET and other relevant organisations; EENET's newsletter in English, Spanish, Portuguese and French; conference papers and reports; and miscellaneous articles by individual practitioners. The site is organised into the following key topics: teacher education; policy; Child-to-Child; parents; deafness; action learning; and early childhood. In June 2001 the contents of the site were captured on a CD-ROM and sent to all those on EENET's mailing list free of charge, thus enabling those who cannot afford to use the Internet to access the information on the site.

2. Information dissemination

Almost 1,500 names of individuals and organisations in 124 countries have been entered on the mailing list. EENET provides information to individuals on request. An index of useful publications is disseminated to all those on the mailing list to ensure that people who do not have access to the Internet are able to access hard copies of documents relevant to their work. EENET also acts as a referral service for education, disability and development issues.

3. Newsletter

EENET's free newsletter, entitled 'Enabling Education', is produced every six to eight months and forms the basis for the exchange of information and ideas about inclusive education. The newsletter is simply and modestly produced in two colours and consists of 16 sides of A4. It is deliberately non-academic and conversational in style. It features stories and accounts of good practice in inclusive education, and details of useful publications and training materials. As far as possible all regions of the world are represented. Although the impetus for the establishment of EENET has come from the field of disability and special needs, the newsletter also features articles relating to a wide range of issues of difference, such as gender, poverty, HIV and/or TB status, race and ethnicity.

4. Family action for inclusion

'Family Involvement in Inclusive Education' is the title of a project initiated in January 1999 to collect stories from parents' groups, which have played a key role in the promotion of a more inclusive approach to education. Stories have been collected so far from South Africa, Lesotho, Bangladesh, Nepal, Romania, UK and Australia. They are available from the web site. A publication is in the pipeline which covers the main issues involved in setting up a parents' group based on the experience of collecting these stories.

5. The Deaf dilemma

EENET has collated information about specific issues related to deaf children and inclusion. The motivation for this is Article 21 in the Salamanca Framework for

Action which states that the educational needs of deaf children 'may be more suitably provided [for] in special schools or special classes and units in mainstream schools' due to their particular communication needs. A seminar was held in 1999 to discuss the particular issues affecting countries of the South, where as few as 1 per cent of deaf children are currently being educated in schools for deaf children, and the vast majority simply do not have access to any form of education. Yet the further development of separate forms of education is simply unaffordable, and arguably undesirable, for the majority of countries. EENET has collected articles reflecting alternative community-based provision in countries as diverse as Afghanistan, Mozambique, Democratic Republic of Congo and Papua New Guinea.

6. Regionalisation

Looking to the future, the main focus for the next few years is to promote the regionalisation of EENET's activities in order to increase the dissemination of information. Preliminary discussions have taken place with regional organisations in Brazil, Hong Kong, China and the Middle East. It is envisaged that each regional agency would take responsibility for a regional mailing list and the collection and publication of stories from their region which can be shared globally. Translation into the major world languages will be a key aspect of the regionalisation process.

7. Action research

'Understanding Community Initiatives to Improve Access to Education' is the title of a new action-learning project coordinated by EENET, which will be completed in early 2003. Funded by the UK Department for International Development (DfID), it is a small-scale project which aims to help people who are involved in community initiatives to increase participation in education to:

- analyse their experience of inclusive practice
- document their learning
- share the lessons with other people.

We have found that there are many barriers that prevent people from sharing their experiences, particularly between cultures. This project sets out to develop ways of overcoming these barriers. Some initial questions include:

- How can people with very different types of knowledge, skills and perspectives be helped to think about, document and learn from their own experience to improve access to learning for all?
- What needs to happen to make this process empowering, particularly for practitioners and people from marginalised groups?

- How can the particular experiences of one community speak to a wider audience and at the same time remain authentic?
- How can 'outsiders' and 'insiders' best work together to improve practice?

No doubt many more questions will be developed during the planning process.

EENET believes that everyone, no matter what their level of formal education or literacy, is capable of being helped to think about and communicate their own experience. This is why we use terms such as 'action-learning' and 'reflective practice'. The intention is that this project should give added value to what people are already doing in the course of their work. The project is significant in a number of ways:

- It has a strong focus on the importance of 'learning from the South'.
- Its aim is to empower people and to improve their projects.
- It will attempt to engage with and throw light on certain tensions and challenges, for example:

    - the relevance of learning across cultures;
    - bridging oral and literacy-based cultures;
    - collaboration and power issues between South and North;
    - exploring how participatory processes can be made fully inclusive.

Conclusion

EENET is a participatory information-sharing network. It aims to do far more than just disseminate information. In capturing the authentic voices of practitioners, it aims to affirm the experience of those struggling to promote inclusion, social justice and democracy.

Until I read your newsletter, it had not occurred to me that the deaf children I teach in a small unit could benefit from being included with their peers in the main school.   (Specialist teacher, Zimbabwe)

EENET gives us an opportunity to know about other countries' solutions to common problems. This stops us from reinventing the wheel, because with information we can achieve a lot by just changing our tyres.
(Coordinator of an information network, India)

Clearly there are many challenges and dilemmas facing EENET as it continues to encourage conversations between practitioners in the field. Balancing the needs of practitioners in predominantly oral cultures with the increasingly rapid and high-tech forms of communication that proliferate in the North is a major concern

(Miles 1999). Linked to this is the dilemma of being based in a Northern university, far from the harsh reality facing those in greatest need of accessible information. The dilemmas we face can be summarised as follows:

- How do we reach the 'hard to reach'?
- How do we overcome barriers to communication?
- How do we avoid Northern domination?
- How do we encourage South-South conversations?
- How do we involve children and young people?

Isolation from information marginalises and further impoverishes excluded groups. The sharing of clear, lively and accessible information and ideas helps to reduce that isolation. Difference is our greatest resource in sharing information globally and promoting more inclusive practices in the education of *all* children.

References

Dakar Framework for Action (1999) *Meeting our Collective Commitments. Notes on the Dakar Framework for Action* (http://www.unesco.org/wef/).

Enabling Education Network (EENET) (1998) *Inclusive Education: Making a Difference.* A report of an International Disability and Development Consortium seminar, Agra. Delhi: Save the Children (UK).

Khatleli, P., Mariga, L., Phachaka, L. and Stubbs, S. (1995) 'Schools for All: National Planning in Lesotho', in B. O'Toole and R. McConkey (eds), *Innovations in Developing Countries for People with Disabilities.* Chorley: Lisieux Hall Publications.

Miles, S. (1999) 'Creating Conversations: The Evolution of the Enabling Education Network', in E. Stone (ed.), *Disability and Development.* Leeds: The Disability Press.

Mumba, P. (1996) 'Democratisation of Primary Classrooms in Zambia: A case study of its implementation in a rural primary school in Mpika', in M. Ainscow and P. Mittler, (eds), *Including the Excluded: Proceedings of 5th International Special Education Congress, University of Manchester.* Delph: Inclusive Technology Ltd.

Mumba, P. (2001) 'Democratisation of the classroom', *Enabling Education*, Issue 5. Manchester: EENET.

Savolainen, H., Kokkola, H. and Alasuutari, H. (eds) (2000) *Meeting Special and Diverse Educational Needs: Making Inclusive Education a Reality.* Helsinki: Ministry for Foreign Affairs of Finland, Department of International Development Co-operation and Niilo Maki Institute.

Stubbs, S. (1995) 'A critical review of the literature relating to the education of disabled children in developing countries', in The Lesotho National Integrated Education Programme. A Masters Thesis. In *EENET Web Site, June 2001 www.eenet.org.uk (CD-ROM).* Delph: Inclusive Technology Ltd.

United Nations Educational, Scientific and Cultural Organisation (UNESCO) (1994) *The Salamanca Statement and Framework for Action on Special Needs Education.* Paris: UNESCO.

United Nations Educational, Scientific and Cultural Organisation (UNESCO) (2001)

Including the Excluded: Meeting Diversity in Education. Example from Uganda. Paris: UNESCO.

Vayrynen, S. (2000) 'UNESCO and Inclusive Education', in H. Savolainen *et al.* (eds), *Meeting Special and Diverse Educational Needs: Making Inclusive Education a Reality.* Helsinki: Ministry for Foreign Affairs of Finland, Department of International Development Co-operation and Niilo Maki Institute.

Section 2

CHAPTER 6

Pastoral care, inclusion and counselling

Henry Hollanders

Introduction

In this chapter our main task is to explore the concept of inclusion from the perspective of pastoral care. Before we get down to this, however, we must devote some space to the corresponding task of exploring pastoral care from the perspective of inclusion. This is necessary because the very term 'pastoral care' may actually be situated more in the realm of *exclusion*, since it reflects constructs that are both socially and culturally determined. Clearly, 'pastoral care' is embedded in both the discourse of religion (in particular, Christian) and the discourse of power. 'Pastor' is the title often applied to Christian ministers who tend their 'flock' as under-shepherds to Christ, who is 'the Great Shepherd of the sheep'. The shepherd is, stereotypically, the caring, but also powerful, figure who leads and directs the sheep. The sheep, for their part, are dependent on him for protection, both from their own foolishness and from the malicious attention of predators. In almost all respects this is now an outdated metaphor, since, for the most part, children in the UK do not live in a pastoral society, and only the minority are brought up in a truly Christian context. Moreover, the concepts that have been developed under the umbrella title of 'pastoral care' in recent years have had little to do with religion (in an institutional sense), and have sought to focus more on personal development than on the imposition of direction from outside. Although a title such as 'Personal, Emotional and Social Care and Development' may be too cumbersome to use, it is more conducive to inclusion, and, probably, more clearly reflects the kind of content and processes currently subsumed under 'pastoral care'. Nevertheless, having made the point, we will revert to the use of the term 'pastoral care' in the rest of this chapter for the sake of convenience.

The present situation

The introduction of the National Curriculum, together with the development of the Literacy and Numeracy Strategies, have had the effect of creating in many teachers a sense of being straitjacketed by statutory requirements. This, together with pressures coming from assessment procedures and performance tables, has compounded the impression that there is little scope for anything other than an intense focus on predetermined content in teaching. While I do not subscribe to the position that creates a dichotomy between 'person-centred' and 'content-centred' education, there is little doubt that this content-centred emphasis has had a major consequence relevant to the subject of this chapter. In practice, if not in intent, attention has been diverted away from emotional care and development, in favour of a more concentrated emphasis on the cognitive development of the child. McGuiness (1998) reminds us that 'in 1979, Her Majesty's Inspectorate published a report (DES 1979) in which they described "the personal development of children" as "the central purpose of education"'. He goes on, however, to point out that 'less than two decades later, testing, vocationalism, central control and, of course, the market place, have given instrumentality centre stage – people as tools and objects, relationships as commodities' (p. 8). This is a strong statement, and perhaps, in the end, too strong. Nevertheless, it is of crucial importance that we should recognise that an educational programme, no matter how professionally devised, carefully prepared and dynamically delivered, will be of very little use if the child does not have emotional, as well as intellectual, access to it. This, of course, is hugely relevant to the debate on inclusive education. Inclusion must mean more than being present in a place of education along with everyone else, being offered the same, or similar, content as that offered to others. To be truly included it is important to *feel included*, and an essential aspect of feeling included is *feeling valued*. Inclusion, in this sense, takes us beyond what might be thought of as special educational needs. It is highly likely that there are many children within our schools who, irrespective of whether or not they are considered to be in need of special educational attention, feel isolated and excluded. Emotional needs may not show up in an overtly disturbed way. Some children may be very 'good', and may learn just enough not to be a cause for concern. If they are generally well behaved and are keeping up, these children are not likely to draw the attention of a hard-pressed teacher. This points us to the possibility of the existence of a kind of 'underground' group of children who, though physically present in the educational system, and generally untroublesome (at least for the moment), nevertheless feel themselves to be emotionally excluded – 'the excluded within'. In an atmosphere that is so geared to a kind of frenetic conveyance of content, the extent and depth of such a sense of emotional alienation, for whatever reason, is unlikely to be gauged in any meaningful way. However, in spite of this, there are some indications of a growing concern among teachers to redress the balance by finding ways of addressing the emotional needs of the children in their care. The practice of circle time, peer support groups and the development of some kind of counselling provision for schools has attracted considerable interest in recent years (Mosley 1996; Lang 1998; Moss and Wilson 1998; McGuiness 1998; Decker, Kirby, Greenwood and Moore 1999). Moreover, a recently published Ofsted document (2000), giving guidance to inspectors on what constitutes an inclusive school, states: 'An educationally inclusive school is one in which the teaching and learning, achievements, attitudes and *well being* of every young person matters . . . The most effective schools . . . identify any pupils who may be missing out, difficult to engage, or *feeling in some way apart from* what the school seeks to provide' (italics added). While this does not explicitly mention the importance of emotional health, the concept of 'well being' goes at least some way towards a more formal recognition of it.

If inclusive education in this broad sense is to be achieved, pastoral care has a crucial part to play. It is to this that we now turn.

What is pastoral care?

While it is possible to produce formal and broad definitions of pastoral care (e.g. Marland 1974; 1989; Dooley 1980; DES 1989; Best 1995), it is, perhaps, more meaningful to go to what it means to those engaged in practice at grass roots level. Best (1995) summarises his research findings on what constitutes pastoral care, by clustering responses from teachers under six headings:

- a bureaucratic structure of status positions and role definitions;
- activities or practices performed by the role incumbents;
- the way in which those practices are carried out;
- the quality of relationships between members of the school;
- the attitudes members adopt towards one another, and the values to which these give expression;
- the ethos or climate of the school as a whole.

From these responses we can discern a number of levels of understanding, each of which points to a valid and important aspect of pastoral care.

Level one

Pastoral care implies a structure of roles taken up by named individuals whose task it is to manage incidents and processes that broadly relate to the care of the pupils. This is likely to include disciplinary procedures, consulting with parents/guardians, liaising with statutory and voluntary agencies, contact with community groups in which the child has a stake, etc. This is the managerial aspect of pastoral care, and it is likely to be taken up by a nominated deputy head, year heads and form tutors.

Level two

Beyond the managerial *function*, pastoral care implies an *attitude* with which the function is to be undertaken. By definition, pastoral care must be caring. Those who undertake the role must do so with an attitude that conveys care, even when tough decisions have to be made and carried out.

Level three

It would be a mistake, however, to see pastoral care solely in terms of roles allocated to certain individuals, no matter how well and caringly they carry it out. It should be the concern of everyone to foster the kind of relationships that are both 'containing' enough to promote good control and discipline, and caring enough to facilitate a sense of empathic mutuality.

Level four

Pastoral care involves the creation of a whole-school ethos in which all are involved all the time. From this perspective pastoral care is not only the responsibility of a named group of people who act in the pastoral role at certain times when they are called upon. It is not even the responsibility of everyone to engage in specific activities from time to time that might be connected in some way with caring for others. Rather, it is the responsibility of everyone, all the time, through all mediums and subject areas, to create an ethos in which all feel valued and included. This is the high task that is at the heart of pastoral care. At this level, those nominated to have the pastoral role will not be seen as solely responsible for the carrying out of pastoral care. A central aspect of their role will be to find creative ways of promoting a whole-school ethos, part of which will be to promote lively debates about issues related to the care of the whole school population. The creation of a whole-school ethos of pastoral care in which all are involved in a committed way, may, in the end, prove to be an impossible task in some settings. Nevertheless, it is a goal that must surely be worth aiming for.

At levels one and two, pastoral care may be largely *reactive* (it is likely to be involved in dealing with 'incidents' and concerns as they arise). At levels three and four it is likely to be both *proactive* (seeking to point to strategies that will prevent at least some issues from arising) and *developmental* (in the sense of facilitating the development of the whole person and profoundly influencing the developmental direction of the whole school (Best 1995)).

For pastoral care to be truly effective it needs to be operating at all four levels, and to be fully engaged in the life of the school reactively, proactively and developmentally.

Some characteristics of a whole-school ethos of pastoral care

To speak of pastoral care as the development of a whole-school ethos is likely to draw the criticism of being too vague to be of any practical use. Here, then, are some suggestions of what such a development might involve:

- There will be clear lines of communication along which proactive and reactive care for all can be quickly and appropriately provided as necessary by well-trained and skilled individuals.
- The need for special care from time to time will be fully accepted without any sense of embarrassment or shame – just part of what it means to be human.
- There will be an emphasis on the importance of listening to each other at every level. The kind of listening that will be fostered will be characterised by genuineness, empathy, and acceptance of the perspectives and feelings of others, even when these are not shared by the listener. This will permeate every aspect of the life of the school.
- There will be a corresponding emphasis on the importance of appropriate expression, usually in words but also in other creative ways. Some may need special help in this direction, particularly those whose inability to express their emotions verbally has resulted in destructive and violent behaviours. This points to the need for the proactive development of an emotional vocabulary, which, alongside the other more specialist vocabularies, should permeate every subject area.
- A sense of being valued will be created. In particular, there will be an emphasis on the value of the individual, of caring and robust relationships, and of community. Such valuing will promote esteem both for self and others.
- An essential aspect of this valuing process will be the valuing of the resources contained within individuals, relationships and the community. Often, to a large degree, these resources are untapped. It will be a central concern of 'whole-school pastoral care' to facilitate achievement (whatever that may mean) by helping individuals and groups to be in touch with, and make use of, the resources that reside in them.
- There will be a sense of safety. Good pastoral care in which all are involved will produce a sense of security and constancy over time which children will come to trust as being reliable even when tested in, perhaps, extreme ways. A kind of 'secure base' (Bowlby 1980) will be created within which good learning can take place, free from harmful and distracting anxieties.
- If a sense of safety is to be created for all, there must be an appropriate exercise

of control. This will be characterised by what Egan (1990) calls 'tough-minded listening', which recognises the need to listen to and respect the person, but which does not shrink from challenge and confrontation when called for. In a school where pastoral care is accepted as the responsibility of the whole community, the exercise of control will also be a communal responsibility. There will, of course, be those who have to take the lead in making and carrying out hard disciplinary decisions. However, where there is a sense of communal responsibility the exercise of control becomes a growth promoting opportunity rather than an oppressive process.

Pastoral care and learning

Good pastoral care is at the heart of education, and is intrinsic to the processes of learning. Following the work of Marton and Saljo (1976), Entwistle (1987) identified three levels of learning: surface, strategic and deep. In surface and strategic learning, the student has the purpose of completing the requirements of a given task, which is usually experienced as being externally imposed. These levels of learning are often associated with assessments of various kinds, but whatever is learned in this way is unlikely to be usefully retained much beyond the time of the assessment. Deep learning, however, is characterised by a genuine desire to understand; to interact with both the content and the facilitator; to relate concepts to experience and previous knowledge; and to come to conclusions that make real sense of the material to the individual. To a large degree, this is learning through insight, and as such it is internalised and becomes part of the learner. If deep learning is to go on, attention must be paid not only to the content, but also to the context of learning. The question here is 'what are the optimum conditions in which deep learning can take place?' In attempting a part answer to this, I want to draw on the work of a philosopher, Martin Buber, and two psychologists, Carl Rogers and L. S.Vygotsky.

The Jewish philosopher, Martin Buber (1961), partly in reaction to the instinct theory of Freud, pointed to the importance of the *'Instinct of Origination'* and the *'Instinct of Communion'* as essential elements in the development of the human personality. The *Instinct of Origination* is manifested in the desire to bring something into being, to produce and shape something – in short, to create. That which is created in this way belongs to the creator, not as a possession, but rather as something that has originated in her/him and gives expression to her/his unique selfhood. The instinct of origination does not mean, of course, that all the components have their origin in the individual, but that the arrangement, the resulting product, has 'been brought forth' from her/him. Thus, for example, the plasticine was given to Alice during a lesson, but through the teacher creating a context which encouraged Alice to have both the naiveté and the confidence to allow the instinct of origination freedom to play, it was shaped by her in a way that was uniquely her own. Used carefully and well, the creative process and the resulting product can become the means by which Alice learns more about herself.

The *Instinct of Communion* is manifested in the desire to relate, to be in touch with another person. It is this instinct that causes us to reach out for that deep contact with another being which Buber (1958) describes as 'I-Thou' relating. This is entirely in keeping with what has become known as the 'object-relations' school of psychotherapy, in which the drive to relate is seen as the prime motivating factor in the development of the human personality, and the way in which relationships have been internalised is considered to determine to a large extent the basic ways in which we approach life (see Winnicott 1990). It is also in keeping with 'attachment theory', expounded originally by Bowlby (1953), but now going beyond his earlier formulations. Here the nature of attachments formed throughout life are a crucial factor in determining the level of anxiety, depression or integration that we experience as we face the ups and downs of life. For Buber, the instinct of communion goes hand in hand with the instinct of origination, and is the essential context in which creative learning takes place. The process of learning goes on in the context of a relationship in which the teacher crosses over to the other side where the child is. From that perspective, she discerns what is needed by the child, goes out 'into the world' to gather it, and then presents it to the child in a way that enables her to work with it to make it her own.

Carl Rogers, the psychologist who played a central role in the development of counselling, spent most of his working life seeking to discover the optimum conditions for personal development (Rogers 1961). His conclusion was that personal growth comes about in the context of a certain kind of relationship in which genuineness, empathy and unconditional positive regard play an essential part. Where such a relationship is formed there is the possibility of new and deep learning taking place – learning about oneself, others and the world (Rogers 1983).

Lev Semyonovich Vygotsky, another psychologist, working from a different perspective to that of Rogers, also pointed to the importance of the relational context in the process of learning. Among other things, Vygotsky was interested in the way learning becomes internalised. He considered that internalisation occurs when 'an interpersonal process is transformed into an intrapersonal one'. He explains this process in the following way:

Every function in the child's social development appears twice: first, on the social level, and later, on the individual level; first, between people (intrapsychologically), and then inside the child (intrapsychologically). This applies equally to voluntary attention, to logical memory, and to the formation of concepts. All the higher functions originate as actual relations between human individuals. (Vygotsky 1978: 57)

Each of the above (Buber, Rogers and Vygotsky), in their own way, point to the crucial importance of the relationship in the process of learning. If deep learning is to take place, full attention must be given to the environment that facilitates it, which is supremely relational. The clear implication of this is that the teacher who is concerned that children should actually learn, cannot be solely concerned with content, or even with method, but must also give careful attention to the development of a facilitating relationship. Moreover, it is only through the development of such a relationship that the teacher is likely to get some idea of what is going on for the child emotionally, and this, in turn, will enable her to understand how best to help her to engage in the process of learning.

It is in this broad sense that it is every teacher's task to be involved in the pastoral care of the child, since it is centrally concerned with the promotion of secure relationships and is, therefore, intrinsic to the process of learning.

Pastoral care and counselling

Counselling is being increasingly seen as one aspect of pastoral care. This, of course, is not new. Throughout the 1970s the development of counselling in schools was the subject of much discussion and debate. Training courses for school counsellors were established at Keele, Reading and Exeter. Bolger (1982) sums up this period thus:

> For ten years or so it [counselling] was a new force in education, a source of controversy, a source of inspiration, a source of theoretical understanding, a source of practical skills. Training courses were established, counsellors were appointed to schools throughout the country, professional bodies of counsellors were formed, research into counselling flourished and pastoral care, the traditional British way of dealing with pupil welfare, backed up by counselling theory became a vigorous movement. (p. 61)

This was not to last, however. Bolger continues:

> Then came recession and cuts in public spending. Development slowed down, came to a halt and then went into reverse. Counsellors reverted to being class teachers, counselling posts were terminated or merged with other positions, counsellors moved into other fields or were made redundant.(p. 61)

The situation now seems to be changing again. The general interest in, and development of, counselling in a number of different contexts (e.g. in primary care and in occupational health settings) has begun to affect the educational scene. There are a growing number of publications on counselling in schools (e.g. Cowie and Pecherek 1994; McLaughlin 1995; McGuiness 1998; Decker *et al.* 1999) indicating renewed interest in what counselling might be able to offer. Full-time counsellors remain rare in secondary education, but are commonplace in further and higher educational institutions. In schools, counselling is being increasingly offered by agencies outside of the school itself, to which pupils can be referred. In some authorities, the Pupil Referral Service offers some counselling provision by using well-trained independent counsellors. Organisations such as 'The Place 2 Be' and Cruse (bereavement counselling) offer counselling to children who may be referred to them by schools which budget for a limited number of sessions per year. That children are prepared to use counselling as a means of gaining some help when in difficulty is evidenced by the large numbers of calls received by organisations such as Child Line.

A fundamental question that needs to be addressed is 'what place might counselling have in a school and what might it offer?' In a brief and partial answer I make the following suggestions.

- *Counselling philosophy joins hands with the philosophy of holistic education.* At best, counselling philosophy upholds the value of the individual without falling into the trap of individualism. It emphasises the importance of the 'inner world' of the child without under-emphasising the importance of social influences and conditions. It offers a value perspective on the self-actualising potential of human beings. In each of these ways counselling may serve as an ally of holistic education, since it is concerned not only with the particular problems of specific individuals, but with the much greater question of what it means to be a person. To have such a voice raised in our schools must surely be of considerable value.
- *Counselling offers a repertoire of skills that can enhance existing roles.* The British Association for Counselling and Psychotherapy makes an important distinction between 'counselling' and the use of 'counselling skills'. Briefly, in the former, two people 'contract' to engage in a specific activity that they understand to be counselling. In the latter, however, a set of skills is used to enhance the existing role of a person, without that person becoming formerly a counsellor. Thus, a doctor will be a better doctor, a social worker a better social worker, and a teacher a better teacher if each adds to their repertoire of skills the skills of counselling. This will not turn them into counsellors, but they will be more likely to fulfil the role that they already have in a more effective manner. The skills of careful active attention giving, listening, and appropriate responding on a number of different levels are among the many skills that the counsellor can offer to the teacher and pupil alike. These skills are particularly important in that they will enable the teacher (and those charged with the managerial role of pastoral care) to work with a child in understanding her particular situation, which may in some instances lead to a referral to an appropriate agency for further help.
- *Counselling offers a specialist activity that may be needed by some pupils.* There are any number of situations in which a child, or a member of staff, may benefit

from a more specialised form of counselling. The experience of a trauma, the loss of some loved person or thing, the bewilderment that comes from being let down in some deep way, anxiety stemming from a felt inability to meet some expectation from a significant other person, bullying and harassment of various kinds, these, and many others, are all situations that might be helped by some sensitive and careful counselling. In such situations it is possible that the initial steps towards help may be taken with a teacher, a teaching assistant or with another child, each of whom might use counselling skills to get to the place where more specialised counselling is undertaken.

Pastoral care and inclusion: Conclusion

Implicit throughout this chapter, and in some places explicit, is the concept that pastoral care and inclusive education share the same vision. Inclusion *needs* the development of 'care-full' relationships. No doubt there is much more to inclusion than the development of good, caring and robust relationships, but one thing is certain – it cannot succeed without them. And, among other things, pastoral care is about the development of such relationships.

Again, no doubt there is more to inclusion than the development of an ethos of emotional care and a sense of being valued. But, also again, it is certain that it cannot succeed without these permeating the whole life of the school. And good pastoral care is about the development of such a whole-school ethos. It is in this sense that pastoral care can be seen to be one of the greatest allies of the project of inclusion.

References

Best, R. (1995) 'Concepts in Pastoral Care and PSE', in R. Best, P. Lang, C. Lodge and C. Watkins (eds), *Pastoral Care and Personal-Social Education*. London: Cassell.

Bolger, A.W. (1982) 'Counselling in Education: Schools', in A.W. Bolger (ed.), *Counselling in Britain: A Reader*. London: Batsford Academic and Educational Ltd.

Bowlby, J. (1953) *Child Care and the Growth of Love*. Harmondsworth: Penguin.

Bowlby, J. (1980) *A Secure Base*. London: Routledge.

Buber, M. (1958) *I and Thou*. Edinburgh: T. & T. Clark Ltd.

Buber, M. (1961) *Between Man and Man*. London: Collins.

Cowie, H. and Pecherek, A. (1994) *Counselling: Approaches and Issues in Education*. London: David Fulton Publishers.

Decker, S., Kirby, S., Greenwood, A. and Moore, D. (eds) (1999) *Taking Children Seriously: Applications of Counselling and Therapy in Education*. London and New York: Cassell.

Department of Education and Science (DES) (1979) *Aspects of Secondary Education in England*. London: HMSO.

Department of Education and Science (DES) (1989) *Report of Her Majesty's Inspectors on*

Pastoral Care in Secondary Schools: An Inspection of Some Aspects of Pastoral Care in 1987–88. Stanmore: DES.

Dooley, S. (1980) 'The relationship between the concepts of "pastoral care" and "authority"', in R. Best, C. Jarvis and P. Ribbins (eds), *Perspectives on Pastoral Care*. London: Heinemann.

Egan, G. (1990) *The Skilled Helper*. Pacific Grove: Brooks/Cole Publishing Co.

Entwistle, N. (1987) 'A model of the teaching-learning process', in J. T. E. Richardson, M.W. Eysenck and W. Piper (eds), *Student Learning: Research in Education and Cognitive Psychology*. Milton Keynes: Open University Press.

Lang, P. (1998) 'Getting Round to Clarity: What Do We Mean by Circle Time?' *Journal of Pastoral Care*, September, 3–10.

McGuiness, J. (1998) *Counselling in Schools: New Perspectives*. London: Cassell.

McLaughlin, C. (1995) 'Counselling in Schools: Its Place and Purpose', in R. Best, P. Lang, C. Lodge and C. Watkins (eds), *Pastoral Care and Personal-Social Education*. London: Cassell.

Marland, M. (1974) *Pastoral Care*. London: Heinemann.

Marland, M. (1989) *The Tutor and the Tutor Group*. Harlow: Longman.

Marton, F. and Saljo, R. (1976) 'On qualitative differences in learning: 1. Outcome and process', *British Journal of Educational Psychology* 46, 4–11.

Mosley, J. (1996) *Quality Circle Time*. Cambridge: LDA.

Moss, H. and Wilson, V. (1998) 'Circle Time: Improving Social Interaction in a Year 6 Classroom', *Journal of Pastoral Care,* September, 11–17.

Office for Standards in Education (Ofsted) (2000) *Educational Inclusion: Guidance for Inspectors and Schools*. London: Ofsted.

Rogers, C. (1961) *On Becoming a Person*. London: Constable.

Rogers, C. (1983) *Freedom to Learn for the Eighties*. Columbus, OH: Merrill Publishing Co.

Vygotsky, L. S. (1978) *Mind in Society: The Development of Higher Psychological Processes*. Cambridge, London and Massachusetts: Harvard University Press.

Winnicott, D. W. (1990) *The Maturational Processes and the Facilitating Environment: Studies in the Theory of Emotional Development*. London: Karnac Books.

CHAPTER 7

Inclusive education and lesbian and gay young people

Jo Frankham

This chapter draws on research conducted with 54 young gay men living in Greater Manchester and Norfolk (Frankham 1996). The work was conducted as part of a study on HIV prevention, hence the focus on male same-sex attraction. Obviously, the specific needs of young lesbians need also to be addressed when considering the development of inclusive practices in this area and a clear priority is to investigate their experiences. Wherever possible I include the needs of lesbian young people in this account, drawing on others' research and anecdotal evidence.

This chapter provides an introduction to the following areas:

1. Background: Growing up lesbian or gay.
2. What are lesbian and gay young people's experiences of school?
3. Starting points for research and action in schools.

The first and second areas concentrate on issues that illuminate something of the complexity of addressing the needs of lesbian and gay young people.

Background – Feelings about being gay or lesbian

Deciding, realising or working out that you are lesbian or gay is not a once-and-for-all business. Neither does it tend to be something you suddenly begin to consider. The people I interviewed talked about feeling they were different sometimes as early as seven or eight years of age. Of course, experiences vary and the context within which people are coming out is changing all the time. It is still the case, however, that being lesbian or gay is socially stigmatised, while simultaneously becoming more visible and acceptable in some quarters. In such a context, most young people continue to experience difficulties with at least their initial feelings of same-sex attraction.

From an early age, the people I interviewed were aware that gay men and women are regularly subjected to abuse and ridicule. Derogatory names emphasise the 'unnaturalness' of being lesbian or gay, their 'perverse' sexual habits and their supposed promiscuity. Often before they know what the words mean, young children will use homophobic taunts towards those regarded as behaving aberrantly. Many young people also report that their parents (most commonly fathers) make anti-gay comments. Heterosexual norms are further reinforced by sex education which tends to concentrate on reproduction, heterosexual relationships and family life (Frankham 1992). In such a context, young people learn that being gay 'is not accepted and it wasn't liked' (Tom). These early lessons also emphasise the *differences* between being gay and being heterosexual rather than the similarities (Herdt 1998). These supposed differences polarise the choices that are apparently available in terms of sexual identity. So if you do not feel you fit the heterosexual norm, there is apparently only one other choice – a choice which is laden with negative connotations and stereotypes.

Many young people talk about further difficulties associated with identifying as lesbian or gay when they do not know what this *means* (except in the negative terms outlined above) either in terms of their own behaviour or in terms of what the future might hold for them. In this respect, some lesbian and gay teenagers feel they occupy an uncomfortable transitional space; they do not belong in the 'straight world', but neither do they know how to join or live in the 'gay world' (Frankham 2001). The young men experiencing such feelings also cite AIDS as provoking further fear and anxiety. Because of the close association that is made between being gay and having AIDS it can seem, as Tariq said, 'that everywhere there's a gay person there's a person with AIDS'. In the absence of general information and advice, many young people experiencing same-sex attraction will spend time considering the origins of their feelings. This may be in an attempt to understand themselves better or because, as Liam said, 'If I can work out what made me gay I might be able to do something about it.'

Clearly there are many more gay and lesbian images in circulation than even five years ago and these are generally welcomed as possible sources of insight into 'being gay'. Soaps with gay characters are often watched avidly, although negative comments from family members and lack of self-regard mean that these images can be experienced ambivalently. Some people also feel that the more positive images seem unrealistic and that their lives are unlikely ever to turn out like that. The Black and Asian young men I interviewed found it even harder to gain reassurance from television programmes or information that was generally available. Tariq was of the opinion that he was 'the only person who's Asian and gay'. Rob described a sense of failing to live up to expectations of Black masculinity: 'They would see you as a coconut – a Black man who's white inside.' Many young people worry about the effect of identifying themselves as lesbian or gay on other people, particularly their parents and close family.

There are a number of related problems associated with saying anything about your feelings at this stage. These problems relate to the stigmatisation of same-sex attraction and to society's tendency to want people to clearly identify and behave as either gay or (preferably) straight. Firstly, an ambivalent position involves, by definition, periods of uncertainty and periods where the person concerned thinks (hopes?) that they are heterosexual. It is also likely to include periods where one is actively trying to deny same-sex attraction. Talking about such attraction would be self-defeating then – one risks reinforcing the very thing one is trying to deny.

Asking parents for information or advice is usually dismissed as a possibility because of their likely reaction. John told me, 'It's them you think of first, but you tell them last.' Concern about disappointing parents is high, and those who turned to them for reassurance discovered their fears were well founded. Parents who were approached at this stage tried to persuade their sons that they *were not* gay, that it was 'just a phase' and that they would grow out of it. In such a context, Francis felt he could not say anything again until he was 'more than 100 per cent sure' of his feelings.

Talk of same-sex attraction among groups of young people is most likely to reinforce negative stereotypes. Most boys dismiss the idea of talking to other boys, even one-to-one, about same-sex attraction. Many of the young men I worked with eventually spoke to a carefully chosen girl about their feelings. Girls do not necessarily find other girls so empathetic when it comes to talking about their same-sex attraction and as Carson (Chapter 18 of this volume) describes, those with learning difficulties can face even more extreme isolation. One of the problems reported with trying to talk about same-sex attraction to peers is the widespread understanding that you are either gay or straight and that you *must* know which it is. Thus it seems that the only tenable way to talk about such feelings is if you actually 'come out' and confirm yourself as gay or lesbian. Given the ambivalence associated with this act it is clear why many people wait until they have left school and left home before naming themselves as lesbian or gay.

Experiences of school

This section provides a brief overview of the following areas:

- What is the informal culture of schools, as it pertains to same-sex attraction?
- What support do young people experiencing same-sex attraction get from teachers at school?
- What coverage of issues around same-sex attraction exists in schools?

'Gay' and less flattering words with the same meaning are used as generic insults by teenagers much as they are by younger children, although verbal bullying of this kind is reported to be more common and vicious among teenage boys than girls.

Some teenagers experience physical as well as verbal bullying and describe how they were ostracised or picked on throughout their school careers. A number of people I interviewed described how bullying had contributed to them dropping out of school altogether. Some studies claim that unhappiness among lesbian and gay teenagers leads to disproportionately high rates of suicide and attempted suicide (Walker 2001).

In such a context, defending anyone who is subject to bullying or calling attention to oneself by talking about same-sex attraction seems untenable. People I worked with described a fear of being shunned – Tariq: 'I thought people wouldn't like me any more. People would change. I'd get beaten up, right, and be considered a freak.' The bullying and name-calling also reinforces fears about what it means to be gay. As Rajpaul expressed it: 'It puts you off coming out and it makes you wonder what sort of person is *in* me.'

People who observe anti-gay abuse, but who are fortunate not to suffer it themselves, generally distance themselves from the person affected. They fear that defence of those who have been singled out for harassment will result in abuse being turned on them. People become aware that they need to 'police' their behaviour, or they risk drawing attention to themselves. This is particularly the case in changing rooms and toilets – sites of some of the most violent bullying that is reported. Many young people will also go along with the norms of heterosexuality – talking about fancying members of the opposite sex and so on – in order to 'fit in'.

Anti-gay taunts, bullying and violence have a number of effects then. They reinforce the feeling that coming out or talking about same-sex attraction is a dangerous and unwise idea. In turn, lesbian and gay teenagers are kept separate from one another because of the difficulties associated with confirming a gay identity and even the implications of being seen with other people known, or assumed, to be gay. And the isolation and assumed 'sickness' of those subject to abuse, reinforces fears about what it means to be gay. On the positive side, those who do come out at school can become an important source of support for others who are experiencing same-sex attraction. The forms of resistance then employed exhibit important alternative behaviours to their peers. Kevin, whose male 'friends' ignored him once he was known to be gay, started 'fighting back' in his last few months at school. When people asked him if he was gay he would reply, 'Why – do you fancy me?' or 'Why, are you?' Basically, he said, he was 'admitting it' and this 'made them feel there's no point in trying to wind me up any more'. Although Kevin was pleased that he could 'counsel' others who thought they were gay, he always discouraged them from coming out – much better, he felt, to 'lead a double life' than go through what he had gone through.

Some teenagers experiencing same-sex attraction talk about how teachers are supportive of them, either directly or indirectly. Some of them feel able to talk to teachers about their feelings and are defended by them in the face of homophobic bullying.

Teachers are only ever approached for support if they have already expressed clear and consistent acceptance of homosexuality. Unfortunately, the vast majority of the young men I spoke to described their teachers as unsupportive or indifferent, or at worst joining in anti-gay abuse. Making anti-gay statements or 'jokes' was regarded as a way teachers – particularly male teachers – would 'score points' with other students. In most cases, teachers ignore same-sex attraction, neither raising the subject themselves, nor responding to the anti-gay abuse that they hear.

Most teenagers do not actually *expect* their teachers to be supportive, although they certainly would like them to be. This is because they feel that teachers are somewhat 'out of their depth' when it comes to tackling even bullying, and some young people's understanding of the law (see below) is that teachers are not allowed to talk about same-sex attraction. As in other contexts, talking to a teacher about bullying might result in a short-term improvement but, 'They're probably going to come back when the teacher's not around and be twice as bad.'

The official curriculum, for the most part, ignores the subject of same-sex attraction. The only time that homosexuality is spoken of regularly in school is in relation to AIDS. In this context, then, young men get some acknowledgement of their existence while lesbianism continues to remain almost totally invisible. The young men I interviewed reported that AIDS education would begin with statements like, 'It's not just a gay disease' or 'Everyone can get it, not just gays and drug users.' Thereafter, the information was framed within an assumed heterosexual norm. It is a cruel irony that when the silence about homosexuality is broken, it is broken with statements that add to the anxiety young gay men already feel about themselves. And the use of the word 'just' was taken as further reinforcement of the derided status of gay men. Andy: 'It's "just" gays that get it – well, that doesn't matter then?' Such statements also imply, of course, that everyone in the classroom is straight.

The assumption of heterosexuality also serves to reinforce the silence of those who think they might be attracted to the same sex because for as long as heterosexuality is assumed, conversations about sexual attraction, per se, are unnecessary. Whom one is attracted to, how one feels about that, others' reactions to those feelings and so on can continue to be seen as irrelevant to the constituency of the classroom for as long as they are all assumed to be straight and 'normal'. According to Watney (1991):

> . . . the question of homosexuality remains in total abeyance. Which is to say that the question of sexuality remains in abeyance, since our respective (UK and US) education systems manifestly fail to acknowledge the actual diversity of human sexuality within the curriculum or outside it. In effect, children are taught that homosexuality is beyond consideration. (pp. 387–8)

Although most of the people I spoke to resented the absence of affirmative statements about same-sex attraction at school, they were also ambivalent about the subject being raised. There was a strong desire for legitimation of their feelings – they spoke often of hoping for reassurance that they too were 'normal'. At the same time, however, they had learnt that discussion of same-sex attraction can act as a goad to those only too willing to be homophobic and in this sense they remained hesitant about recommending its inclusion into the curriculum. Some of the young men I spoke to were perhaps also aware of the difficulties of being confronted with information that they would really rather not have, the associations with AIDS that I discuss above, for instance, or merely the reminder that their feelings were as they were. Those who were already being picked on for being gay also predicted feeling very exposed if the topic was raised. This ambivalence illustrates a key challenge in this area: young people experiencing same-sex attraction want such attraction to be spoken of but at the same time (generally) do not want to speak of it themselves and may feel very uncomfortable when others do so.

Starting points for research and action in schools

There is some positive news in terms of legislation that applies in this area. The age of consent for gay men has been equalised and although the Government has failed to repeal Section 28, repeal has been discussed (and achieved in Scotland).[1] In addition, new guidance on 'Sex and Relationship Education' is explicit for the first time about 'inclusion' of those experiencing same-sex attraction:

> It is up to schools to make sure that the needs of all pupils are met in their programmes. Young people, whatever their developing sexuality, need to feel that sex and relationship education is relevant to them and sensitive to their needs. The Secretary of State for Education and Employment is clear that teachers should be able to deal honestly and sensitively with sexual orientation, answer appropriate questions and offer support. (DfEE 2000: para. 1.30)

Perhaps inevitably, the *Guidance* 'treads a tightrope' (Epstein, O'Flynn and Telford 2001) in this area, 'attempting both to stress the desirability of marriage to please the churches and those on the Right, and simultaneously expounding a more liberal view about individual sexuality, in order to keep its election pledge to those lesbian and gay rights campaigners, broadly on the Left' (p. 5). Nonetheless, each tiny shift is to be welcomed while also being clear about its somewhat derisory

---

1 Section 28 does not actually preclude discussion of same-sex attraction in schools but has been interpreted this way. Guidance – Circular 12/88 – states: 'Section 28 does not affect the activities of school governors, nor of teachers. It will not prevent the objective discussion of homosexuality in the classroom, nor the counselling of pupils concerned about their homosexuality.' Nevertheless, repeal continues to be required if this area is to become less confused in terms of people's *understanding* of the law.

nature. One of the many challenges in this area is finding even *starting points* for action and, at least, the new guidance refers to the needs of lesbian and gay young people.

Given this legal situation and given the circumstances of young people (as outlined above), what might inclusive education mean in this context? Before proceeding to such an ambitious question, I believe I need to underline aspects of the nature of schooling and the challenges we face in this area to set the *context* for an educational agenda. I also wish to underline the nature of the proposals (if proposal is not too strong a word) that I make. My ideas are tentative rather than prescriptive; I want to suggest some 'broad brush' issues for exploration as much as putting forward concrete strategies for action. Frustrating as this may be, this seems the only realistic approach in such a contested, challenging and poorly understood area. Broadly speaking I believe we need first to *understand* much more about schooling as it relates to the production of sexualities and only then can recommendations for change become more confident. This also means that any attempted change needs to be accompanied by support for the students and teachers most directly involved and also by careful research on the intended and unintended consequences of those changes.

My first general point, then, relates to the nature of education; as Epstein (*ibid.*) and many others have made clear, schools are 'a key site for the *production* of compulsory heterosexuality' (p. 3). That is, the formal and informal curricula of schools produce and reinforce versions of 'normal' (hetero)sexuality underlined by the ostracism and marginalisation accorded to the 'other' in this context (i.e. the lesbian or gay person). As Atkinson (2001) describes:

> The trouble is we *do* teach homosexuality from children's earliest experiences of school: through the absence of its representation in discussion, study, inquiry or subject-matter; through the policing and perpetuation of heterosexual norms and assumptions; and through the blind eye we turn, collectively, to heterosexist and homophobic practices. (p. 12)

Thus we have first to explore the contours of schooling that naturalise and police *hetero*sexualities and then make these contours visible. (Why are all 'relationships' assumed to be heterosexual? Why do girls play different sports to boys? Why are various forms of behaviour (being a lad) acceptable in boys but not in girls? And so on.) In this way the curriculum can open up debate about the *limitations* on heterosexual masculinities (what does it mean to be a 'real man'?) and on heterosexual femininities (how are girls schooled in being a member of the 'fairer sex'?). Then we can begin to open up understandings of the construction of *homo*sexualities, and thereby expose the ways in which *these* are produced and constrained. (What associations are made between gay men and heterosexual femininity? What associations are made between lesbians and heterosexual masculinity? Why? And so on.)

In this way we get questions about gender and about sexual *identities* onto the school agenda. The questions 'What are we?' and 'How have we come to "know" what we are?' would figure large in such an approach. In 'asserting the variety in practices, behaviour and identities which are subsumed under the title "heterosexual" ' (Jackson 1999) and under the title 'homosexual' we can perhaps find *new* ways of speaking about heterosexuality and homosexuality. Such questions need to be approached with a particular orientation, of course – they are not questions asked in the expectation of a definitive answer but, rather, questions posed in the aspiration that they provoke thinking and debate. Such attempts might begin to open up a key issue in this area. We have both to acknowledge people's desire/need/imperative to claim a sexual identity while recognising that the binary heterosexual/homosexual that drives this desire is one that needs to be undermined. In other words we have somehow to work with and outwith identity, if the choices for young people are to be extended beyond silence on the one hand and committing to an absolute, essential, committed identity on the other. This challenge is exemplified in this chapter – binary notions of sexuality have been reinforced as I have delineated the straight from the gay. And the terms 'gay', 'lesbian', 'straight' also imply a homogeneity which does not exist and reinforces ideas such that there is 'a gay lifestyle' or that young people can learn what 'it means to be gay'. What these tensions underline, of course, is that the very ways we have of talking sexuality are implicated in the versions of sexuality that we need to challenge.

A further challenge and contradiction in this area relates to the curriculum area in which change is assumed to be located, i.e. sex education. To continue to speak only of same-sex attraction in sex education is to reinforce an unfortunate elision between sexuality and sex. Opportunities in other parts of the curriculum for discussion of homosexuality (e.g. English literature) are equally important. However, it may be that those most willing to attempt the research and development required in this area already work in personal and social education. They perhaps also feel less constrained than some teachers by the Standards agenda which has come to so dominate both curricula content and pedagogical approach in British schools. As I suggested above, working in this area will call for attention to both content *and* process in equal measure. McNeill (1988) makes clear that increasing centralisation of curricula and emphasis on effectiveness measures has resulted in US teachers organising classrooms as sites of consumption rather than education. With the emphasis on content and control, education becomes reduced to the transmission of information. Addressing gender, power and the social construction of sexualities will require, of course, changes in content, but without attending to approach any significant changes in this area will continue to elude us.

In terms of content, I suggest we need a radical review of the components of sex education curricula. At present these consist, more or less, of information about conception, contraception and disease prevention. An important parallel strand of learning (curricular and extra-curricular) is in what it means to fall in love and find 'fulfilment' in a relationship. An example of an alternative orientation to the curriculum is available through processes of textual analysis and deconstruction. This could be applied, for instance, to the discourses (or languages) of love and of risk/disease. While unprotected penetrative sex is equated with 'sharing oneself' and is regarded as a sign of commitment (among both homosexual and heterosexual couples) such notions will continue to collide with advice in the area of HIV prevention and 'protection'. Through these discourses, young people learn entirely contradictory lessons about penetrative sex – it signifies trust when equated with love, but they somehow have to invoke *distrust* when observing HIV prevention advice (can you ever be sure of your partner's HIV status?). To examine the meanings of penetrative sex and why HIV prevention literature tends to consist of 'rules' (e.g. *always* use a condom), would be to acknowledge the contradictory nature of these messages. Young people need opportunities to understand the constraints there are on safer behaviour (such as the contradictions outlined above, and questions of gender and power) and begin to develop alternative ways of talking about love and safety which incorporate each other.

Of course, there are much more superficial changes which need also to take place such as adapting existing policies on bullying to include homophobic abuse. Although such changes are largely cosmetic they do signal important *principles* to students, parents and teachers and establish a context within which more fundamental changes may be contemplated. Similarly, teacher training that acknowledges the existence of lesbian and gay young people and clarifies the legal situation will contribute to changes in attitude and willingness to consider broader shifts in practice among some new teachers. Part of the problem in relation to suggesting more fundamental changes is that:

> Without radically altered sex education programmes in schools, it is unlikely that more widely held heterosexist views will ever be challenged and yet it is necessary to secure that challenge first before such programmes will be allowed. (Epstein *et al.* 2001: 7)

As I have already mentioned, the problem then becomes 'where to start'; the world needs to change before the sex education curriculum can change but the world will not change without radical changes in the sex education curriculum. My somewhat tentative response to this challenge is to recommend change on many fronts simultaneously.

It will be clear by now that my thinking about inclusive education and lesbian and gay young people does not rely on an approach that simply incorporates their needs into the mainstream. Such an approach would leave existing practices more or less unchanged except that further material on 'other' sexualities might be added onto or into the curriculum. This approach, necessarily then, is based on misunderstandings of the nature of the 'problem', for it is only in relation to changes in the *mainstream* that change appropriate to the needs of lesbian and gay young people will take place. This signals a vital first step in this area – to shift the focus *away* from those thinking about same-sex attraction and towards all students and teachers in the school.

References

Atkinson, E. (2001) *Education for Diversity in a Multisexual Society: Negotiating the Contradictions of Contemporary Discourse.* Paper presented at BERA, Leeds, September 2001.

Carson, I. (2002) 'An Inclusive Society? One young man with learning difficulties doesn't think so!' (Chapter 18 of this volume)

Department of Education and Employment (DfEE) (2000) *Sex and Relationship Guidance.* London: DfEE.

Epstein, D., O'Flynn, S. and Telford, D. (2001) *Innocence and Experience: Paradoxes in Sexuality and Education: Handbook for Lesbian and Gay Studies.* London: Sage.

Frankham, J. (1992) *Not Under My Roof: Families Talking about Sex and AIDS.* Horsham: AVERT.

Frankham, J. (1996) *Young Gay Men and HIV Infection.* Horsham: AVERT.

Frankham, J. (2001) 'The open secret: limitations on the expression of same-sex desire', *Qualitative Studies in Education* 14(4), 457–69.

Herdt, G. (1998) 'Gay and lesbian youth, emergent identities and cultural scenes at home and abroad', in P. M. Nardi and B. E. Schneider (eds), *Social Perspectives in Lesbian and Gay Studies in Education.* London: Routledge.

Jackson, S. (1999) *Heterosexuality in Question.* London: Sage.

McNeill, L. (1988) *Contradictions of Control.* London: Cassell.

Walker, P. H. (2001) 'Sexual identity, psychological well-being and suicide risk among lesbian and gay young people', *Educational and Child Psychology,* 18(1), 47–61.

Watney, S. (1991) 'Schools Out', in D. Fuss (ed.), *Inside/Out: Lesbian Theories, Gay Theories.* London: Routledge.

But teachers have successfully been borrowing from and applying psychology for years. The majority of teachers I have worked with are 'psychologically literate', and can draw upon a sophisticated knowledge base covering, for example: learning theories; child development; types of assessment; intelligence; motivation; behaviourism; listening skills; counselling; self-management; social skills; self-esteem; meta-cognition; etc.

Teachers engage with psychologists and others in talk of intervention at different levels: those that target the child; those that target the environment; and increasingly, those that invite them to reflect on their own behaviours, attitudes and expectations.

Without the luxury of a clinical setting, the benefit of a 50-minute 'therapeutic hour', or control groups with which to compare results at their disposal, teachers manage to incorporate a great many psychological tools, theories and principles into their work. The best teachers are skilled action researchers, constantly noticing and adjusting, planning, implementing and evaluating what works and with whom.

So, don't be afraid to raid this set of simple, flexible therapeutic principles. The ideas underpinning SFBT are ripe for plundering!

The 'miracle'

You could see SFBT as a set of techniques about how to do therapy. I did at first, and there was a real danger that SFBT was about to go the way of most of the other 'packages' I had been trained in: tried it for a bit; didn't use it often enough to remember or internalise it (rather like my holiday Spanish); reverted to tried and tested methods.

I was working in a secondary school. The Special Educational Needs Coordinator (SENCO) had consulted me about a Year 8 pupil, Matthew, who was disruptive, difficult to engage, verbally aggressive to other pupils and some teachers. One teacher, particularly, was concerned about this lad. The teacher felt Matthew was bright at his subject, English, and had the potential to do well. The SENCO felt she had 'run out of ideas'. The curriculum was well matched to Matthew's abilities in reading and spelling, which she had assessed, and at an appropriate interest level. The teacher was well organised, his lessons were interesting, he was popular with pupils. Matthew's parents were cooperative and supportive of school. They diligently filled in home-school diaries, praised Matthew's 'good' days, monitored his reports, talked to him, withheld privileges as agreed, attended meetings and so on. Did I think Matthew might have Attention Deficit Hyperactivity Disorder (ADHD)? Could I offer some counselling to try and understand what his problem was?

As a first step, I agreed to observe an English lesson. As expected, it was well planned and well managed. The teacher ignored the lesser excesses of Matthew's behaviour, reminded him of classroom rules, frequently 'touched base' with him, praised him when he was on task and generally employed sound behaviour management techniques. It took a lot of teacher time and energy, and still Matthew interfered with the work of others, got out of his seat, made noises, swore audibly and produced little work. Towards the end of the lesson the teacher, whom I felt had demonstrated admirable patience (maybe because I was sitting in?), raised his voice, told Matthew that his behaviour was entirely unacceptable, that he would have to report to the head of year, and that this was the fourth time in as many lessons that this had happened. Matthew retorted, 'Why don't you all just get off my back and leave me alone!' The class was dismissed, and Matthew charged out of the room, knocking a fellow pupil's books flying as he passed.

I had a chat with the teacher who, fortunately, had some non-contact time.
    'Well, what do you think?' he asked.
    I was not about to waste his time discussing more precise behaviour targets, or reinforcement schedules. This man was teaching English very competently to 26 young teenagers while being constantly irritated and having his efforts undermined. Yet he remained positive about Matthew. He was concerned and wanted to help.
    'How do you know he is bright?' I asked.
    'Well, get him talking about something he likes and he's away. Good vocabulary, develops arguments fully, articulate, imaginative.'
    'When does that happen?'
    'You know, when we finish a few minutes early, have a bit of free time, I'll kick off a discussion or get one of the kids to.'
    'And his behaviour at those times?'
    'Like talking to an intelligent, polite young adult.'

I decided I would offer to see Matthew individually, and said I would make an appointment for the next couple of weeks.
    'Any advice between now and then?' the teacher asked, 'Anything I could try?'
    'What you're doing is good, fine, but it's not working is it?' I was almost thinking aloud. 'Perhaps you could just do something different.'
    'Like what?' Before I could reply, he went on, 'Maybe I should just get off his back, try a different tack.'
    'Well, that's Matthew's suggestion. It's better than anything I can come up with at the moment!'

We met again in two weeks, prior to my appointment with Matthew. Although we had parted jokingly, I felt guilty that I had not been able to offer this teacher something more concrete and substantial, and I was not looking forward to our conversation revisiting the same set of problems.

'He's been really good, it's a bloody miracle!' the teacher enthused, 'He's a changed lad.'

'What on earth did you do?' I asked.

'Well, not much really.'

'Go on,' I prompted. I knew there was something to be learned from reflecting on this teacher's behaviour in relation to Matthew.

The next lesson after our meeting, the teacher explained, he had initiated a short private conversation with Matthew as the class took out their books, pens and so on. It went like this:

Teacher: 'See your team won again on Saturday.'

Matthew: 'What?'

T: 'I see United won again on Saturday. Did you go?'

M: 'Oh. Yeah.'

T: 'See Giggs scored.'

M: 'Sir, he is so awesome. It was a brilliant goal. He never stopped working. Did you go, sir?'

T: 'No, you can never get a ticket. Saw it on TV later.'

The whole exchange lasted less than 20 seconds. The teacher got the lesson off to a start without further ado. Within minutes he took a 'bit of a risk', in his words, and asked Matthew to read out loud a passage from a book. When he had attempted this strategy before, Matthew had showed off by changing words to make it seem rude, and adopted silly voices. This time, he read the passage straight, and accurately.

'Nice one, Matthew. Thanks.' Two seconds of praise, acknowledgement of a strength. No fuss.

The teacher kept up his good-natured, brief exchanges with Matthew throughout that week and the week after. He spotted opportunities for Matthew to demonstrate his academic strengths. Matthew's participation in lessons improved noticeably. The teacher modestly said that he had similar, occasional interactions with most pupils. He felt it important to relate to them as individuals; it was just that his exchanges with Matthew had come to be dominated by Matthew's problems.

Upon reflection soon after, I realised that what the teacher and I were doing was implementing some of the assumptions and techniques of SFBT.

1. The system involving Matthew and his teacher was 'stuck'. By invoking only a

small change, a solution was set in motion.

2. Pupils are pupils and problems are problems. The teacher made a conscious effort to let Matthew know he saw him as a person by engaging in *problem-free talk*.

3. Some of the solution was already visible. There were *exceptions* to Matthew's unacceptable behaviour, described by the teacher as their 'free time' discussions. The teacher learned from these exceptions and set the context for them to occur more frequently.

4. Matthew had a preferred vision of the future, what SFBT terms a *miracle picture*. In an almost throw-away remark, Matthew had communicated this to us: 'Why don't you all just get off my back and leave me alone!'

Matthew's case may have been the happy confluence of a little knowledge and intuition coming together in the consultation between his teacher and myself. Solutions are rarely so easy, but it rekindled my interest in SFBT. I began to see SFBT not merely as a set of therapeutic techniques, but as a way of talking with clients (teachers, parents, children, etc.) that is associated with change and solutions rather than focused on problems and deficits.

This approach has much to offer in non-therapeutic milieus such as classrooms, because it is really about the language we use and the conversations we have.

Solution focused approaches

History

The history of SFBT is well documented in the literature (e.g. O'Connell 1998). If you are interested, but do not have much time, information sheets, of usually no more than one or two sides, are available from the Brief Therapy Practice (contact details at end of chapter). I would like to acknowledge these information sheets as a major source in what follows.

I will not dwell on detail here, save to illustrate how the central tenets evolved. SFBT has its roots in family therapy, and the work of Milton Erikson. Erikson aroused interest in the therapeutic community because his approach aimed to disrupt clients' problem patterns rather than gain insight or understanding into the causes of their problems. This approach seemed to generate new possibilities for clients. Two researchers, John Weakland and Paul Watzlawick, who had happened upon Erikson's work, set up the Mental Research Institute (MRI) of Palo Alto in the United States and developed what they described as 'problem resolution brief therapy'. The idea central to this approach was that problems are maintained by clients' unsuccessful attempts at resolving them. They therefore attempted to get clients to stop doing what wasn't working and do something different instead.

Steve de Shazer further expanded the ideas developed at the MRI. De Shazer was particularly interested in the principle of finding out what clients do that works, and having them do more of it. This was the beginning of SFBT. You might recognise the work done with Matthew and his teacher in the above.

Underlying assumptions

Original sources (e.g. DeJong and Berg 1998), are written with reference to 'client' and 'therapist' or 'worker'. I will attempt here to describe the underlying assumptions, and some specific techniques of SFBT, with reference to 'pupil' and 'teacher'. In doing this I do not imply that incorporating such assumptions and techniques into classroom interactions can or should substitute for skilled therapeutic intervention as practised conventionally in a clinical setting. Rather, I wish to demonstrate that teachers may inform their practice – add to their toolkit – through an understanding and knowledge of SFBT. Through judicious and creative reflection, teachers can deploy aspects of SFBT in meeting the challenge of including children with EBD.

i) Attempting to understand the causes of a problem is not a necessary, or even useful step towards a solution.

It is human nature to try and understand why a problem is occurring. Many individual therapies devote time, effort and analysis to the search for insights into the root causes of problems. This approach is strongly influenced by scientific and medical models of rigorous assessment or diagnosis, classification and treatment. If we can find out what's wrong, we can treat it. If we can understand a problem, we will be able to generate strategies to alleviate it. But pupils' problematic behaviours seldom resemble diseases, and the factors that contribute to them are rarely as predictable as viruses and bacteria.

In their book *Interviewing for Solutions* (1998), Peter DeJong and Insoo Kim Berg describe an exercise used with groups of students undergoing training in one of the helping professions. I have used the same exercise myself with groups of teachers and trainee psychologists. Students are given a brief pen picture of Rosie, someone with a range of problems, and are then asked to collectively interview her, asking the questions they think are necessary to help. A real or imaginary pupil can easily replace Rosie if you want to try this at work. The exercise usually goes well, with students asking a lot of questions. What is interesting is the type of questions asked. They can generally be categorised as follows:

- Questions about problems
- Questions about mistakes
- Questions about causes
- Questions about feelings
- Questions about solutions

De Jong and Berg believe that even newcomers to the caring professions have 'absorbed a problem-solving approach about how best to help others'. Therefore, it is no surprise that teachers opt for this approach as the model of choice.

There is no doubt that this approach works in certain situations. But reflect for a while on the amount of time, effort and energy you have spent with pupils trying to 'get to the bottom of things': the numerous talks at break or after school; the time you've spent discussing the problem with colleagues; the hours you've given to thinking about the Matthews and Rosies at home, searching for the key to understanding that you hope will bring about a solution, a change.

Now reflect upon the product of these labours. How often have they paid dividends? Do you judge them to be the best use of your time when measured against outcomes? If you feel perhaps not, you may consider joining me in a paradigm shift. By this I mean to let go of the problem-solving model as the dominant body of theory and research that guides your practice, and adopt a solution-building approach.

ii) Successful work depends on knowing where the pupil wants to get to. Once this is established, your task is to find the quickest way there.
The pupil will have an idea of how they envisage life without the problem, and how they will know that a solution has been reached. They are likely to need help, however, in articulating their vision, and in establishing clear goals. SFBT has developed a number of useful questions to help in this process, which we will come back to in the section on 'techniques' (goal setting).

iii) However fixed a problem pattern may seem, there are always exceptions, when the pupil is doing some of the solution. The most economical way of building upon this is to have the pupil do more of 'what already works'.
This is one of the key ideas central to SFBT. In SFBT, exceptions can be seen as the beginning of a process that disintegrates the power the problem seems to wield over the pupil's, and often the teacher's, life. We will look at questions that are useful for eliciting exceptions in the 'techniques' section.

iv) Problems do not represent underlying pathology; they are just something the pupil would rather do without. In most cases, then, the pupil will be the best judge of when the problem has been resolved.
Obviously, certain behaviours may be caused by organic conditions; abuse; or substance abuse, for example. These should be investigated thoroughly and appropriately where evidence suggests they may contribute to a pupil's behaviour. The main point here, though, is that labels such as 'conduct disorder' and 'disaffection' do not necessarily provide effective guidance for working with pupils. The time and effort spent in trying to assess or diagnose them could be used to build solutions.

v) Only the smallest of changes may be necessary to set in motion a solution to the problem. Since change in one part of a system leads to change in other parts it is not necessary to gather exhaustive information from all those associated with the pupil.
Do something different. This is technically known as a 'pattern intervention'. They can be surprisingly effective. One teacher, who had been operating a whole-class behaviour management system, told me that the class never earned enough merits to get their 'crisps and cola' party on Friday afternoon. After a particularly bad day, she thought she might treat herself to a long bath, some chocolates and a glass of wine that night to make up for it. She reflected that if she felt that way, the kids might, too. She impulsively shared with the class that it had been a horrid day, and maybe they should just treat themselves and start anew tomorrow. The long strived for crisps and cola came out of the storeroom, and they treated themselves, chatted about everything but problem behaviour, and went home with smiles on their faces. The next day the class were great.

A technique of SFBT that helps pupils identify small changes they feel confident they can make is 'scaling'. Scaling questions will be reviewed in the next section.

vi) It is the teacher's role to determine the pupil's unique way of cooperating with solution building, and to empathise and work with this. This is a more useful approach than describing lack of progress as 'resistance', for example, as this impedes the development of cooperation between pupil and teacher.
The teacher must acknowledge and mobilise the child's resources, nurturing them so that the child feels empowered to take control of the problem and build solutions.

Techniques

The only way to really get to grips with the techniques of SFBT, and to discover ways of using them in your classroom, is to go on a training course and practise often! Even then, don't get hung up on the wording of 'the miracle question' or scaling questions and think it's too complicated, as I did. Integrate its principles into your practice, as you do so many other knowledge bases. You will not do harm if you use it sensitively, and certainly cause less distress than repeatedly focusing on problems, which can be actively unhelpful to pupils who will come to see themselves as 'problems', and whose self-esteem will be damaged.

I promised to describe some of the techniques employed in SFBT in order to 'flesh out' the principles described above.

Pre-session change

Not mentioned so far, but an interesting and powerful agent for change in a therapeutic context. Something happens the moment a client decides to take action about a problem. They become active in relation to the problem, and a process of change is underway. So, in the first session, a therapist would usually ask something like, 'What differences have you noticed between requesting an appointment and coming here today?'

In schools, pupils may not often self-select for help with problems and problem behaviour, though it has been known. Some schools employ counsellors, or have 'quiet places' to which pupils can self-refer. Many teachers will have experienced pupils approaching them 'to talk'.

With a seemingly intransigent pupil exhibiting severe behavioural problems, though, what can we draw from this technique? You are probably ahead of me in thinking that maybe the head teacher, head of year, or whoever, rather than dealing with the problem on the hoof could arrange a future appointment with the pupil a couple of days hence and propose to the child that they will try to find solutions to the problem behaviours then. This should not be posed as a threat, but an undertaking to do work. It would be legitimate in this case to ask the pupil, 'What differences have there been in your behaviour between (Monday) and today?' Chances are that there may have been changes for which the pupil is totally responsible, and thus we are tapping into the pupil's resources already. We can follow up with exploratory questions such as, 'How did you manage that?' and acknowledge the resources the pupil has in finding solutions to the problem.

Problem-free talk

There is always a danger that we will address the problem rather than the person. In so doing we run the risk of losing sight of the pupil's skills, competencies, resources and strengths. We need to connect with these to bring about solutions. Nobody ever got better by exploring his or her deficits.

Problem-free talk is not about discussing the weather before launching into an exploration of the shortcomings of the person. It is about actively listening to what the pupil's interests, strengths and skills are. One teacher I worked with discovered, simply by asking what kind of morning a boy had had so far, that he had been up at 6 a.m. to take the dogs for a walk, then done a paper round before breakfast, and got to school on time. She acknowledged and mentally noted his resources and strengths in accomplishing this. He was organised, had energy and commitment. He could manage his time. Not surprisingly, when pupils are made aware that we know there is more to them than the sum of problem behaviours they present to us, they seem freer to talk about what they wish to change.

Exception finding

No unacceptable behaviour, or problems experienced by teachers in relation to pupils' behaviour, happens all the time. There are always times when part of the solution is happening. Questions that can help in eliciting exceptions might be:

- Tell me about when it's not happening.
- Tell me about when it happens less.
- When does it bother you least?
- When do you control the urge to . . .?

These contrast with frequently asked questions that put pupils on the spot, such as

- Why did you do that?
- You do know the school rules, don't you?
- How do you think the rest of us feel when you behave like that?

Such questions rarely provide insights and guidance as to ways forward upon which we can act. Most pupils cannot reply, or give monosyllabic answers. They know they are not really being engaged in finding a way forward, but feel they are being berated.

Exception-finding questions offer hope, and propose an agenda of belief that solutions already exist and can be built upon. To develop a prescription for action, though, once exceptions have been identified you might need to put flesh on the bones by asking further questions such as:

- What are you doing differently at those exception times?
- What are others around you doing differently?

Goal setting

If work towards solutions is to be brief, and empowering for pupils, then goals must be clear and meaningful. This can be achieved by involving pupils actively in setting those goals. SFBT has developed a framework of questions that are facilitative in this respect:

- How will you know that this plan has worked?
- How will you know that this problem is over?
- How will your parents know that it is OK to stop worrying?
- How will Mr Lonsdale know when the aggression problem is solved?
- If you went home tonight and a miracle happened while you were asleep, so that these problems were resolved, how would you know when you woke up? What would be different? What would you be doing differently? What would others be doing differently that would make you think a miracle had happened?

The 'miracle question' and other goal-setting questions unlock energy and allow the pupil to entertain a world in which the problem no longer exists, a preferred future. This is not mere fantasy, however, and supplementary conversations with pupils can make the miracle more concrete:

- Who would be the first to notice a miracle had happened?
- What would they notice first?

If the pupil is sceptical about a miracle happening, you can ask how confident they are about the possibility of a 'miracle' happening, or what they would settle for instead that would be good enough.

Goal-setting questions kick off conversations with pupils that allow them to envisage, inhabit and explore a future without the problem. You have to help them understand what it would be like, what they would be doing and what others would be doing. Through this they define clear and meaningful goals for change.

Scaling

Scaling questions are a very flexible tool in solution focused work. They enable change to be measured and provide feedback to the pupil about her or his ability to change and move forward. They are useful in identifying exceptions and goals:

- On a scale of 0–10, with 0 representing the worst that things have been and 10 the way you want them to be, where are you today?
- What are you doing that means you are at (3) and not 0? (Very few pupils ever say they are at 0; if they do you can ask them how they are managing to come to school and talk with you when things are so bad. You are actively seeking out the pupil's resources and strengths.)
- So, if you're at 3, tell me what you will be doing when you know you're at 4.
- How will things be when you're at 10?
- So what have you been doing to move up two points since last week?

Conclusion

There are those who caution against using solution focused approaches with children who have suffered rejection and loss, and we should heed their warnings. It would be entirely inappropriate in a classroom setting to elicit the preferred future of a bereaved child, a child who has been taken into care, a child who has suffered abuse or a child caught up in an acrimonious divorce. They are likely to answer that they want their parent(s) back. And then what do you do?

But what do you do anyway? Act as if nothing were wrong? Tell them you are always there if they want to talk? So long as you are honest in saying to the child that you cannot change things outside school, you can engage them in finding solutions for problems in school.

One teacher who had attended several training courses in SFBT wanted to talk with me about a child who had been placed in foster care. The child's behaviour was causing problems. She was bullying and being bullied. She was refusing to work, and running out of class. We decided that the teacher would talk with the child and explain that while she could not help with the situation at home, she wanted to help with things at school, to make matters better.

By setting the parameters within which solution focused work could occur, solutions began to emerge and the bullying began to resolve. This teacher had not, and could not have, solved all the young girl's problems, but she had made a difference that benefited the girl, her classmates and the teacher herself. The girl began to be reincluded in the life of the school. She was not excluded, as happens to so many children taken into care.

SFBT in its purest form is effective in addressing the most challenging social behavioural problems. There is a substantial body of literature supporting its efficacy in dealing with families and individuals beset by drug abuse, crime, marital problems and the stresses of caring for dependents. Thus, we need to engage and interact with it. It represents a growing body of research-based knowledge which teachers can adapt in meeting the challenge of including all children in mainstream schools.

Information source

Trainers and sources of information in SFBT:

Brief Therapy Practice
4d Shirland Mews
London
W9 3DY

Solutions@brieftherapy.org.uk
www.brieftherapy.org.uk

References

Ainscow, M. (2001) *Understanding the Development of Inclusive Schools.* Conference proceedings, Manchester University.

Cassidy, S. (2001) 'Time to open a new set of doors', *The Independent,* 10 May 2001.

Centre for Studies on Inclusive Education (CSIE) (2000) *Index for Inclusion: Developing Learning and Participation in Schools.* Bristol: Centre for Studies on Inclusive Education.

DeJong, P. and Berg, I. K. (1998) *Interviewing for Solutions.* Pacific Grove, CA: Brooks/Cole.

Hayden, C. and Dunne, S. (2001) *Outside Looking In: Children's and Families' Experiences of Exclusion from School.* London: The Children's Society.

O'Connell, B. (1998) *Solution Focused Therapy.* London: Sage.

Rosenholtz, S. (1989) *Teachers' Workplace: The Social Organisation of Schools.* London: Longman.

Senge, P. M. (1989) *The Fifth Discipline: The Art and Practice of the Learning Organisation.* London: Century.

CHAPTER 9

Can nurture groups facilitate inclusive practice in primary schools?

Andy Howes, Judith Emanuel and Peter Farrell

How can schools change so that children who can be identified early on as likely to fail can learn to succeed? In many LEAs, nurture groups are being explored as one answer to this question. In this chapter, we investigate nurture groups as an example of a pragmatic inclusion strategy, looking to see under what circumstances they may constitute a school development that helps staff and children to accommodate each others' needs, a form of early intervention that enables more children to participate fully in mainstream classrooms. We draw on case studies of nurture groups set up recently in different LEAs.

There is a great deal of interest in nurture groups at the moment, and practitioners with substantial experience are involved in sharing good practice through courses and over the Internet (http://www.nurturegroups.org/). Nurture groups have been acknowledged in the Green Paper *Excellence for All Children* (DfEE 1997) as a promising approach to early intervention for children with social and emotional difficulties (Cooper, Arnold and Boyd 2000), whose developmental level puts them at risk of failure in mainstream class.

The original model, called the 'Boxall model', consists of classes of 10–12 pupils, aged 4–6 in mainstream schools, staffed by a teacher and learning support assistant. Children usually attend the nurturing group full-time while registering with their classes and joining the class for some activities. Children rejoin their classes after between two and four terms. Other models of nurture groups have also been developed some involving older children (Cooper *et al.* 2000).

Nurture groups start where children are at emotionally and place emphasis on the individual needs of the child, the involvement of parents and the rest of the school. Over the course of approximately one year children in nurture groups have the opportunity to go through development stages they are thought to have missed. The underlying theory supporting the concept of nurture groups is attachment theory (Bennathan and Boxall 2000). The model assumes that the child's problem stems from not having developed emotional security and social skills due to not having had the opportunity for 'normal attachment' to adults in preschool years. An opportunity to build trusting relationships with adults is provided by two adults working cooperatively in a learning environment that is homely, which can help to build up the child's social and emotional capacity to operate and learn successfully within the mainstream school. If successful, the nurture group enables children to avoid a route through school leading to exclusion and permanent EBD provision, with all the potentially damaging consequences for life chances that route involves.

On a day-to-day basis though, a nurture group is not an inclusive mode of provision. Children are withdrawn each day from their mainstream class over a long period of time, separated from peers whose potentially positive influence on them is thereby reduced. The formation of a separate group which interacts little with peers may lead to labelling and a perception by the rest of the school that they are a group of children whose behaviour warrants their isolation. The nurture group may reduce the sense of responsibility of other staff to reflect on and adapt their classrooms and teaching styles in the light of the needs of the children they work with. In a mixed-age class with such a range of learning and behavioural needs, the National Curriculum might prove too demanding.

There is therefore a legitimate tension surrounding the development of such provision in a school. As staff in a school begin to recognise that they are unsuccessfully meeting the needs of some of the children in the locality, the opening of a nurture group is not in itself an answer. But can it be part of the answer, and if so, how? That is the question which we explore now through three case studies, each of which describes something of the context of the nurture group, shows how basic principles have been interpreted in practice in that context and focuses on a particular aspect of the process of learning.

The nurture group in context: three case studies

Case study I – a learning opportunity

The first case study describes how a school as a whole is systematically learning to better meet the needs of children in the local community through the development of a nurture group. The setting is a small community school hidden away in the middle of an estate of largely council-owned maisonettes. About 40 per cent of pupils are known to qualify for free school meals, and a significant proportion of families experience a high level of stress; nearly all are white. The nurture group here was established in February 2001, one of several measures designed by the school and LEA to strengthen the school itself to meet the needs of its community. There are also plans to better utilise the school site for community facilities.

The school has been through a difficult period in recent years. Early in 1999 it went into special measures with whole-school weaknesses mainly involving management, behaviour and progress in learning; the staff were very demoralised. In September 1999 the intake in reception was just 12. Following the appointment of a new head teacher, the LEA made available considerable support for the school, including the temporary provision of a school improvement teacher, additional classroom assistants and funding to re-equip the nursery/Year 1 classroom. The school came out of special measures following HMI's visit in summer 2000. Amid the celebrations, the head and LEA staff looked for ways to shore up the transformation, and agreed to the allocation of Standards Fund money for the development of a nurture group. The governors agreed, and a working party was established with governors, educational psychologist, school improvement officer, head teacher and a university researcher involved with the school in action research. In developing a policy document, the team borrowed heavily from literature from Enfield and Cambridge, and the group was established in line with the model developed by Bennathan and Boxall (2000). A light and airy room was allocated to the group, and equipped with lounge, kitchen and dining areas as well as several locations for play.

Before the nurture group was established, there had been a sense of frustration from Key Stage 2 staff that it would not involve children whose needs they were finding it difficult to meet. In addition, parents of some children at the school had expressed concern that the group would be stigmatising. One term after the opening, however, the nurture group is increasingly being seen by other staff as a school resource, and the attitude of parents, both of children who are in the group and those who are not, has been extremely positive. Significantly, the nurture group teacher is also assistant deputy head, and has established strong working relationships with staff and parents.

Nine children from reception to Year 2 attend the nurture group for nine sessions a week. The staff have created a learning environment which is attractive, stimulating and continually changing. They rapidly developed and embedded a range of positive behaviour strategies, creating an enthusiastic and cohesive social group by emphasising positive interactions, such as inviting children to give stickers to another child who has been nice to them. The group has breakfast together, in line with the model, and the rich interactions around the table are evidence of how all members of the group are learning to participate. But the creation of a group has some unintended consequences; staff have noticed how the boys tend to act as a gang on the playground, their mutual support sometimes exacerbating minor conflicts. This problem has been alleviated by moving some older boys to the Key Stage 2 playground that they will use next year.

The head teacher has created a forum for reflective learning from the establishment of the nurture group with a monthly meeting involving the nurture group staff, the head, university staff from Manchester, the teacher from whose class most of the children come, the governor with responsibility for SEN and a parent governor. In this forum, the effect of the nurture group on the school at large is under scrutiny. A video has been made which shows children and staff in the group engaged in the main activities of the day, and includes interviews with staff from whose classes the children come. This has proved to be an effective and relatively non-threatening way of stimulating reflection among the school staff. As an example, the practice of affirming positive behaviour was mentioned in one video interview, and this has become an area of whole-school policy development involving the whole staff.

Plans to increase collaboration between the Key Stage 1 teachers were made at the meeting in April 2001, so that responsibility for differentiated lesson plans is now shared between them. Reflection on progress in June provoked a discussion of the nurture group curriculum, and a policy decision to give priority to the affective curriculum at the expense of covering literacy and numeracy at the speed of other classes where necessary. The nurture group is becoming a within-school case study of educational practice and priority in this context, to the potential benefit of all marginalised children in the school.

Case study II – the nurture group as a nurturing resource

The second case study relates to a school where concerns about inclusion have led to changes in the organisation of the nurture group, in particular a move from full- to part-time provision. This case study started when the nurture project had been running for two months and ended when it had been running for six months.

The school is a two-form entry infants school in a predominantly white inner-city area. Approximately 70 per cent of children are entitled to free school meals and 30 per cent are on the SEN register. The area has a regeneration project and the Standards Fund administered through the LEA and the regeneration project jointly provided the funding for the nurture group. The staffing includes a teacher, a learning support assistant and a playworker to cover dinner times.

The school's bid for a nurture group was accepted in September 2000 and they were advised to set up as quickly as possible. Staff were recruited and the room set up in November 2000 with limited information about nurture projects, no LEA guidelines and before training was available. The school had considerable autonomy in setting up the group and worked closely with two other schools setting up nurture provision in the local area and officers from the LEA and regeneration project.

The initial focus was to reduce exclusions, to improve achievement in the school as a whole and, in regard to the group, to improve the behaviour, learning, attendance and punctuality of the children selected so as to ultimately reintegrate them into their classes. Initially four boys were selected to join the group on a full-time basis. It was soon recognised that the aim of freeing up teachers from children whose behaviour was demanding of time and energy had some negative effects. 'Difficult' children selected for the nurture group were in danger of becoming the 'responsibility' of the nurture group staff. This was not seen to be in line with the ethos of nurturing projects or inclusion and would make reintegration to mainstream classes harder.

The nurture group teacher supported by the head teacher and other staff was able to reflect on this and she adapted her role and work accordingly. Both she and the teachers in the two other schools with the support of the LEA and regeneration officer decided to move to part-time provision at the beginning of 2001. After six months there were two groups with boys and girls, one with five children and the second with seven, and it is anticipated that the numbers will continue to increase. Part-time provision has meant that more children could be involved, and made it possible to separate them from particular peers where this has made for a more constructive experience. It also meant that mainstream teachers had a greater involvement with the children while they were in the nurture group thereby maintaining responsibility for them, and hopefully this will reduce problems in relation to reintegration.

The nurture group teacher has made it a strong priority to make the school community feel that the nurture group is a resource for everyone through a range of activities. She runs nurture group provision for seven sessions a week and 11 of the 12 children attend half these sessions and one all of them. One session a week is dedicated to joint activities with mainstream classes; for example, the nurture group and reception performed plays for each other; and there is a weekly design and technology class for one mainstream class including nurture group children from that class and staff. One afternoon a week was set aside for 'Star of the Week' from each class and a friend. It is hoped through this that every child in the school will have an opportunity to spend time in the nurture room and there will be no stigma attached to children who spend time in the room.

At the time the study ended, children in the group no longer need constant supervision at playtime, although a member of nurture group staff continues to do playground duty providing support to children in the nurture group as and when it is needed. The role of the playworker was extended. She runs a midday club in the nurture room two days a week for six children identified by teachers and lunch-time organisers on the basis of incident sheets, in order to prevent more serious problems developing. The groups are coordinated by the nurture group teacher and this ensures liaison between her and the Senior Lunchtime Organiser. Some attend once and others twice weekly.

The nurture group teacher has also run INSET sessions for other staff and developed handbooks for them, informing them about nurture groups. Interviews with a teacher and the head teacher suggested that their understanding had changed as the nurture groups had changed. The nurture group teacher is increasingly seen as a role model and as having an advisory role in terms of behaviour management. The nurture room was seen as a place where strategies could be developed for each child which could then be carried out in the classroom.

Case study III – a shared nurture group

This group was set up in an infants school in October 2000 with funding from the Standards Fund, and is staffed by a teacher and two teaching assistants. In one key respect it differs from the Boxall model and the first two case studies, in that pupils from all over the borough are eligible to attend, and indeed all but one of the pupils come from schools some distance away. All pupils attend the group on a half-time basis. One group attends in the morning and one in the afternoon. After going to their local mainstream school for registration, the morning group are collected by taxi and brought to the school housing the nurture group. The children return to their mainstream school in the afternoon.

Schools wishing to refer a pupil have to provide information to an admissions panel that meets at least once a term. This comprises the nurture group teacher, the Principal Educational Psychologist, a SENCO, the manager of the behavioural support team and the Principal Special Educational Needs Officer. Having agreed to admit a pupil, the nurture group teacher visits him or her in their mainstream school and completes the Boxall Profile with the child's teacher. All pupils are expected to be at the School Action Plus stage (previously Stage 3) of the Code of Practice.

HMI have reported on the excellent quality of the work in the group in the recent Ofsted report on the infants school in which it is based. The structure of the half day is familiar to the pupils and seems to have a calming effect on them. Their behaviour and emotions can be extremely volatile, but they seem to value the support given by the staff, who are forever on the lookout for opportunities to praise and encourage them. There is an Action Plan for the management of the group as a whole and detailed individual education plans for each of the pupils, with graphs that clearly display each pupil's progress.

Every Wednesday afternoon nurture group staff each visit a different mainstream school to talk to staff and to work with the nurture group child. This helps them to maintain contact with the mainstream school attended by the children and to get a first-hand picture of their behaviour and learning within that setting. Almost daily written communication takes place between the staff in the group and the mainstream school, which greatly helps to coordinate work plans. Generally staff in the mainstream schools considered that the liaison between them and the nurture group staff was excellent. They appreciated the notes and comments that were communicated on a daily basis, and they felt that the staff in the group were approachable and willing to offer advice on their visits. Effective liaison was facilitated by the fact that the nurture group teacher is well known and respected among teachers in the borough.

Most of those involved in supporting these pupils consider that they already have major emotional and behavioural difficulties. Although the aim is for eight pupils to attend each session, numbers were much smaller than this in the first few months, three in the morning and two in the afternoon although recently the numbers have grown slightly. Up to now the majority of pupils have been in Year 2 and hence will shortly move on to a junior school. There is one Year 1 child who attends in the morning and a reception pupil in the afternoon group.

It is possible that when the group was first established, schools understandably referred their most seriously disturbed pupils; many come from families where there has been a history of problems. Their behaviour suggests that they are extremely insecure, uncertain of themselves and of their abilities; they have major difficulties in making relationships, they are prone to display temper tantrums and they can be excessively violent. The nurture group teacher felt that the balance of the group was wrong – 'too much B (behavioural disturbance) and not enough E (emotional problems)'.

Perhaps not surprisingly, staff in the mainstream schools were extremely positive about the provision. Essentially they felt that the group provided a breathing space for the mainstream class as it allowed them to get on with the business of teaching the rest of their pupils without having to manage an extremely disturbed child at the same time. They then felt able to incorporate the pupil for the remaining half-day session although this still caused some problems for them and the rest of the pupils. Staff also appreciated the skills and abilities of the nurture group staff and felt that they were able to offer helpful suggestions about how to work with the pupils.

Given that the group has only been in operation a few months, it is difficult to draw firm conclusions as to pupils' progress. There are encouraging indications from Boxall profiles that were completed four months from the start of the group, but pupils continue to demand very sensitive and skilled handling from the staff and it appears extremely unlikely that they will be able to resettle into their mainstream class when they enter Year 3 next year, without further specialised help. It is more probable that they will need support for many years and the LEA are establishing alternative mainstream-based provision.

The LEA has learnt from this first year. In future, pupils admitted to the group will not include such a concentration of disturbed children, and they will be younger, from reception or Year 1, allowing more time for the intervention to be effective.

What can we learn from these three examples of nurture groups?

Reflecting on the experience represented by these case studies, we revisit the question: can nurture groups facilitate inclusive practice in primary schools? The following table summarises some of the key points from the three case studies and suggests a number of topics which deserve careful attention in considering the development of a nurture group as a means to more inclusive practice.

Table 9.1 The three nurture group case studies

	Case study 1	Case study 2	Case study 3
Provision	full-time	full- becoming part-time	part-time
Institutional intake	children from one school only	children from one school only	children from all over the LEA
Size	9 children	5 and 7 children and planning to increase	3 and 2 children (a.m./p.m.)
Age	mainly Years 1 and 2	mainly Years 1 and 2	mainly Year 2
Links with mainstream teachers	daily (staff room) and monthly meeting	daily (staff room)	structured weekly visits
Key learning points to date	value of systematic reflection by school staff for developing collaboration	part-time as a means of increasing whole-school involvement and minimising the difficulty of reintegration into mainstream class	consequences of referring very disturbed children to the group
Funding	external and fixed-term	external and fixed-term	external and fixed-term

The most central issue that is relevant to the impact of nurture groups concerns the extent to which all staff are involved, in particular the links that exist between the staff and students who work in the nurture group and the rest of the school. Case studies show how setting up and maintaining a nurture group can involve the development of whole-school policy and practice to the benefit of a large number of staff and children, although this is far more difficult where more than one school sends children to the group.

If the nurture group is not properly connected into the school, it potentially faces an unintended consequence of any isolated social group: labelling of the members of that group by those outside it. The concern has been expressed that children in nurture groups could be seen by their peers and by staff in the mainstream class as naughty children, such that the group acts as a 'sin bin' for the school.

Where whole-school development is possible, case studies demonstrate that it can extend to areas of curriculum planning, staff learning new approaches to behaviour management and positive discipline, and the development of a more positive attitude towards families under stress and the children. Important, practical and sometimes sensitive issues may come to the fore through such whole-school dialogue. Through observations of nurture group practice, the issue of physical contact with children (occasional hugs etc.) has been raised in one of these schools and discussed among the whole staff for the first time, aware as they are both of children's need for such reassurance and affection, and of the extreme caution needed to avoid any possibility of sexual abuse.

Is there an ideal composition for a nurture group, in relation to inclusion? Three interrelated factors are relevant here: the size of the group, the age of the children and the mixture of emotional and behavioural difficulties they present. The small group in case study III could not be larger, given the level of disturbance that these particular children bring to the group; but it is at least uncertain that they can be resettled into full-time mainstream provision, which is the test of an effective nurture group. The first two case studies give some indication of a manageable range of size for children, the majority of whom are expected to resettle into their classes.

In respect of age, if the Boxall model of two to four terms is adhered to, children should have ideally entered the nurture group in Year 1, even if this implies that children have not reached Stage 3 (School Action Plus) of the SEN Code of Practice. Younger children appear to benefit most from the nurture group; moreover, they will thereby leave the group before Year 3, avoiding further complications with transition arrangements into the Key Stage 2 curriculum and wider social group.

Another issue raised through the comparison of groups is an opportunity cost of the nurture group: what do children lose out on through long periods of full-time separation from their peer group who can cope in the large class? On the other hand, if part-time provision is adopted as a compromise, what evidence is there that this reduced intensity of input can be effective in addressing their needs? At present, we do not know enough about how nurture groups work in practice to be able to provide a reasoned answer to this question: a long-term research study will be necessary to learn more about the psychological states of individual children, or the composition of the social groups for whom nurture groups can be effective. At present it could be argued that attachment theory, on which nurture groups are based, is little more than a theoretical fig leaf to cover the absence of adequate explanations of the effect of nurture group membership.

These case studies also raise the issue of resourcing. As the table indicates, funding for these groups is external to the school, largely from the LEAs' Standards Fund. In certain contexts, nurture groups might be a useful temporary provision through which teachers, head, support staff and community regain confidence that a school can effectively provide educational opportunity for all the children in the local community, in which case temporary funding would be appropriate. In other cases though, the loss of an established nurture group may be a severe loss to a school's capacity to meet community needs. If nurture groups are not to be simply another educational fad of yesteryear, then schools and LEAs must look beyond the immediate financial horizon and put arrangements in place to secure the sustainability of nurture group funding.

Perhaps the key issue for a school considering a nurture group can be summed up in the question: who is being expected to change as a result of this initiative? A pragmatic, inclusive answer might be both children and staff: children in respect of their ability to cope with the demands of the mainstream curriculum in a large class, and mainstream staff in respect of their ability to reduce those demands for vulnerable children through their effective management of the classroom environment. If a nurture group is a means to achieving these changes, it should be judged a triumph.

References

Bennathan, M. and Boxall, M. (2000) *Effective Interventions in Primary Schools: Nurture Groups* (2nd edn). London: David Fulton Publishers.

Bishop, A. and Swain, J. (2000) 'The bread, the jam and some coffee in the morning – perceptions of a nurture group', *Emotional and Behavioural Difficulties* 5(3).

Cooper, P., Arnold, R. and Boyd, E. (1999) *The Nature and Distribution of Nurture Groups in England and Wales.* The Nurture Group Project, University of Cambridge, School of Education.

Cooper, P., Arnold, R. and Boyd, E. (2000) 'The Rise and Rise of Nurture Groups', University of Cambridge, School of Education Newsletter, No. 6.

Department for Education and Employment (DfEE) (1997) *Excellence for All Children: Meeting Special Educational Needs.* London: DfEE.

Enfield Education Group (1999) *Nurture Groups in Enfield: Policy and Operational Guidelines.*

Lucas, S. (2000) 'The nurturing school: the impact of nurture group principles and practice on the whole school', *Emotional and Behavioural Difficulties* 4(3).

The Nurture Group Project (2000) *Meeting the Needs of Young Children with EBD: The Role of Nurture Groups,* University of Cambridge, School of Education. http://www.educ.cam.ac.uk/nurture/brochure.html (21/11/00)

CHAPTER 10

The impact of domestic violence on children: implications for schools

Anne Rushton

Lucy – a pupil

A secondary school was in the middle of a critical incident. One of the pupils, Lucy we will call her, was in hospital having taken an almost lethal cocktail of tablets. The school's child protection coordinator was reproaching herself for not doing more for Lucy and her mother whom she had learned was experiencing escalating domestic violence perpetrated by Lucy's father. Lucy had shared something of what was happening at home with this teacher and there had been a three-way discussion between Lucy, her mother and teacher in which different strategies to tackle the abuse had been discussed. Lucy's mother, however, was reluctant to confront her partner's behaviour for fear of reprisals. Lucy's teacher was becoming increasingly anxious, as the impact on Lucy was so obvious to see in her behaviour and academic performance in school.

In the event, child protection deliberations were overshadowed by the overdose incident. The teacher visited Lucy in hospital and was struck by Lucy's apparently light mood considering the ordeal of the previous two days. After a little gentle probing, Lucy described the coming round from unconsciousness to see her father sitting at her bedside. He was in floods of tears and begging her to forgive him, promising her that he would never lay a finger on her mother again . . . and Lucy believed him.

Introduction

The exposure of children and young people to domestic violence can have a major impact on development and learning. It can also affect children's capacity to participate fully and be included in school life. Hence the issue is important for schools that wish to develop more inclusive policies and practices.

Children gauge the level of threat to them by the reactions of significant others. If they come to realise that adults cannot, or do not, choose to protect them, the next logical step is to find ways to protect themselves. Garbarino (1999), writing about why boys become violent, observes that maltreated children often develop externalising survival strategies that are antisocial and/or self-destructive, yet the underpinning emotion is fear. Similarly, Dodge, Pettit and Bates (1997) found that children who are maltreated are much more likely than non-maltreated children to develop a chronic pattern of challenging behaviour. However, not all children in their study became violent. Being maltreated teaches children to adapt their behaviour and thinking to the harsh fact that the adults who are caring for them are the same people who can hurt, neglect, terrorise, ignore, isolate, corrupt, degrade and exploit them and those they love. Children in this situation learn how the social world works through the lens of their abuse and in the case of domestic violence, also through watching others suffer.

Two decades of research, now extensively reviewed (Kolbo, Blakely and Engelman 1996; Margolin 1998; Kashani and Allan 1998; Hughes and Graham-Bermann 1998; Edelson 1999) on children's experience of witnessing domestic violence normally perpetrated on their mother by her partner/spouse has provided clear evidence of a negative impact on behavioural, emotional and cognitive functioning in exposed children. It affects attitudes and children's long-term outlook on life.

Domestic violence manifests itself as a series of painful and often confusing interactions between key people in a child's inner circle with unpredictable and highly traumatic episodes generating feelings of terror, loss, helplessness and inevitably extreme stress. The connection between the terrifying act of assaulting a mother and emotional abuse of her children has become increasingly apparent (Hart and Brassard 1990; Rossman and Rosenberg 1997; Rossman, Hughes and Rosenberg 2000). The effect has been compared to that observed in children exposed to war (Terr 1991; Herman 1992; Black, Newman, Mezey and Harris Hendriks 1995) where the ongoing and unpredictable nature of the traumatic events so powerfully impacts on a child's development. The difference between domestic violence and war is in its existence within the intimacy of a child's family life.

Lucy's teachers had observed that Lucy was increasingly distant in class. She was often observed staring into space and she had to be frequently returned into the lesson. She was failing to complete tasks in class and to hand in homework. Lucy was often found loitering in the toilets and she had several times left the school in the middle of the day. When apprehended, her reaction could be unpredictable. On one occasion, she started shouting at the teacher and the shouts became screams. It took two members of staff an hour to calm her down.

At this point, she talked about what was happening at home.

Long and Fogell (1999) state:

> Schools have a central role to play in supporting all children through adverse and difficult events. Our task in school is to make a difference where we can make a difference. It is not always possible or appropriate for a class teacher to work with children's families. We do not have the power to change their home circumstances but we can ensure that the school environment is emotionally supportive for all children, and especially those who are most vulnerable. (p. 26)

This chapter looks further at the nature of domestic violence; describes research evidence of the impact of living with domestic violence on children's development and emotional well-being; and considers how inclusive schools might respond to the significant negative consequences on pupils' educational performance and behaviour of exposure while contributing to their resilience and future mental health.

Domestic violence: the picture

Definition

Hester, Pearson and Harwin (2000) define domestic violence as:

> . . . any violent or abusive behaviour (whether physical, sexual, psychological, emotional, verbal, financial, etc.) which is used by one person to control and dominate another with whom they have or have had a relationship. (p. 14)

Woman's Aid Federation England (WAFE) (1992) offer a more gendered version, recognising the high level of perpetration by men on their female partners (over 90–95 per cent of reported cases) and point out that domestic violence is not necessarily inherently *physically* violent. WAFE cites threats, intimidation, manipulation, isolation, keeping a woman locked in, deprived of food and money, or using (and abusing) her children in various ways to frighten her or force compliance as typical strategies utilised by male perpetrators.

Prevalence

The UK has no national data concerning the extent of domestic violence (Hester *et al.* 2000; McGee 2000) but findings from the British Crime Surveys (Mirrlees-Black 1995) concentrating on the physical aspect of perpetration and other criminal dimensions such as stalking and rape, indicate that abuse of women by their male partners is widespread. In some relationships, onset of violence may occur at the point of marriage, when the partner becomes pregnant or during the divorce/separation phase of a relationship. Domestic violence, in fact, contributes to a significant number of divorces, very often continuing and even escalating after the divorce/separation and domestic violence is often present in the lead-up to the murder of a female partner (De Becker 1997).

Estimates of the prevalence of domestic violence suggest that one in nine or ten women experience the impact of domestic violence (Mirrlees-Black 1995; Stanko *et al.* 1998). However, much domestic violence remains hidden and therefore fails to be recorded. In addition, not all disclosed domestic violence is deemed to amount to the commission of a criminal offence (Hester *et al.* 2000) regardless of the implications for those on the receiving end.

There is evidence of interpersonal violence in some same-sex relationships, of women being violent towards their male partners and of two-way violence in heterosexual couples. However, research (e.g. Nazroo 1995) suggests that there are qualitative gender differences in the way violence is used in relationships. Male violence is much more likely to lead to serious injury and to generate high levels of stress in the home. It is also more often associated with strategically applied power and control tactics that generate fear, confusion and degradation in the recipient.

Children's exposure to domestic violence

Women often report that their reasons for staying in an abusive relationship are related to fear for their safety and that of their children. The intimidation over time and the lack of opportunity to validate experiences outside the family can lead to immobilisation and a belief that there are no alternatives. Conversely, other women report that a reason for leaving an abusive relationship is their children's safety and well-being. The presence of children in a family makes women more vulnerable to domestic violence and many children are present or in the next room when abuse is perpetrated (Hughes 1992).

Abusers have a profound impact on the emotional climate in which children grow up and the presence of domestic violence is predictive of a prevailing parental style where power-control dynamics predominate. Abusers very often appear not to be aware of, or care about, the cost to their children of the ongoing experience.

Lucy's father had intermittently abused her mother for many years. Lucy's mother recalls that the first time was when he kicked her in the stomach on discovering that she was pregnant with Lucy. Lucy told her teacher that her dad was unpredictable:

> **'Sometimes he is great fun and then when it's not going his way, he just turns nasty. He calls my mum awful things and pushes her about. Once she made him a really nice meal and he said she was wearing too much make-up, so he threw the meal at her.'**

McGee (2000) highlights that children experience domestic violence in a range of ways including being abused themselves. There are strong links between domestic violence and physical abuse of children and some evidence that the more severe the abuse of the partner, the greater the severity of the associated child abuse (McClosky *et al.* 1995; Appel and Holden 1998). As strategic application of power and control and the maintenance of secrecy exist in sexual abuse and domestic violence perpetration, it is not surprising that domestic violence is often present in families where there is known sexual abuse.

Impact of domestic violence on children

Domestic violence and chronic trauma

Findings from working with children who have been involved in traumatic situations such as suicide in the family, parental murder, child abuse and natural disasters (e.g. Briere 1992; Black *et al.* 1995; Yule 1998 for summaries) have made it possible to measure the real cost of being traumatised as a child. Children, like adults, suffer more intensely and persistently when a person causes the trauma and being close to the incident intensifies this.

Certain symptoms of post-traumatic stress are particularly profound in children. Terr (1991) suggests that these could include repetitive dreams and nightmares; flashbacks; joyless play; a feeling of going mad; over-activity and irritability; impaired concentration and memory; bed-wetting and soiling; and self-abuse among them. If these endure over time after the incident, a child can be considered as suffering from a clinically diagnosable condition – post-traumatic stress disorder (PTSD). PTSD can become extremely debilitating affecting relationships, the ability to learn and may trigger major physical and mental illness.

Lucy's behaviour in school indicated that she was post-traumatically stressed. She had also told her teacher that she could not sleep and that sometimes she felt 'like she was going mad'.

Pynoos and Eth (1986) reported post-traumatic stress symptoms in 80 per cent of a large sample of uninjured child witnesses of domestic violence. Children cited in later research on domestic violence (e.g. NCH 1994; McGee 2000) typically display in the descriptions of their behaviour, the signs of its existence. Yet children exposed to domestic violence often do not attract supportive responses afforded to children experiencing one-off traumatic incidents.

Children rarely have the option of either *actual* flight or fight in traumatic circumstances, but for them, as for adults, the physiological and emotional responses take over. Trapped by overwhelming feelings, and an ability to achieve a state of calm, children often freeze psychologically (dissociate), so that they do not have to feel any more (Putnam 1997). This strategy works in the short term, but at a cost. One of the emotions specially targeted in this way is fear. Children can often appear to be completely devoid of this as well as hurt and anger in apparently intolerably frightening and harrowing situations.

Other children become locked into 'flight' mode as evidenced by their over-arousal, agitation and inclination to flee situations. Yet others in 'fight' mode appear overly aroused, aggressive and hostile and may become involved in the violence themselves. Pupils in all of these states will be familiar to teachers.

Children's responses to domestic violence according to age

According to Edelson (1999) exposed preschool and nursery-aged children are more often described by their mothers as affected by the violence than are their older peers. This may be because very young children more directly demand time and energy from their caregivers. From studies of children in refuges, we know that signs of failure to thrive (an indicator of neglect) are common.

Younger primary-aged children worry about being abandoned and may fear their deep feelings. They frequently make erroneous connections between their behaviour and that of their adult carers. Believing that the violence at home is their fault, they may act in a manipulative and overly demanding manner in an attempt to reduce the tension within the family. Some children believe they have to protect the non-perpetrating parent by either getting involved or trying to avoid any build-up of the precursors to an episode of violence. They may refuse to attend school in order to look after and/or protect their abused parent.

As childhood progresses, patterns of behaviour become established and gender role models are increasingly influential. Any violent, aggressive conduct disordered behaviour establishing itself at this point will be difficult to eradicate later (e.g. Kazdin 1997). Adolescents are extremely vulnerable to the impact of domestic violence. Struggling towards a sense of their own identity, they may become a focus for the violence themselves. They are generally more guarded and protective of their families and may try to manipulate their parents with complex ploys. Conversely, dissociated from the level of violence in the house, they can become apathetic or even collude with the perpetrator. Adolescents under pressure display a range of extreme behaviours such as escape into drug or alcohol abuse and criminal activities. Eating disorders may surface and they may run away from home, or leave home early. They are also vulnerable, as we have seen in Lucy's case, to depression and attempted suicide.

Gender and domestic violence

The relationship between a child's gender and response to exposure to domestic violence is not straightforward and it would seem from a range of studies that the differences between boys' and girls' reactions to domestic violence are less than the similarities. Both tend either to internalise or externalise their feelings in the extreme and are as likely to experience confusion, anger, depression as well as misbehaving at home and school (Morley and Mullender 1994).

However, the impact of gender socialisation should not be dismissed as unimportant for the individual child. Many boys, for instance, tend not to be able to visualise themselves as victims. The experience of direct or indirect abuse may convey to a boy that he is not masculine enough, and he may try to reduce tension through excessive or extreme behaviour. In controlling emotions in order to feel masculine, he might only allow himself to show anger. The consequences in the classroom are all too frequently seen. Traumatised girls, on the other hand, may need help to move from a gendered submissive position, connect with feelings that are more assertive and to realise that they are not to blame. The most robust finding across studies in relation to difference in boys' and girls' response to domestic violence cited by Hester *et al.* (2000) is a greater propensity by boys to condone or accept violence towards women.

Social impacts

For all children, domestic violence within a family provides a negative social model for conflict resolution and communication within intimate relationships. Children exposed over time have been found to be less sensitive interpersonally and less attentive to social cues. They find it difficult to identify the emotions of others. Not surprisingly, they seem more inclined to adopt aggressive solutions to interpersonal problems and 'read' others as having hostile intent (Dodge *et al.* 1990, 1997). Dawud-Noursi *et al.* (1998) report that children exposed to domestic violence and physical abuse were teacher-rated lower than comparison peers on measures of peer functioning.

Implications for schools

Promoting resilience

Some children exposed to adverse life events cope in ways that seem not to negatively affect their development. Many of the identified 'protective' factors reside within the individual, but their very existence and expression is influenced by access to social and environmental opportunities. Smith (1997) in summarising a number of studies suggests that resilience gives a child access to more competent and functional ways to handle the vulnerability imposed upon them. Factors that emerge as protective in the sense that they may serve to reduce the long-term impacts include:

- sustained positive self-esteem
- adaptability
- organised thinking and effective problem solving
- good social skills
- access to a supportive peer network
- secure attachments
- feeling part of a community (e.g. extended family, school).

It is argued that by teaching children some of these key skills adults, including teachers, can facilitate children's resilience. Grotberg (1997) lists teaching effective communication and problem solving and showing children how to handle their own negative thoughts and behaviour alongside the encouragement of autonomy and independence as ways of helping children become more resilient. A role for schools is clearly apparent.

In her introduction to Bristol City Council's Emotional Literacy Hour Pack for schools, Goss (2000) outlines the importance of emotional intelligence (the ability to recognise, understand, handle and appropriately express emotions) for children's academic achievement in school and in the promotion of their mental health. The emotional literacy curriculum covers developmental progression from preschool to adolescence and includes the following components:

- talking about feelings
- listening skills
- self-awareness
- managing feelings
- empathy
- goal setting
- problem solving
- decision making.

Keeping pupils safe

Disclosure of domestic violence often carries serious risk for the exposee, particularly if they are also being directly abused. Here there is a tendency to consider the level of perceived severity of the incident. There may be judgements made about whether physical perpetration is more damaging than emotional abuse and/or whether this is a 'one-off' incident. Child protection deliberations may be triggered, but there is often uncertainty about how to respond.

It can be argued that exposure to domestic violence is *always* emotionally abusive and therefore inevitably a child protection issue for schools. Hester *et al.* (2000) state:

- Domestic violence is an important indicator that a child may be at risk of abuse (physical and/or sexual).
- The effects on children of living with domestic violence – both direct abuse and witnessing such violence – may be deemed to constitute 'significant harm' (Children Act 1989).
- All children living in circumstances of domestic violence may be deemed 'in need'.

McGee's study (2000) of 48 mothers and their children who had experienced domestic violence found that in this sample, teachers were willing to discuss the violence at home with children, but in quite a number of cases, this information was not shared with the non-perpetrating parent or the information passed on to other agencies such as Social Services. Children reported that they would have liked more information about where they could go for help and how to deal with matters safely.

Hester *et al.* (2000) suggest that an effective safety strategy is to consult children about their experiences on a regular basis and to be seen to take issues around domestic violence very seriously. As domestic violence manifests in many ways, it is vital that safety is uppermost in the mind of any teacher involved in such discussions.

Therapeutic responses in schools

McGee's study (2000) showed that schools had been playing a part in the support system for over half of the 48 families. While the study is small-scale, the issues raised by these mothers and children are key for inclusive schools:

- Mothers turned to schools in desperation; they had no one else to turn to.
- Recognising the impact of the violence on their children's academic performance and behaviour, they hoped that teachers would understand and that school would set up support for their children.
- They needed to address fears, such as the possibility of the children being snatched from school by a violent ex-partner and have contingency plans in place.

Repeated moves to escape the violent partner leads to children moving schools. Not an easy experience for children at the best of times, moving for a child already traumatically stressed further compounds the impact. Clearly, the support and understanding of teachers is vital. Black *et al.* (1995) highlight the importance to a child's recovery of being able to talk about their experiences. Signalling to a pupil that the issue is difficult to discuss is likely to lead to the assumption that it is taboo and/or the adult does not want to deal with it. It is helpful for a child to know that what is happening is not their fault.

Canada and the USA have developed a wide range of services to support exposed children. The UK has been much slower in response, particularly in bringing therapeutic opportunities into schools. Voluntary agencies such as Barnardo's, the NSPCC and NCH Action for Children are developing therapeutic work, as are court mediation and court welfare services to name a few. Relate has recently launched a service for children in school called 'Time to Talk'. Teachers can call upon a trained counsellor to come to school and spend time with a troubled child.

There is now extensive experience of running programmes for children and adolescents exposed to domestic violence and feedback from children is positive. Group work which focuses on breaking the secrecy; assigning responsibility for the perpetration; safety planning; and expression of feelings alongside self-esteem building and opportunities to relax work well. Perhaps more could be done in schools in this vein by tapping into support services such as educational psychology, behavioural support teams and Child and Mental Health Service resources.

Spalding (2001) has reported about the Quiet Place Project in Liverpool schools which was established out of an earlier project working with children showing signs of social, emotional and behavioural difficulties. Quiet Places have been set up in a number of primary schools in Liverpool (and subsequently further afield and in special and secondary schools) in which a range of therapeutic activities are carried out by trained therapists. The environment is designed to be calming and tension-reducing for children whose life experiences generate powerful and painful emotions. These initiatives warrant further investigation in relation to domestic violence.

Preventative approaches – the role of schools

Many writers argue that prevention approaches to violence are the way forward and that schools, both primary and secondary, make an ideal point of focus. They provide access to large numbers of children who are experiencing or who are at risk of experiencing inter-parental violence and it enables access to the next generation of parents.

Violence awareness and safety skill development are being undertaken in many American schools. Wolfe and Jaffe (1999) cited in Rossman *et al.* (2000) argue that *all* children need to know about domestic violence in order that they are never in a position of isolation and that they may be able to safely assist peers should the need arise. This approach also encourages a corporate responsibility and may influence children and adolescents' own behaviour in their developing relationships.

Some education authorities have developed curriculum materials for use in schools. Manchester schools, for instance, have access to a series of packs to aid teachers in supporting children and carers who are experiencing domestic or dating violence, teaching about domestic violence as a social issue and empowering young people to develop relationship skills (Manchester Education Committee 1996).

Conclusion

For Lucy and many young people like her, domestic violence is a significant life experience affecting all areas of development. The way a school responds to vulnerable pupils can have a profound effect on their level of physical safety as well as emotional well-being. However, in today's climate, where the standards agenda is so prevalent, this represents a considerable challenge for schools and LEAs. It is therefore important for governments around the world to take an active role in supporting schools in developing policies and strategies to help children who experience domestic violence to cope with the trauma and to become stable adults.

References

Appel, A. E. and Holden, G. W. (1998) 'The co-occurrence of spouse and physical child abuse: review and appraisal', *Journal of Family Psychology* 12, 578–99.

Black, D., Newman, M., Mezey, G. and Harris Hendriks, J. (eds) (1995) *Psychological Trauma: A Developmental Approach.* London: Gaskell, Royal College of Psychiatrists.

Briere, J. (1992) *Child Abuse Trauma: Theory and Treatment of the Lasting Effects.* Newbury Park, CA: Sage.

Dawud-Noursi, S., Lamb, M. E. and Sternberg, K. J. (1998) 'The relations among domestic violence, peer relationships and academic performance', in C. Feiring and M. Lewis (eds), *Families, Risk and Competence,* Mahwah, NJ: Erlbaum, 207–26.

De Becker, G. (1997) *The Gift of Fear: Survival Signals that Protect Us from Violence.* London: Bloomsbury.

Dodge, K. A., Bates, J. E. and Pettit, G. S. (1990) 'Mechanisms in the cycle of violence', *Science* 250: 1678–83.

Dodge, K. A., Pettit, G. S., and Bates, J. E. (1997) 'How the experience of early physical abuse leads children to become chronically aggressive', in C. Cicchetti and S. L. Toth (eds), *Developmental Psychopathology: Developmental Perspectives on Trauma,* Vol. 9, Theory Research and Intervention. Rochester, NY: University of Rochester Press, 263–88.

Edelson, J. L. (1999) (ed.) 'Special focus on interventions and issues in the co-occurrence of child abuse and domestic violence', *Child Maltreatment* 4(2), 22–9.

Garbarino, J. (1999) *Lost Boys: Why our Sons Turn Violent and How We Can Save Them.* New York: The Free Press.

Goss, J. (2000) 'Introduction', in *The Emotional Literacy Hour: Teaching for Achievement in Bristol Schools. Bristol City Council.* Bristol: Lucky Duck.

Grotberg, E. (1997) 'The International Resilience Project', in M. John (ed.), *A Charge Against Society: The Child's Right to Protection.* London: Jessica Kingsley.

Hart, S. N. and Brassard, M. R. (1990) 'Psychological maltreatment of children', in R. T. Ammerman and M. Herson (eds), *Treatment of Family Violence: A Source Book*. New York: Wiley, 77–112.

Herman, J. L. (1992) *Trauma and Recovery: The Aftermath of Violence – From Domestic Abuse to Political Terror*. New York: HarperCollins.

Hester, M., Pearson, C. and Harwin, N. (2000). *Making an Impact: Children and Domestic Violence. A Reader*. London: Jessica Kingsley.

Hughes, H. (1992) 'Impact of spouse abuse on children of battered women', *Violence Update* 1, 9–11.

Hughes, H. M. and Graham-Bermann, S. A. (1998) 'Children of battered women: impact of emotional abuse on adjustment and development', *Journal of Emotional Abuse* 1(2), 23–50.

Kashani, J. H. and Allan, W. D. (1998) *The Impact of Family Violence on Children and Adolescents*. Thousand Oaks, CA: Sage.

Kazdin, A. E. (1997) 'Conduct disorder across the life-span', in S. S. Luthar and E. Zigler (eds), *Developmental Psychopathology: Perspectives on Adjustment, Risks and Disorder*. Cambridge, MA: Cambridge University Press.

Kolbo, J. R., Blakely, E. H. and Engelman, E. (1996) 'Children who witness domestic violence: a review of the empirical literature', *Journal of Interpersonal Violence* 11, 282–93.

Long, R. and Fogell, J. (1999) *Supporting Pupils with Emotional Difficulties: Creating a Caring Environment for All*. London: David Fulton Publishers.

McClosky, L. A., Figueredo, A. J. and Koss, M. P. (1995) 'The effects of systematic family violence on children's mental health', *Child Development* 66, 1239–61.

McGee, C. (2000) *Childhood Experiences of Domestic Violence*. London: Jessica Kingsley.

Manchester Education Committee (1996) *Working with Young People on Domestic Violence Issues*. Manchester: MEC.

Marans, S. and Adelman, A. (1997) 'Experiencing violence in a developmental context', in J. Osofsky (ed.), *Children in a Violent Society*. New York: Guilford, 202–22.

Margolin, G., (1998) 'Effects of domestic violence on children', in P. K. Trickett and C. J. Schellenbach (eds), *Violence Against Children in the Family and Community*. Washington, DC: American Psychological Association, 57–102.

Mirrlees-Black, C. (1995). 'Estimating the extent of domestic violence: findings from the 1992 British Crime Survey', *Home Office Research Bulletin* 37, 1–18.

Morley, R. and Mullender, A. (1994) 'Domestic violence and children: what do we know from research?' in A. Mullender and R. Morley (eds), *Children Living with Domestic Violence: Putting Men's Abuse of Women on the Childcare Agenda*. London: Whiting and Birch Ltd, 24–42.

National Children's Home (NCH) (1994) *The Hidden Victims – Children and Domestic Violence*. London: NCH Action for Children.

Nazroo, J. (1995) 'Uncovering gender differences in the use of marital violence: the effects of methodology', *Sociology* 29(3), 475–94.

Putnam, F. W. (1997) *Dissociation in Children and Adolescents: A Developmental Perspective*. New York: Guilford.

Pynoos, R. S. and Eth, S. (1986) 'Witness to violence: the child interview', *Journal of the American Academy of Child and Adolescent Psychiatry* 25, 306–19.

Rossman, B. B. R., and Rosenberg, M. S. (1997) 'Psychological maltreatment: a needs analysis and application for children in violent families', in R. Geffner, S. B. Sorenson and P. K. Lundberg-Love (eds), *Violence and Sexual Abuse at Home: Current Issues in Spousal Battering and Child Maltreatment.* Binghampton, NY: Haworth.

Rossman, B. B. R., Hughes, H. M. and Rosenberg, M. S. (2000) *Children and Interparental Violence: The Impact of Exposure.* Philadelphia, PA: Brunner/Mazel.

Smith, G. (1997) 'Psychological resilience', in *Turning Points.* London: NSPCC.

Spalding, B. (2001) 'A quiet place: a healing environment', *Support for Learning* **16**(2), 32–41.

Stanko, E. A., Crisp, D., Hale, C. and Lucraft, H. (1998) *Counting the Costs: Estimating the Impact of Domestic Violence in the Borough of Hackney.* London: Crime Concern.

Terr, L. C. (1991) 'Childhood traumas – an outline and review', *American Journal of Psychiatry,* **148**, 10–20.

Wolfe, D. A. and Jaffe, P. G. (1999) 'Prevention of domestic violence: emerging initiatives'. Paper presented at the annual Asilomar Conference on Children and Intimate Violence. Pacific Grove, CA. Quoted in B. B. R Rossman, H. M. Hughes and M. S. Rosenberg (2000) *Children and Interpersonal Violence: The Impact of Exposure.* Philadelphia, PA: Brunner/Mazel.

Woman's Aid Federation England (WAFE) (1992) *A Woman's Aid Approach to Working with Children.* Bristol: WAFE.

Yule, W. (1998) 'Post-traumatic stress disorder in children and its treatment', in T. W. Miller (ed.), *Children of Trauma: Stressful Life Events and their Effects on Children and Adolescents.* Madison, CT: International Universities Press, 219–43.

Section 3

CHAPTER 11

Checking individual progress in phonics

Rea Reason and Sue Palmer

Introduction

Educational inclusion implies full participation in the literacy curriculum. Where children make slower progress, it is particularly important to ensure differentiated planning so that the children have the opportunity to learn reading and writing at their own pace. In this chapter we shall argue that the National Literacy Strategy (NLS) sets very ambitious targets in phonics and that there are children needing to progress more slowly. In order to enable teachers to adjust the pace and content of teaching, we have developed a curriculum-based test that enables them to check individual progress in phonics. Our results show that children learn at widely differing rates with some speeding through all targets while a substantial minority need a repetitive approach based on principles of consolidated learning.

The chapter starts with a theoretical account of the role of phonological processing in learning to read. This leads to a consideration of word level targets and the opportunities for inclusion within the National Literacy Strategy. We conclude with a description of Checking Individual Progress in Phonics (ChIPPs) – a curriculum-based test for monitoring children's progress in this area of learning.

The role of phonological processing in learning to read

Written English language is a phonetic code. Each phoneme in a spoken word is represented by a grapheme in a written word. Although numerous studies have shown that early phonological skills training has beneficial effects on reading development (e.g. Cunningham 1990; Duncan and Johnston 1999), other training studies have shown that phonological awareness on its own, although necessary, is not sufficient. Phonological skills training and phoneme-grapheme correspondence instruction are both necessary components for maximum benefit (Berninger,

Abbot, Zook, Ogier, Lemos-Britten and Brooksher 1999; Bus and van Ijzendoorn 1999). Malicky and Norman (1999) have suggested that, rather than phonemic awareness per se, what seems to be essential to learning to read is that children develop an understanding of the connections between oral and written language. At the macro level this involves an understanding that written words represent words in oral language. At the micro level it involves understanding that letters, or groups of letters, in written words stand for individual sounds in spoken words.

The majority of new readers come to school with neither the skill to hear the individual sounds in words nor the knowledge that written words represent spoken words and even more rarely with the knowledge that the letters in the written word represent the sounds in the spoken word. Those who do not receive explicit instruction in the link between spoken and written language can begin to make false assumptions about written language. Many children believe that they must remember the whole word, rather than decode the word one sound at a time. They do not understand the fundamental intention of written English language. Once children begin to memorise whole words as a primary reading strategy, they have developed a bad habit which will make learning to read and spell correctly more difficult.

Skilled word reading involves rapid and automatic mapping of letter strings on to the most likely pronunciation. Skilled readers do not read words, or letters in words, as pictures, but are rapidly and automatically phonologically decoding all the elements within them (Adams 1990; Greaney, Tunmer and Chapman 1997; Share and Stanovich 1995). However, young beginning readers may have to resort to processing the visual cues in the letter strings as an aid to reading before they have learned grapheme-phoneme correspondence (Ehri and Wilce 1985; Gough, Juel and Griffith 1992). This use of visual cues may help them to read very familiar words such as 'dog' with the tail on the end, but does not give them a strategy with which to read new or unfamiliar words (Share 1995; Share and Stanovich 1995).

Phonological decoding of the print on a page involves identifying the sound that the letters or combination of letters represent, holding each sound in memory in a sequential manner until all the sounds have been identified and storing them in such a way that they can be blended together to form a word (Adams 1990). For skilled readers this is done silently, quickly and effortlessly. For the child who is just beginning to learn to read, this is often done slowly, overtly and takes great effort. The temporary storage of material that has been read is said to depend on working memory (Baddeley 1990; Cantor and Engle 1993; Gathercole and Baddeley 1993; Just and Carpenter 1992) which must take account not only of storage for later retrieval, but also of the demands of partial storage of information related to several levels of text processing (Conway and Engle 1994; Miyake, Just and Carpenter 1994; Swanson 1999).

Phonological recoding in working memory involves accessing the phonological representation of the visual stimuli and manipulating this in preference to the visual representation (Palmer 2000a; 2000b). Children with phonological recoding difficulties can be expected to have problems with acquiring alphabetic reading skills because these recoding difficulties make it hard to utilise knowledge of letter-sound correspondences or onset rhyme analogies in decoding words (Hanley, Reynolds and Thornton 1997). Specifically, phonological recoding inefficiencies make it difficult to perform simultaneous or rapidly sequential identification, comparison and blending processes that are required to identify words by phonological decoding strategies (Torgesen and Burgess 1998).

The National Literacy Strategy and Inclusion

The influence that special education has had on the development of the curricular framework of the NLS has perhaps not been recognised sufficiently. No more are there polarised debates about teaching methods that focus either on language experience or structured cumulative approaches. It is clear that children need both. Within the NLS, text level work ensures that children understand and enjoy the very purpose of reading and writing – communication – while sentence and word level work provide the more structured elements within the framework. In some ways general education can now be regarded as a part of special education rather than vice versa.

There are, of course, areas of concern: first, to what extent can children with learning difficulties participate in and learn during the 'hour' and, second, how can they start to reach the very ambitious learning targets set out in the framework? The guidance on special educational needs within the NLS makes it very clear that, with rare exception, every child will participate in the 'hour' and that additional support should become an integral part of the NLS framework.

Whole-class interactive teaching provides the rationale for the shared reading and writing activities of the NLS. All the children are exposed to these activities for a much longer time than they would be during individualised instruction. They listen to the teacher, they respond together to the teacher, they observe the models of the other children and they take turns to respond individually. If we learn to read through reading then, overall, the NLS whole-class activities can provide many more planned opportunities to read.

But being 'exposed' to reading does not necessarily mean that all children will learn to read. If those with learning difficulties are to benefit from the 'hour', then the starting point has to be that all teachers develop their skills of noticing individual differences and adjusting the level of questioning and the responses required. With guided group reading and writing there can, of course, be better opportunities for differentiation than with whole-class teaching.

Perhaps most important is the common language of the NLS that enables class and support teachers to work together. Support teachers now have a central role in preparing children for classroom activities through their assessments, targets and additional teaching as necessary. The information provided by support teachers enables class teachers to adjust their teaching to individual needs.

This way of working assumes, of course, that we have the prerequisite teacher time, expertise and resources. Far from 'doing away' with special needs support, the NLS requires that all those involved, including classroom assistants and parents, have a good understanding of teaching and learning within the NLS. The NLS extends far beyond the 'hour' and children with special needs can now be prepared for the whole-class lessons during supported individual and group work. This can include more deliberately planned and repetitive approaches outlined in Palmer and Reason (2001).

Phonics within the National Literacy Strategy

In line with the research reviewed above, word level targets contain a heavy emphasis on the development of children's phonological competencies and word recognition skills based on 'phonics'. The reception year starts with activities to encourage and consolidate the development of the children's phonological awareness, i.e. the discrimination of sounds in words. Even at this stage, it is possible to notice those children needing more assistance and practice with these important precursors to learning to recognise grapheme/phoneme correspondences.

It is important to note, however, that the learning of lists of words that share particular letter patterns does not necessarily 'generalise' to the reading and writing of continuous text (Reason 1998). Children might be able to read and spell the words as lists while still not using this information for the purposes of written communication. In order to encourage the transfer of learning from lists, the NLS includes approaches such as the reading and construction of sentences containing the words and the linking of reading and writing activities in order to reinforce the learning.

Teachers following the NLS framework are expected to know what the particular phonics targets are for the class or the group so that familiar patterns can be pointed out and reinforced when reading together continuous text. In this way, words containing selected patterns are taken from the texts being read, practised in lists as necessary and then reread in the context of the text. This is illustrated in teaching examples contained in the NLS training video on phonics within word level work. In addition, the subsequent *Progression in Phonics (PiPs): Materials for Whole-class Teaching* (DfEE 1999) provides a selection of games that make the learning of phonics both active and participatory.

Cognitive research now also supports what many teachers have been doing for years. In terms of connectionist modelling (Snowling 1998; Reason 1998), readers need both phonological and semantic information to be able to cope with all types of printed word. We can read, for example, 'eat a mint' and 'drink a pint' without any confusion about the pronunciations of mint/pint because we have learnt to read these words in the context of meaningful text. So continuous text with a rich and varied content plays a central role in furthering overall literacy development. The more children read, the better they get at reading. Shared and guided reading of interesting material requires culturally relevant contents which are also appropriate for the purposes of learning phonics.

Developmental longitudinal research (Rego and Bryant 1995; Lazo, Pumfrey and Peers 1997) has demonstrated how children combine semantic, syntactic and phonological knowledge in a complex and interdependent way when learning to read. The research has been translated into practice within the 'searchlight model' of the NLS showing that knowledge of context, phonics, grammar and word recognition converge to help the learner read and spell the text. With regard to the phonics component, the framework for teaching states that pupils should be taught to:

- discriminate between the separate sounds in words;
- learn the letters and letter combinations most commonly used to spell those sounds;
- read words by sounding out and blending their separate parts;
- write words by combining the spelling patterns of their sounds.

(DfEE 1999: 4)

Children need to understand that some phonemes are represented by graphemes consisting of one letter, others have more than one letter; many phonemes can be represented by more than one grapheme, while some graphemes can represent more than one phoneme. In addition, children need to develop skills that allow them to manipulate the phonemes in different parts of words for reading by analogy in order to enable them to decode new words unaided.

Over-ambitious targets

The NLS framework provides a cumulative sequence of word level targets starting from oral/aural activities and ending with complex phonics. The reception year places emphasis on the securing of a confident knowledge of phoneme/grapheme correspondences in line with research regarding the importance of knowledge and experience at school entry of rhyme, alliteration and letter sounds. However, Year 1 Term 3 and Year 2 Term 1 targets require a pace that has been regarded as over-ambitious by many teachers (Pietrowski and Reason 2000). Although there is repetition of targets in subsequent terms, the danger is that the targets will not receive the careful and systematic coverage required to ensure that children have really learnt them. In the light of experience, we may need to reconsider the detail and sequence of phonic knowledge covered in the transition from Year 1 to Year 2 and the possibility of an extension of this work into Year 3 to ensure thorough and confident learning of the targets.

As shown by Palmer and Reason (2001), a substantial proportion of the children do not reach the phonics targets specified by the framework. Figures 11.1 to 11.5 show the increasing numbers of children in Years 1 and 2 who are struggling with the progressively more complex targets within the phonics sequence. The vast majority can read some simple c-v-c words (consonant-vowel-consonant words such as 'cat') by the end of Year 1, although, as can be seen in Figure 11.1, there are a small percentage of children even at the end of Year 2 who are struggling to read even one simple c-v-c word.

In contrast, Figure 11.5 shows that almost half of Year 2 are able to read the majority of words containing complex vowel digraphs, with nearly 10 per cent of Year 1 pupils at the same stage even though such words are not included in their phonics targets.

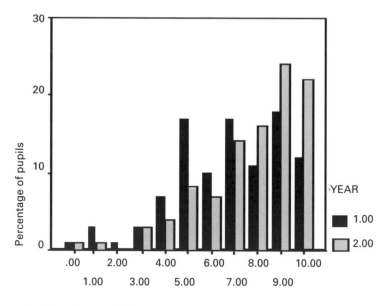

Figure 11.1 Number of children reading c-v-c words correctly (n = 200)

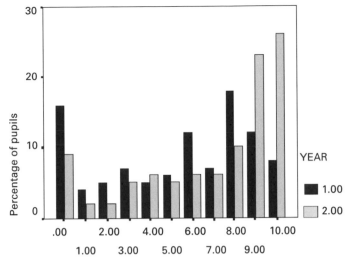

Figure 11.2 Number of children reading consonant digraph words correctly (n = 200)

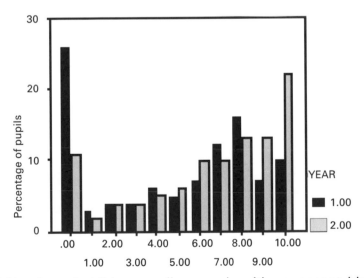

Figure 11.3 Number of children reading words with consonant blends at the beginning *or* end correctly (n = 200)

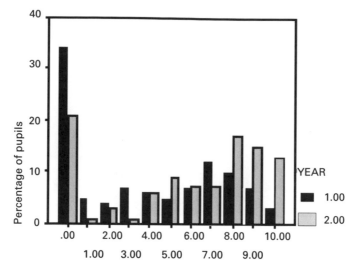

Figure 11.4 Number of children reading words with consonant blends at the beginning *and* end correctly (n = 200)

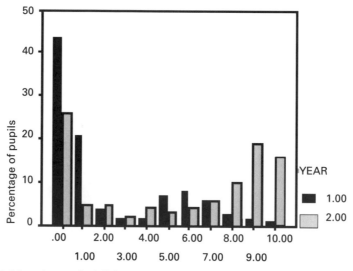

Figure 11.5 Number of children reading words with complex vowels correctly (average for final three sets of words) (n = 200)

In recognition of these problems and on the basis of pilot studies currently in progress, the National Literacy Strategy is introducing resources to all schools involving additional help to children in Year 1 (Early Literacy Support). It has already introduced Additional Literacy Support to children in Year 3 (aged seven to eight years) and plans for Further Literacy Support are underway. While we do not yet have systematic evaluations of these initiatives, there can be debates as to their rationales, methods and staffing. Nevertheless, the initiatives can provide the opportunities we need for introducing more deliberate monitoring of progress to determine the persistence of literacy difficulties in line with the practices recommended in Reason, Frederickson, Heffernan, Martin and Woods (1999).

Assessment for learning

The report on assessment arrangements by the Curriculum and Assessment Authority (DfEE 2001) is entitled 'Assessment for learning' and draws together information from many sources including theories of motivation and the psychology of learning. It is based on a number of research studies which point out certain common features related to successful learning. The features are:

- that teachers provide feedback to pupils that is developmental and indicates how the work could be improved or taken forward;
- that teachers use information from assessing pupils' progress in learning to adjust their teaching;
- that pupils are aware of the goals of their activities in terms of what they are intended to be learning;
- that pupils are actively involved in assessing their own progress and in making decisions about what to do next;
- that teachers regard it as important to use assessment to increase pupils' motivation and self-esteem.

The National Literacy Strategy can meet many of these requirements. We have, for example, observed literacy hours where the goals of the lesson are explained to the children at the beginning and then reviewed with them at the end of the lesson. However, in the light of the ambitious phonics targets discussed above, there is a need to develop methodology that enables teachers to 'assess to teach', i.e. to adjust their teaching in response to the pupils' progress. Below we shall describe one such approach.

The rationale and content of ChIPPs

ChIPPs (Checking Individual Progress in Phonics) was devised as a curriculum-based test (Palmer and Reason 2001). We assumed that the phonics curriculum could be mapped out as a set of hierarchical stages where earlier ones were needed in order to progress to the later ones. It was then possible to find out what each child could do in relation to this progression so that we could plan what he/she needed to learn next. Unlike curriculum-based tests such as Standard Assessment Tasks (SATs) within the English National Curriculum, ChIPPs informed teaching from the very start and then checked on progress after a period of teaching.

The content of ChIPPs was based on *Progression in Phonics (PiPs): Materials for Whole-class Teaching* (DfEE 1999) which specified the progression in terms of seven steps as described in Table 11.1. On the left-hand side of the table are described the skills of sound discrimination, segmentation and blending and on the right-hand side the knowledge of letters that should be taught, in parallel, at each step.

Steps 1 to 3 contain primarily oral/aural skills involving rhyme and the 'hearing' of phonemes in initial and final position. Children are also taught to recognise a few letters, i.e. phoneme/grapheme correspondence. ChIPPs focuses on Steps 4 to 7.

As can be seen from Table 11.1, steps 4 to 7 require children to blend and segment (read and spell) an increasing number of phoneme/grapheme correspondences.

Table 11.1 Progression in phonic skills and knowledge (from DfEE 1999: 6)

Step	Skill in:	Knowledge of letters:
1	hearing and discriminating general sounds, speech sounds and patterns	
2	hearing phonemes /s/, /m/, /k/, /t/, /g/, /h/ in initial position	s, m, c, t, g, h
3	hearing phonemes /s/, /m/, /k/, /t/, /g/ in final position	ss, ck, l, n, d, k, sh, ch
4	hearing phonemes /a/, /e/, /i/, /o/, /u/ in medial position CVC blending and segmenting, reading and spelling	a, e, i, o, u, f, qu, b, r, j, p, th, ng
5	C(C)V(C)C blending and segmenting, reading and spelling	v, w, x, y, z
6	CVC blending and segmenting, reading and spelling	ai, ee, ie, oa, oo, or, ar, ir, oi, ou
7	CVC blending and segmenting, reading and spelling	ay, a-e, ea, igh, y, i-e, ow, o-e, oe, ew, ue, u-e, oy, ow, er, ur, aw, air, ear, oo

While continuing with oral/aural activities, Step 4 introduces blending and segmenting, i.e. reading and spelling c-v-c words such as cat, red, bin, dog, mud. Step 5 contains consonant blends and digraphs at the beginnings and ends of words (e.g. frog, hand, vest, brush, thing). Step 6 contains ten vowel phonemes (digraphs ai, ee, ie, oa, oo, or, ar, ir, oi, ou). Step 7 contains vowel digraphs and trigraphs (ay, a-e, ea, igh, y, i-e, ow, o-e, oe, ew, ue, u-e, oy, ow, er, ur, aw, air, ear, oo).

ChIPPs assumes that the early auditory stages of phonemic awareness (Steps 1 to 3) have been learnt, i.e. that the children can:

- discriminate and remember sounds in words
- appreciate the rhythm and rhyme in words
- identify initial phonemes in words.

The test also assumes that children have learnt to recognise at least some written single letters (graphemes) so that they can start to blend the words in Set 1 of ChIPPs. If they struggle with Set 1, then suggestions are made in this manual as to tests-to-teach that involve checking children's phonemic awareness and the single letter sounds that they can recognise.

ChIPPs consists of seven sets of words and non-words of increasing difficulty in two parallel tests. The progression in both versions is as follows:

Set 1: Consonant-vowel-consonant (CVC) words with a, e, i, o, u as the medial vowel (e.g. bat, jup, fog, rek, vix)

Set 2: CVC words with consonant digraphs ch, sh, th, ck, ss, ll at the beginning *or* end of the word (e.g. chum, dash, gock, mell)

Set 3: CVC words with consonant clusters (e.g. br, st, dr, tw) at the beginning *or* end of the word (e.g. brag, just, twid)

Set 4: CVC words with consonant clusters at the beginning *and* the end of the word (e.g. block, grasp, slept, dwolt, truct)

Set 5: Words with vowel digraphs ai, ee, oa, oo, or, ar, ir, oi, ou (e.g. mail, join, keet, soat, lort)

Set 6: Words with vowel digraphs ay, ea, y, o-e, ew, u-e, ow, ur, air, aught (e.g. way, plode, skew, town, smead)

Set 7: Words with vowel digraphs a-e, igh, i-e, oe, ue, oy, er, aw, ear (e.g. bright, flerk, clear, droy, plue)

Differentiated planning

In trialling ChIPPs with children at the end of Year 1 (aged about six years) and in their second term of Year 2 (aged six to seven years) we found that children fell broadly into the five groupings below.

1. There are children who struggle with the CVC words in Set 1. Some sound out each letter (e.g. s-a-t) and cannot then blend the phonemes into a word. They may have learnt to recognise single letter sounds without yet developing an understanding that the sounds need to be blended in order to make words. Alternatively, their attempts at blending are so laborious that they do not succeed. A few children may lack the phonemic competencies or knowledge of single letters needed to read CVC words.

2. The children can read the CVC words in Set 1 but there are differences in fluency. Some sound out letter by letter (e.g. s-a-t) and then blend, some combine elements (e.g. s-a sa, sa-t sat or s-at sat) and some read the word without hesitation (e.g. sat). They have not yet learnt the consonant digraphs and clusters required for Sets 2 and 3.

3. Many children can read the consonant digraphs and clusters at the beginnings and ends of the words in Sets 2 and 3. When these letter combinations appear both at the beginnings and at the ends of words, as in Set 4, the task has often become more difficult. Some sound out each letter (e.g. b-r-a-g), some combine elements (e.g. br-ag) and some read the word without hesitation (e.g. brag).

4. Some children can read many but not all of the vowel digraphs in Sets 5, 6 and 7. They can do this in different ways. The key skill to look for is fluency. Some sound out and blend each element (e.g. t-ai-l) and others are much more fluent.

5. There are some children who zoom through all seven sets of ChIPPs so easily and effortlessly that one wonders whether phonics is really a skill to be built up by practice. They should have no difficulties with the majority of monosyllabic words and are likely to have transferred this knowledge also to polysyllabic words.

The results from ChIPPs help to target and differentiate learning in the classroom. Usual teaching programmes can be examined to decide which children need what kind of content and what kind of emphasis. This can then inform whole-class teaching and, during group work, children making similar progress can be taught together.

Taking whole-class progress as a starting point, the results from ChIPPs link with a broad approach that does not require additional detailed record keeping. The results also identify those children making the slowest progress who may be entitled to additional help such as the Early Literacy Support or the previous Additional Literacy Support provided within the English National Literacy Strategy.

Some children making slower progress will need a step-by-step approach that provides increased repetition of a specified task. On the basis of the teacher-designed tests-for-teaching described in the manual, teachers can decide together with the children what to practise and create a record system for frequent (daily) checks of progress and for later checks to see whether the learning has been retained. We have called this 'consolidated learning'.

Conclusion

ChIPPs can facilitate differentiated planning and teaching in the primary classroom. These plans and methods also apply to children making slower progress. The curriculum-based test enables teachers to:

- Assess before teaching by finding out what children already know in order to plan what they need to learn next.
- Monitor progress by using the two parallel versions to undertake an assessment, retest following a period of teaching and plan further teaching on the basis of the retesting.
- Make individual plans by observing children's strategies in blending the phonics elements and adjusting teaching to take account of those differences. Some children need a more repetitive approach and for them the tests-for-teaching, based on the banks of words in the manual, can help in the planning and monitoring of more detailed programmes.

References

Adams, M. J. (1990) *Beginning to Read: Children Thinking and Learning about Print.* Cambridge, MA: MIT Press.

Baddeley, A. D. (1990) *Human Memory: Theory and Practice.* Hove, UK: Lawrence Erlbaum Associates.

Berninger, V. W., Abbott, R. D., Zook, D., Ogier, S., Lemos-Britten, Z. and Brooksher, R. (1999) 'Early intervention for reading disabilities: teaching the alphabet principle in a connectionist framework', *Journal of Learning Disabilities* 32, 491–503.

Bus, A. G. and van Ijzendoorn, M. H. (1999) 'Phonological awareness and early reading: a meta-analysis of experimental training studies', *Journal of Educational Psychology* 91, 403–14.

Cantor, J. and Engle, R. (1993) 'Working memory capacity as long-term memory activation: an individual differences approach', *Journal of Experimental Psychology: Learning, Memory and Cognition* 19, 1101–14.

Conway, A. and Engle, R. (1994) 'Working memory and retrieval: a resource-dependent inhibition model', *Journal of Experimental Psychology: General* 123, 354–73.

Cunningham, A. E. (1990) 'Explicit versus implicit instruction in phonemic awareness', *Journal of Experimental Child Psychology* 50, 429–49.

Department for Education and Employment (DfEE) (1999) *Progression in Phonics (PiPs): Materials for Whole-class Teaching.* Reading: National Literacy Strategy.

Department for Education and Employment (DfEE) (2001) 'Review of assessment arrangements: assessment for learning', *Paper by Curriculum and Assessment Committee of the QCA (06/01).*

Duncan, L. G. and Johnston, R. S. (1999) 'How does phonological awareness relate to non-word reading skill amongst poor readers?' *Reading and Writing* 11, 405–39.

Ehri, L. C. and Wilce, L. S. (1985) 'Movement into reading. Is the first stage of printed word learning visual or phonetic?' *Reading Research Quarterly* 20, 163–79.

Gathercole, S. E. and Baddeley, A. D. (1993) *Working Memory and Language Processing.* Hove, UK: Lawrence Erlbaum Associates.

Gough, P., Juel, C. and Griffith, P. (1992) 'Reading, spelling and the orthographic cipher', in P. Gough, L. Ehri and R. Treiman (eds), *Reading Acquisition*. Hillsdale, NJ: Lawrence Erlbaum Associates, 35–48.

Greaney, K. T., Tunmer, W. E. and Chapman, J. W. (1997) 'Effects of rime-based orthographic analogy training on word recognition skills of children with reading disability', *Journal of Educational Psychology* 89, 645–52.

Hanley, J. R., Reynolds, C. J. and Thornton, A. (1997) 'Orthographic analogies and developmental dyslexia', *British Journal of Psychology* 88, 423–40.

Just, M. and Carpenter, P. (1992) 'A capacity theory of comprehension: individual differences in working memory', *Psychological Review*, 99, 122–49.

Lazo, M. G., Pumfrey, P. D. and Peers, I. (1997) 'Metalinguistic awareness, reading and spelling: roots and branches in literacy', *Journal of Research in Reading* 20(2), 85–104.

Malicky, G. V. and Norman, C. A. (1999) 'Phonological awareness and reading: an alternative interpretation of the literature from a clinical perspective', *Alberta Journal of Educational Research* 45, 18–34.

Miyake, A., Just, M. and Carpenter, P. (1994) 'Working memory constraints on the resolution of lexical ambiguity', *Cognitive Neuropsychology* 33, 175–202.

Palmer, S. E. (2000a) 'Phonological recoding deficit in working memory of dyslexic teenagers', *Journal of Research in Reading* 23, 28–40.

Palmer, S. E. (2000b) 'Development of phonological recoding and literacy acquisition: a four-year cross-sequential study', *British Journal of Developmental Psychology* 18, 533–55.

Palmer, S. and Reason, R. (2001) *ChIPPs: Checking Individual Progress in Phonics*. Windsor: NFER-Nelson.

Piotrowski, J. and Reason, R. (2000) 'The National Literacy Strategy and dyslexia: a comparison of teaching methods and materials', *Support for Learning* 1(2), 51–7.

Reason, R. (1998) 'How relevant is connectionist modelling of reading to educational practice?' *Educational and Child Psychology* 15(2), 59–65.

Reason, R., Frederickson, N., Heffernan, M., Martin, C. and Woods, K. (1999) *Dyslexia, Literacy and Psychological Assessment*: Report by a Working Party of the Division of Educational and Child Psychology, The British Psychological Society. Leicester: The British Psychological Society.

Rego, L. B. and Bryant, P .E. (1995) 'The connection between phonological, syntactic and semantic skills and children's reading and spelling', *European Journal of Psychology in Education* 8(3), 235–46.

Share, D. L. (1995) 'Phonological recoding and self-teaching: *sine qua non* of reading acquisition', *Cognition* 55, 151–218.

Share, D. L. and Stanovich, K. E. (1995) 'Cognitive processes in early reading development: accommodating individual differences into a model of acquisition', *Issues in Education* 1(1), 1–57.

Snowling, M. (1998) 'Reading development and its difficulties', *Educational and Child Psychology* 15(2), 44–58.

Swanson, H. L. (1999) 'Reading comprehension and working memory in leading disabled readers: is the phonological loop more important than the executive system?' *Journal of Experimental Child Psychology* 72, 1–31.

Torgesen, J. K. and Burgess, S. R. (1998) 'Consistency of reading-related phonological processes throughout early childhood: evidence from longitudinal correlational and instructional studies', in J. L. Metsala and L. C. Ehri (eds), *Word Recognition in Beginning Literacy*. London: LEA, 161–88.

CHAPTER 12

What do we mean when we say 'dyslexia' and what difference does it make anyway?

Kevin Woods

This chapter considers the use of the term 'dyslexia' in educational practice and a recent attempt by the British Psychological Society (BPS) to propose a useful 'working definition' set within the context of a model of literacy learning. Implications of the definition for teaching and assessment practices and the promotion of educational inclusion are considered.

The term 'dyslexia'

> 'When I use the word,' Humpty Dumpty said . . ., 'it means just what I choose it to mean – neither more nor less.'
> 'The question is,' said Alice, 'whether you can make words mean so many different things.'
> 'The question is,' said Humpty Dumpty, 'which is to be the master – that's all.'
> (Carroll 1872, *Through the Looking Glass*)

This quotation reflects something of the difficulties that have surrounded the use of the word 'dyslexia' both within and between educational, medical and academic communities over the last two decades. The literal meaning of the word 'dyslexia', (derived from Greek; 'dys' meaning difficulty and 'lexis' meaning 'words'), is 'difficulty with words'. This has been extrapolated mainly, though not exclusively, to aspects of reading and spelling, rather than oral language. Though a substantial amount of high-quality research has been generated on the subject, firm resolutions about definition and identification, which are meaningful across disciplines, have not yet been reached (Rutter 1998). At the same time, the term 'dyslexia' has entered the realms of popular language and so its meaning is not the preserve of professionals alone (Woods 1998). Prolonged, and sometimes confusing, debate about definition has been a source of difficulty and distraction, not only for the academic community attempting to advance knowledge on the subject, but also for teachers, psychologists and policy makers concerned with addressing children's needs for progress, participation and inclusion (Elliott 1990; Tonnesson 1997; Woods 1998). If addressing children's needs at school is, to a large extent, dependent upon the coordinated efforts of teachers, parents, learners and other specialists (e.g. speech therapists, psychologists), particularly in the case of 'vulnerable' children such as those with literacy learning difficulties, then a common understanding about the nature of the learner's difficulties is likely to be an important and recurrent issue. For example, teachers may ask themselves, 'What is my role in identifying dyslexia?', 'What should I be looking for?', 'How, if at all, is dyslexia different from ordinary reading/writing difficulties?' or 'How should I teach a child with difficulties of a dyslexic nature?' This in turn may create difficulties for work with parents and learners, some of whom may be asking the same questions. It is perhaps because of these sorts of interpersonal dynamics that attempts to avoid the term 'dyslexia' by those educationists concerned about the stigmatising and pedagogically unhelpful effects of 'labelling' children or the principles of resource allocation in relation to ill-defined labels or dubious diagnostic processes, have been neither viable nor effective (Elliott 1990; Woods 1998). In 1998, the BPS commissioned a Working Party of academic and specialist educational psychologists to survey relevant research and current practice, and to make recommendations, following consultation, about the concept of dyslexia and the principles of educational psychology assessment related to this concept (BPS 1999a). The BPS (1999a) Dyslexia Working Party's report identified two particular sources of confusion concerning the definition of dyslexia. First, a definition, in the scientific sense, would need to begin with a small number of clear features and keep separate any consideration of causal factors. So, for example, although phonological processing difficulties may be commonly identified as a cause of literacy learning difficulties, it would remain essentially separate from an identification of dyslexia per se.

Second, the concept of dyslexia has had a close association with concepts of 'intelligence', 'special educational needs' (SEN) and 'specific learning difficulties'. Dyslexia has often been identified by lower literacy skills in relation to higher 'intelligence', perhaps because of its facility in creating a subgroup for special study or provision where the area of interest/concern (literacy learning difficulties) actually exists on a continuum (Pumfrey and Reason 1991). It may be also that the rapid and arguably ill-conceived development of the SEN agenda through the 1980s and 1990s (Solity 1991; Wolfendale 1993; Dyson 1994; Armstrong 1995), combined with the conspicuous and continuous nature of literacy learning difficulties and convenience of literacy and intelligence measures, conspired to consolidate this link (Connor 1994; Woods 1998). The BPS (1999a) Dyslexia Working Party states, however, that:

The relationship between intelligence and reading is . . . complex and more likely to be multifaceted and curvilinear rather than a simple linear relationship. (p. 37)

Therefore, aspects of 'intelligence' may have different influences for different learners depending upon a range of other factors, and generalisations about the relationship between literacy learning and intelligence may be open to criticism on theoretical grounds.[1]

Furthermore, the report points to a considerable body of research evidence, from many countries and with children of different ages, which supports the conclusion that children with reading difficulties of different intelligence quotient (IQ) levels perform similarly on a variety of reading and spelling measures (BPS 1999a; Vellutino, Scanlon and Reid-Lyon 2000). Therefore, whatever the relevance of 'intelligence' (however this may be defined or measured) to other aspects of the learner's experiences at school, there is not the evidence at present to use that concept in distinguishing a group of children who are learning literacy more slowly.

The concept of 'specific learning difficulties' in relation to literacy learning has, in educational practice, been operationalised either by linking literacy learning difficulties to higher 'intelligence' to create a subgroup of children considered to have SEN (the 'discrepancy' understanding), or by providing a functional analysis of what exactly learners cannot do in relation to the tasks of reading and writing (the 'skills deficit' understanding). The former understanding is subject to the above criticisms of assuming a simple linear link between literacy learning and the concept of intelligence; the latter understanding is more in keeping with what is perhaps the essential behavioural feature of any dyslexia definition, namely, 'difficulties with literacy learning'.

Based upon the work of the Committee of the Health Council of the Netherlands (Gersons-Wolfensberger and Ruijssenaars 1997), the BPS Dyslexia Working Party proposed a 'working definition' of dyslexia shown in Figure 12.1 below. This definition embodies the core feature of 'literacy learning difficulties', does not include causal factors[2] nor exclude on the basis of intelligence measures, accords with the 'skills deficit' understanding of 'specific learning difficulties', as well as enabling an appropriate separation of the dyslexia concept from that of SEN.

---

1 Note that the commonly found positive correlation of about 0.6/0.7 between literacy and intelligence (IQ) measures taken across large populations conceals a wide variation between individual learners regarding literacy/intelligence measures. Also, correlation does not imply causation and other factors, such as economic advantage, may better account for variation in both literacy learning and measured intelligence (Turner 1997; Howe 1997).

2 Note that a whole chapter within the BPS (1999a) report is devoted to considerations about causal factors. This aspect is, therefore, not ignored, but rather separated out from actual defining features.

> *'Dyslexia is evident when accurate and fluent word reading and/or spelling develops very incompletely or with great difficulty. This focuses on literacy learning at the word level and implies that the problem is severe and persistent despite appropriate learning opportunities. It provides the basis for a staged process of assessment through teaching.'*
>
> (BPS 1999a: 18).

Figure 12.1 A working definition of dyslexia

The first sentence of this definition contains the essential identifiable features of the condition, as required by any process of scientific enquiry, and the remainder of the definition provides an appropriate educational and psychological context.

The definition is described as a 'working definition' in contrast to what might be termed an 'operational definition'. The present 'working definition' does not attempt to justify particular significant or functional cut-off points on the continua of reading and spelling measurements. Indeed, Tonnesson (1997) has pointed out that it may in fact be difficult to identify non-arbitrary cut-off points for reading and spelling measures below which dyslexia is said to be evident. Also, the BPS (1999a) 'working definition' for dyslexia does not indicate exactly what literacy measurements might be made and why (e.g. word reading within or out of text; fluency over shorter/longer time period; reading comprehension and/or reading accuracy).

In conclusion, it could be argued that the BPS (1999a) dyslexia report has made considerable progress towards clarifying some of the previous fundamental problems in the way that we have used, and responded to the word dyslexia. The report is, however, lengthy and theoretically complex in parts. The next challenge for research-practice collaborators must be to evaluate and develop the potential of the BPS (1999a) dyslexia report for influencing and permeating educational assessment, intervention and policy.

Implications of the British Psychological Society's (1999a) dyslexia report

Research interest now focuses upon how teachers and educational psychologists might view the BPS (1999a) dyslexia report in relation to their literacy planning and teaching, and in particular, how persistence and severity (as identified in the dyslexia working definition) will be monitored and evaluated as part of a process of assessment through teaching. The following three subsections consider the possible impact of the report upon assessment, definition and SEN policy.

Assessment implications

Regan and Woods (2000) highlight the BPS (1999a) dyslexia report's focus upon monitoring persistence and severity of word reading and spelling difficulties through a staged process of assessment through teaching that provides appropriate learning opportunities. 'Assessment through teaching' entails the monitoring of learner progress through a cycle in which teachers notice individual learner performance and then adjust teaching programmes accordingly as far as possible. This process is challenging to teacher resources and may also require specific skills development (QCA 2001). The structure of the National Literacy Strategy (NLS) (DfEE 1998) provides the overall framework through which teachers will identify and make provision for children's difficulties with word reading and spelling. There are some concerns, however, that the NLS framework may be too prescriptive and ambitious in its target setting for children's word reading and spelling, with the possibility that some children may be left behind or receive instruction for skills already learnt (Piotrowski and Reason 2000; Barrett, Reason, Regan, Rooney, Stothard, Williams and Woods, submitted). From an analysis of generally available teaching methods and materials, Piotrowski and Reason (2000) found that many generally available literacy learning schemes do in fact provide a comprehensive model of reading and spelling development with a clear progression of phonological targets, but with an under-emphasis on principles of 'assessment through teaching'.

In order to address these issues, a group of psychologist-researchers based at Manchester University have developed and piloted a literacy planning framework for use by teachers (and learning support assistants where appropriate) (Barrett *et al.*, in press). The literacy planning framework is designed to assist teachers, using a combination of NLS and other general literacy scheme resources, in planning for the needs of individual learners within the group teaching situation and to incorporate careful consolidation on word level targets where necessary. Elements within the literacy planning framework include:

- opportunity for teachers to reflect upon the way in which lessons will be planned and adapted to accord with a comprehensive model of literacy learning and their own observations of the learners;
- an emphasis upon involving learners in evaluating and recording their own word reading and spelling progress;
- maximising communication and learning opportunities by explicitly drawing together the actions and perceptions of all those with a concern in the learners' progress, including the learner;
- teaching of phonic targets according to assessment information about each child in the teaching group, with teaching planned to maximise 'inclusion' by interaction and participation;

- Opportunities for children to consolidate and, where necessary, revise, phonic skills.

Figure 12.2 below shows the outcomes of using Barrett *et al.*'s (in press) literacy planning framework for a Year 4 pupil. This required initial joint assessment work by an educational psychologist and a support teacher using Additional Literacy Support (ALS) materials of the NLS.

Paul is a Year 4 child where there is concern about his spelling progress and motivation for literacy learning. In addition to some whole-class teaching in literacy hour, he receives daily small group teaching from a teacher using ALS materials.

The educational psychologist's phonic assessments formed the starting point for planning for each child in the group. ALS lessons were adapted accordingly to avoid the noticed effects of 'one size fits all' ALS lesson plan structure where some children could be left behind while others may be repeating learning objectives they had already consolidated. Additional resources for over-learning of word level reading and spelling ('Easylearn phonics') were found from a phonic skills package in the school resources bank. These were chosen for their simple and appealing presentation, as well as the range of activities at each level of difficulty. Most often children in the group were able to work together in pairs or threes on selections of activities and games appropriate to shared word level targets.

Timed reading sheets ('race games') from the scheme were to be adapted to reinforce, and test accuracy and fluency of, the phonic targets being worked on by each child. Race game sheets would be available to the children to practise with a partner in class and at home, and the children themselves shall record the numbers of words read accurately in the one-minute time allowance by colouring a block graph on the 'race game' sheet.

Both the ALS teacher and the educational psychologist thought that the ALS materials separated reading from writing to an extent that was not optimal for word level learning and underutilised onset-rime approaches. Adaptations to the ALS materials, sentence dictation exercises focusing on the phonic targets and use of Phonological Awareness Training (PAT) materials (Wilson 1997) were incorporated into the literacy plans for the group.

Twice-weekly timed sentence dictation exercises were designed to monitor and compare the children's accuracy and fluency of phonic target spelling in context.

A teacher-to-teacher notebook was devised for communication between the ALS and the class teacher in order to enable best literacy planning, curriculum access and reinforcement opportunities in class.

Certificates incorporating the actual word targets learnt for word reading (race game) and spelling (sentence dictation targets) achievement would be made available through the class teacher as part of the whole-class reward system.

Figure 12.2 Initial assessment outcomes from a teacher-psychologist collaboration using a literacy planning framework

The use of approaches such as the literacy planning framework illustrated in Figure 12.2 above may have implications for the role of support and assessment professionals, such as educational psychologists, in the identification and assessment processes relating to dyslexia. The focus on assessment *by* external specialists shifts to 'assessment *with*', bringing the advantage of classroom relevant dialogue and effective, jointly planned intervention. Through this, educational inclusion is promoted by bringing school-based and externally led assessment and intervention closer together and more accessible to all learners in the teacher's group. With the transparency of the BPS (1999a) working definition of dyslexia, and its clear link to learning opportunities, there may be less need for diagnostician's waiting lists. As the assessment role becomes less restricted, educational psychologists may be able to extend collaborations with teachers to promote more actively their wider role with schools, alongside literacy advisers and consultants, in developing strategies for consolidating and monitoring progress and investigating specific causes of literacy learning difficulties (e.g. Solity and Bull 1987; Frederickson, Webster and Wright 1991; Frederickson, Frith and Reason 1997; Palmer and Reason 2001).

It is worth noting, however, that teacher-psychologist assessment collaborations, despite their advantages, may be more time-consuming at individual case level and go against the grain for some when a discrete, distinctive or confirmatory contribution is expected (Regan and Woods 2000).

Identification: views on the working definition of dyslexia

Regan and Woods (2000) espoused the importance of shared understandings as a basis for joint work with teachers and so examined directly 36 teachers' understandings of the working definition and its assessment implications.

Though the teachers' pre-existing definitions of dyslexia included a wide range of features including phonological awareness problems, perceptual problems, sequencing problems and memory difficulties, the simplicity of the BPS (1999a) dyslexia report's working definition attracted approval. The clear description of features in the working definition makes it easy to understand and communicate:

'Yes it's less complicated . . . I think the general public would understand it a whole lot better . . . it takes away some of the confusion – can we use the "D" word or not? – And then parents say is he dyslexic and you don't really feel confident about what to say.' (Teacher comments from Regan and Woods 2000: 340)

On the other hand, teachers expressed some reservations about a possible lack of discriminatory power:

'I think it's too broad to be useful . . . Every single child with learning difficulties would fit within it.' (Teacher comments from Regan and Woods 2000: 341)

This has been a common concern by readers of the report. There are, however, certain other considerations to be made on this point. First, it may not follow that all children with literacy learning difficulties would be identified as having difficulties of a dyslexic nature. The BPS (1999a) dyslexia report suggests that:

> . . . the psychologist will consider whether there are other areas of concern for the child, extending beyond the working definition, which will need to be addressed and which may suggest a better fit with some other descriptor(s). (p. 62)

For example, it may not be parsimonious to identify dyslexia where a child's literacy learning difficulties exist alongside a number of significant difficulties in other skill areas. Similarly, it may not be appropriate to identify dyslexia where there are significant receptive and expressive language difficulties.

Second, clarification of the concept of dyslexia in less exclusive terms may not necessarily lead to more applications of the label to individual learners. Pilgrim (2000) suggests that in the process of clarifying the diagnostic process, psychologists may move (somewhat paradoxically) to a position of understanding 'diagnosis' to be less helpful because:

> Categorical descriptions are more reductionist, impersonal and stigmatising. (p. 303)

Drawing upon recent BPS (1999b) 'Guidelines for the use of diagnostic classifications in professional reports provided for the courts', Pilgrim (2000) proposes a more sophisticated model, in which psychologists may provide *formulations* based on psychological models and theories. In other words, psychologists may be more inclined to give a more useful and accurate functional description of 'what is going on here and why' rather than applying a general term which, while being useful to some extent for comparison to similar cases, might tend to conceal pertinent case details. Pilgrim (2000) also highlights the developing emphasis, in an increasingly democratic society, upon the empowerment of the client in those social processes that concern and affect them:

> With our clients we should negotiate the meaning . . . in a way that sensitively places behaviour and experience in its biographical and social context. (p. 304)

Third, it is not entirely clear what the concern to maintain the rarity of the term 'dyslexia' is about. Is it a concern that the number of dyslexia identifications will increase or that there will no longer be a subgroup of children with literacy learning difficulties who are excluded from the dyslexia subgroup (often termed 'general' or 'garden variety' poor readers instead) (Vellutino *et al.* 2000)? Yet given the confusions in the conceptualisation of dyslexia (BPS 1999a), it is not surprising that there is at present considerable variation in dyslexia identification rates, and so perhaps previous experience of identification should not be anticipated as a reliable guide to future identification rates or processes (Pumfrey and Reason 1991). Also, an increase in dyslexia identification might have some advantages. First, it might reflect a welcome reduction in the exclusion of some children from the dyslexia category because of the previous theoretically unsound focus on their measured intelligence in relation to their literacy learning difficulty. Second, the more inclusive, and perhaps extensive use of the term dyslexia might reduce stigma or mystique attaching to the label and promote constructive responses through mainstream education. Third, with an increased identification of dyslexic difficulties, the term could not be seen as automatically synonymous with SEN. This might be beneficial to the development of the latter concept, which is criticised as labouring under a circular definition and being insufficiently validated (Solity 1991; Woods 1998; Dyson 1994; BPS 1999a). The BPS (1999a) dyslexia report asserts that dyslexia and SEN are essentially separate matters and so each must develop its own distinct identity and validity.

Indeed a more inclusive use of the term 'dyslexia' may depend very much upon evidence-based clarifications on the nature of SEN. Many educational practitioners and parents consider children with difficulties of a dyslexic nature to have different educational needs depending upon other factors, such as measured IQ:

> 'But what are we going to call these children who fit the traditional concept of dyslexia – are they also just dyslexic, or are they severely dyslexic, because often their needs are quite, quite different from many of the other kids I could think of, who really don't have as much general intelligence in a variety of areas.' (Teacher quotation from Regan and Woods 2000: 341)

It will be important to clarify, with practitioners, parents and learners, exactly what kinds of differences are thought to exist and to ascertain through research, whether such differences can be said to exist in all cases and whether indeed any differences relate to features of dyslexia (reading and spelling difficulties) or to aspects of what may be thought of as SEN (e.g. curriculum participation/personal adjustment factors). At present there is little evidence to support the suggestion that children with difficulties of a dyslexic nature require qualitatively different literacy teaching programmes to other children who require carefully progressive teaching of the phonic code within the context of appropriate written and oral language experience (Reason 1998; Piotrowski and Reason 2000). There may be underlying lay assumptions about the 'frustrations' experienced by those more able children with difficulties of a dyslexic nature, or about notions of special provision to compensate for thwarted 'academic potential', that need to be explored and investigated when considering more comprehensive constructions of special educational needs (Connor 1994; Woods 1998). This work will require collaboration between practitioners, researchers, parents and learners, and as much emphasis upon dissemination as upon research investigation (Woods 1998).

Dyslexia and policy for special educational provision

The BPS (1999a) dyslexia report proposes that:

> Formulation on the matter of a learning difficulty . . . is essentially a separate, and more extensive, endeavour than formulation on the matter of dyslexia. (p. 57)

In the section dealing with SEN, the BPS (1999a) dyslexia report highlights access to curricular opportunities as an important consideration. This emphasis may indeed be in keeping with the original aim of the Warnock Report (DES 1978) which sought to separate 'conditions' from functional considerations about children's needs in school. This aim, it could be argued, has remained largely unfulfilled as legislation has continued to maintain a weight of references to descriptions of behavioural categories (e.g. DfEE 1994; DfES 2002). To the extent that literacy learning progress per se, as well as curriculum participation, may be viewed as one part of educational needs in some circumstances (e.g. literacy levels below levels for certain expected functions), the BPS (1999a) report points out that:

> The features of the definition (severity, persistence) may inform . . . judgements regarding severe and long-term special educational needs. (p. 69)

A greater emphasis upon the views and experiences of literacy learners themselves in the determination of their own educational needs might also be predicted (Hobbs and Todd 2000; Pilgrim 2000; DfES 2002). Detailed evaluation of both curricular participation and the experiences of the learner are promising areas for developing joint work between teachers and support workers which could be the focus of future research.

Conclusion

> If we do not know quite what we are looking for, or why, it is not surprising that the methods we use to achieve this nebulous end result are both ill-defined and diverse. They are likely to be subject to professional fashions, and without a clear rationale underpinning them, likely to be subject to marked fluctuations in popularity. (Elliott 1990: 24)

We may now begin to move away from this state of affairs. The BPS (1999a) dyslexia report has clarified the way in which the term 'dyslexia' has been used in educational practice and provided a new 'working definition' which is both transparent and robust. The definition can accommodate a variety of causal explanations and emphasises the importance of assessing progress against careful instruction. It provides a clear and practical starting point for the development of collaborative literacy and SEN assessment paradigms involving teachers, educational psychologists, learners and parents. Collaboration is a key feature of inclusive educational settings (Booth, Ainscow, Black-Hawkins, Vaughan and Shaw 2000).

Future research should evaluate and disseminate the utility of the definition, especially in relation to its impact upon classroom teaching and assessment practices, and its influence upon formulations about SEN.

References

Armstrong, D. (1995) *Power and Partnership in Education*. London: Routledge.

Barrett, M., Reason, R., Regan, T., Rooney, S., Stothard, J., Williams, C. and Woods, K. (in press) 'Co-researching the concept of "noticing and adjusting"', *Educational Psychology in Practice*.

Booth, T., Ainscow, M., Black-Hawkins, K., Vaughan, M. and Shaw, L. (2000) *Index for Inclusion: Developing Learning and Participation in Schools*. Bristol: Centre for Studies in Education.

British Psychological Society (BPS) (1999a) *Dyslexia, Literacy and Psychological Assessment: A Report by a Working Party of the Division of Educational and Child Psychology (DECP) of the British Psychological Society*. Leicester: the British Psychological Society.

British Psychological Society (BPS) (1999b) 'Guidelines for the use of diagnostic classifications in professional reports provided for the courts', *The Psychologist* 12(9), 465.

Carroll, L. (1872) *Through the Looking Glass*. Cited in British Psychological Society (1999a) *Dyslexia, Literacy and Psychological Assessment: A Report by a Working Party of the Division of Educational and Child Psychology (DECP) of the British Psychological Society*. Leicester: the British Psychological Society.

Connor, M. (1994) 'Dyslexia (SpLD): assessing assessment', *Educational Psychology in Practice* 10(3), 131–40.

Department for Education (DFE) (1994) *Code of Practice on the Identification and Assessment of Special Educational Needs*. London: DFE.

Department for Education and Employment (DfEE) (1998) *The National Literacy Strategy*. London: DfEE.

Department for Education and Skills (DfES) (2002) *Code of Practice on the Identification and Assessment of Special Educational Needs (Revised)*. London: DfES.

Department of Education and Science (DES) (1978) *Special Educational Needs: Report of the Committee of Enquiry into the Education of Handicapped Children and Young People (The Warnock Report)*. London: HMSO.

Dyson, A. (1994) 'Towards a collaborative learning model for responding to student diversity', *Support for Learning* 9(2), 53–60.

Elliott, C. D. (1990) 'The definition and identification of specific learning difficulties', in

P. D. Pumfrey and C. D. Elliott (eds), *Children's Difficulties with Reading, Spelling and Writing.* Basingstoke: Falmer Press.

Frederickson, N., Frith, U. and Reason, R. (1997) *Phonological Assessment Battery (PhAB).* Windsor: NFER-Nelson.

Frederickson, N., Webster, A. and Wright, A. (1991) 'Psychological assessment: a change of emphasis', *Educational Psychology in Practice* 7(1), 20–29.

Gersons-Wolfensberger, D. J. M. and Ruijssenaars, W. A. J. J. M. (1997) 'Definition and treatment of dyslexia: a report by the committee on dyslexia of the Health Council of the Netherlands', *Journal of Learning Disabilities* 30(2), 209–13.

Hobbs, C. and Todd, L. (2000) *Consulting with Children.* Newcastle/Bradford: University of Newcastle/Bradford Educational Psychology Service.

Howe, M.J.A. (1997) *IQ in Question: the Truth about Intelligence.* London: Sage.

Palmer, S. and Reason, R. (2001) *Checking Individual Progress in Phonics (ChIPPs).* Windsor: NFER-Nelson.

Pilgrim, D. (2000) 'Psychiatric diagnosis: more questions than answers', *The Psychologist* 13(6), 302–5.

Piotrowski, J. and Reason, R. (2000) 'The National Literacy Strategy and dyslexia: a comparison of teaching methods and materials', *Support for Learning* 15(1), 51–7.

Pumfrey, P. and Reason, R. (1991) *Specific Learning Difficulties (Dyslexia): Challenges and Responses.* Windsor: NFER-Nelson.

Qualifications and Curriculum Authority (QCA) (2001) *Review of Assessment Arrangements: Assessment for Learning.* London: QCA.

Reason, R. (1998) 'Effective academic interventions in the United Kingdom: does the "specific" in specific learning difficulties (disabilities) now make a difference to the way we teach? An evaluation ten years on', *Educational and Child Psychology* 15(1), 71–83.

Regan, T. and Woods, K. (2000) 'Teachers' understandings of dyslexia: implications for educational psychology practice', *Educational Psychology in Practice* 16(3), 333–47.

Rutter, M. (1998) 'Dyslexia: approaches to validation', *Child Psychology and Psychiatry* 3 (1), 24–5.

Solity, J. (1991) 'Special needs – a discriminatory concept?' *Educational Psychology in Practice* 7(1), 12–19.

Solity, J. and Bull, S. (1987) *Special Needs: Bridging the Curriculum Gap.* Milton Keynes: Open University Press.

Tonnesson, F. E. (1997) 'How can we best define dyslexia?' *Dyslexia* 3, 78–92.

Turner, M. (1997) *Psychological Assessment of Dyslexia.* London: Whurr.

Vellutino, F. R., Scanlon, D. M. and Reid-Lyon, G. (2000) 'Differentiating between difficult-to-remediate and readily remediated poor readers: more evidence against the IQ-achievement discrepancy definition of reading disability', *Journal of Learning Disabilities* 33(3), 223–38.

Wilson, J. (1997) *Phonological Awareness Training (PAT).* Aylesbury/London: Buckinghamshire County Psychological Service/University College London.

Wolfendale, S. (1993) 'Thirty years of change: children with special educational needs', *Children and Society* 7(1), 82–94.

Woods, K. (1998) 'Dyslexia: questions from a social psychology perspective', *Educational Psychology in Practice* 13(4), 274–8.

Section 4

CHAPTER 13

Specialist teachers and inclusion: a case study of teachers of the deaf working in mainstream schools

Wendy Lynas

Specialist teachers and inclusion: are they compatible?

Specialist teachers of 'special needs' pupils are not always traditionally welcomed into mainstream schools as key figures in the development of inclusive schooling. They may be criticised for detracting from the true spirit of inclusion. It is alleged that their focus on individual 'special' children sustains the medical model of disability by reinforcing the idea of deficit within the child (Ainscow 1999). Within the medical model, children who appear unable to learn 'normally' are prescribed special treatment from specialist practitioners in order to make good the deficit: the children must be changed if they are to benefit from education. Inclusive education, on the other hand, is premised on the social model of disability which, when applied to education, locates the source of difficulties within the child's educational environment rather than within the child.

The social model prescribes change. Not on changing the child to help her/him fit into the 'normal' classroom but on rethinking and changing the whole school's teaching and learning environment so that it can genuinely welcome *all* children and accommodate pupil diversity. The burden of responsibility for transforming the school environment to meet the needs of all learners rests primarily, according to inclusive educators, with those who work within the mainstream school (Ainscow 1999). Ordinary school teachers, it is argued, need to sit down together and reflect on their practices in order to work out ways of creating a learning environment which allows for the participation of all the young learners in their local area. The recently published *Index for Inclusion* (Booth, Ainscow, Black-Hawkins, Vaughan and Shaw 2000) offers detailed guidelines on developing inclusive practice in schools and, perhaps predictably, makes scant reference to specialist teachers of pupils with disabilities or learning difficulties. The authors clearly do not assign a significant role to specialist teachers in working towards the goals of 'creating inclusive cultures', 'producing inclusive policies' nor 'evolving inclusive practices' (Booth *et al.* 2000). The *Index* directs its advice towards staff in schools and bids them 'to build on their existing knowledge about what impedes learning and participation in their schools. . .' and asks them to examine 'the possibilities for increasing learning and participation in all aspects of their school for all their students'. While there is considerable emphasis in the *Index* on developing collaborative cultures in schools, between 'staff, governors, students, parents', specialist educators are not explicitly included in this collaboration.

It is, however, quite reasonable to claim that specialist teachers can be helpful to schools charged with the task of catering for 'all-comers'. They have insights, developed over the years, about the barriers to learning caused by a variety of conditions and circumstances and their accumulated knowledge of techniques and strategies for overcoming barriers to learning are considerable. Unfortunately, specialists are clearly mistrusted by inclusive educators for the reasons offered in much of the writings of those who might be termed 'inclusionists', e.g. M. Ainscow and T. Booth (UK), R. Slee (Australia). Specialist teachers, it is claimed, sustain the idea of categories of special need and thereby confer stigmatising labels on categorised special needs children, thus creating inequalities among pupils (Ainscow 1997). It is argued that specialist teachers, in order to justify their presence in mainstream schools, must, of necessity, draw attention to their specialist skills and knowledge (Dyson 1991) and this will serve to undermine the efforts of 'ordinary' teachers to cater for diversity, thus creating inequalities among teachers. It is also argued that a significant presence of specialist teachers in schools leads to the idea that the education of children who have any kind of problem in learning are being 'taken care of' and, therefore, there is no need for change: the status quo is maintained and the learning environment unreconstructed (Ainscow 1999).

In the eyes of inclusionists, specialist teachers, far from contributing to the process of 'including all', are seen as a barrier to change and an impediment to the development of inclusive practice. So, inclusionists would be extremely sceptical of the suggestion that *specialist teachers can be the driving force towards inclusion.* Despite this scepticism, the aim of this chapter is to show exactly that. Using the example of current practice in the mainstream education of hearing impaired pupils, I believe I can demonstrate that specialist teachers can be the trigger to inclusive practice. Using the example of teachers of the deaf in Britain, based on recent research evidence, I hope to show that this particular group of specialist teachers not only work towards the goal of including deaf children within mainstream education but also act as a force for the development of inclusive practices within the school to the benefit of all children.

Recent research of teacher of the deaf practice in mainstream schools

To support my argument that teachers of the deaf work in inclusive rather than segregating ways, I will be using the findings of three recent research studies with which I have been involved.

One research project (Lynas 1999) included observations of practice where teachers of the deaf were supporting nine profoundly deaf 6- to 7-year-old children in mainstream schools. The second study, supported by the Teacher Training Agency (TTA), involved observations of practices employed by teachers of the deaf in support of 52 hearing impaired pupils in mainstream primary and secondary schools in England and Wales (Hopwood and Lynas 2000). The third investigation included observations of teachers of the deaf in 30 or so mainstream schools throughout the UK which had been judged to be examples of 'good practice': the aim of the project was to identify key features of good practice in deaf education (Powers, Gregory, Lynas, McCracken, Watson, Boulton and Harris 1999). All in all, more than 100 teachers of the deaf featured in the three investigations.

While the studies revealed a variety of practices, common features emerged and it is on the basis of what the support practices had in common that the case is made for the crucial role of specialist teachers of the deaf in moving towards inclusive education.

Before discussing the research findings, I should perhaps point out that provision within the mainstream is normal practice in deaf education in the UK and has been for many years, long before the term 'inclusion' came into currency. This is despite the barriers to educational development caused by a substantial and permanent hearing loss. Preference for mainstream rather than special school education for deaf children reflects not so much idealistic notions of inclusion but a pragmatic belief among deaf educators that the ordinary school offers deaf children more challenge and stimulus for academic, linguistic and social development than the special school for the deaf (Dale 1984; Harrison 1993). The current position is that around 90 per cent of deaf children in the UK attend either their local school or a resource-base within a nearby mainstream school and they are supported by specialist teachers of the deaf, most of whom have never worked in a special school context.

Research findings: developments towards inclusion in deaf education

High aspirations

Despite the deaf child's potential learning difficulties, aspirations were found to be high and this finding is confirmed elsewhere (Webster and Webster 1997).

The deaf children featuring in the studies were expected to have access to the curriculum and to 'achieve', like any other child, according to their intellectual ability. Deafness per se was not considered to be a justification for lower attainments. The goals of education were, therefore, similar to those for normally hearing pupils and in that sense the aim was to offer an equal education.

The deaf child – a special pupil?

However, offering an equal education did not mean, to the teachers of the deaf featuring in the investigations, offering the 'same' education. There is no doubt about the belief of teachers of the deaf in deaf pupils' 'specialness', nor indeed their own 'specialist' status. The one year or equivalent of specialised training in language acquisition, audiology, communication strategies – verbal and sign, encourages the conviction that deaf children's special needs are complex, that they are vulnerable in learning and that they need 'qualified teacher of the deaf support' (McCracken 1999).

Individual focus leads to a focus on the school environment

That the teachers of the deaf featuring in the investigations focused in the first place on their 'special' pupil did not prevent those teachers from paying heed to the environment of the school. It was this focus on the individual that drew attention to features of the school environment. Before the deaf child sets foot in the school the teacher of the deaf, using her/his specialist knowledge, typically visits and observes the school to examine the acoustic environment, teaching styles and the ethos of the school. Usually, none of these features are perfect from the point of view of the deaf learner. And it seemed to be up to the teacher of the deaf to take a proactive initiative in improving matters. It was not the case, according to the research observations, that initiatives came from the mainstream teachers as 'reflective practitioners'. Mainstream teachers were more than happy to take the advice of the specialists and they eagerly sought guidance from them.

The acoustic environment

The successful inclusion of the pupil who is a hearing-aid user depends crucially on the acoustic environment of the school. The following examples from the research studies on the activities of teachers of the deaf illustrate the lengths to which they go in order to improve acoustic conditions and reduce reverberation and background noise:

- fund-raising activities to get carpets, curtains, acoustic tiles for a classroom or hall;
- negotiating for the installation of a 'sound field' system in the deaf pupil's

classroom, which has the effect of damping down background noise and thereby making the teacher's speech more audible;

- persuading the head teacher to replace an overhead projector with a hum with a silent one;
- organising an engineer to reduce the noise generated by the central heating system;
- negotiating a change of location of the class to be attended by the deaf child so that the classroom is not next to the playing field or the infant playground;
- creating opportunities to address all staff and all pupils to promote 'noise awareness' so that problems of noise are minimised, e.g. classroom doors to be kept closed; a 'keep your voices down in the corridors' rule.

The above examples demonstrate a concern to ease the life of the deaf pupil in a mainstream environment but what I trust will be clearly apparent is that such changes to the school environment improve conditions for *all* pupils. All children benefit from a reduction in distracting noise and in being able to better hear their teachers and each other.

The teaching and learning environment

At least as important as the physical environment is the teaching and learning environment. The teachers of the deaf featuring in the investigations did not expect mainstream teachers to be knowledgeable about deafness, to understand, for example, how hearing aids work nor be aware of the many accommodations they might adopt which can 'make all the difference' to the deaf child's access to the curriculum. They did not take it as given that staff and pupils in a school will be interested in deafness nor enthusiastic about having a deaf pupil or deaf classmate. The research studies confirmed a belief on the part of teachers of the deaf that it is their job to engender and maintain interest and enthusiasm for the pupil who is deaf and to share their knowledge and skills with their mainstream colleagues in facilitating the deaf child's education.

Changing the learning environment: mainstream teachers

Through the practice of regular inservice training and through ongoing liaison and discussion, all the teachers of the deaf observed sought to 'up-skill' and empower their mainstream colleagues. Teachers of the deaf negotiated time, regular sessions, for a day or half-day or lunch-hour to give talks/workshops to staff in schools. They used a wealth of illustrative materials – videos, audiotapes, audiograms, etc. – to inform school staff about deafness, the educational implications of deafness, hearing aids, communication strategies and so on. Teachers of the deaf might observe classroom teaching and then advise on good practice from a deaf pupil's point of view. Teachers of the deaf visited schools regularly and frequently to liaise with teachers and discuss problems. Examples from the research studies give an indication of the new skills of mainstream teachers resulting from this liaison and inservice work:

- mainstream teachers are sufficiently familiar with the deaf child's personal hearing aids that they can change batteries, replace leads or tubing, decide if the aid is faulty;
- mainstream teachers know how to use the radio aid transmitter appropriately: they know when to switch the transmitter on or off, hand over to another pupil, etc.;
- mainstream teachers develop habits of teaching that support the deaf child's access to information. For example:

  - they face forwards when talking to the class;
  - they do not pace up and down when talking;
  - they pay attention to the deaf child's seating position and make sure the deaf child can see the teacher's face in the light not against the light;
  - they repeat or reformulate pupil utterances from the floor so that the deaf pupil can have access to pupil contributions;
  - where the deaf child has signed interpretation, the teacher pauses to wait for the interpreter to finish;
  - they 'go slowly' and speak clearly when introducing new or unusual vocabulary and they offer alternative words, terms, explanations of 'difficult' vocabulary;
  - they use repetition and give opportunities for pupils to articulate a new word;
  - key words/points in a lesson are written on the board;
  - they signal a topic and demand the attention of all in the class before launching into the topic;
  - instructions for class or homework are repeated.

These are just a few examples from the practices observed, and the list of mainstream teachers' accommodations to a deaf pupil is extendable. Some of the practices represent new skills. But most, it could be argued, represent 'good teaching' and benefit all pupils in the class. Undoubtedly it is this kind of good teaching that transforms the locational integration of the deaf pupil into genuine participation: to inclusion, in other words. And the overall improvements were initiated not by mainstream teachers reflecting on how they were going to reconstruct the learning environment but by the specialist teachers motivated by a desire to get things right for the 'special' pupil.

The teachers of the deaf who featured in the studies were perceived as a resource for mainstream teachers enabling them to feel confident in taking responsibility for the deaf pupil in their class. The following citations from mainstream teachers featuring in one of the studies confirm this point:

> 'I felt terrified. I nearly died when M (deaf child's mother) said she was sending him here. We've learned so much since then. We honestly couldn't do without T's (teacher of the deaf) support.'

> 'The teacher of the deaf helps enormously in encouraging staff to be as helpful as possible . . . the visiting teacher of the deaf is key to the success . . . pointing out things we'd never thought about . . . the school have taken him (deaf child) on lock, stock and barrel . . . you can't underestimate her importance . . . she gently nudges staff along . . . to be better while reassuring.' (Head teacher)
> (Powers *et al.* 1999)

In addition to the practice of 'working through the mainstream teacher', teachers of the deaf offered more tangible and direct support in the form of extra visual or written materials, some of which were found to benefit non-deaf pupils in the class. The National Curriculum, the Literacy Hour, the Numeracy Hour have made the school day at both primary and secondary level a lot more predictable so that the teachers of the deaf can more easily plan work with class teachers. And it is to mainstream teachers that teachers of the deaf turn to learn more about the curriculum and ways of presenting it. With these added insights, teachers of the deaf can offer to team-teach for certain sessions and plan together the script of those lessons paying attention to the likely difficulties to be encountered by the deaf and indeed other vulnerable children in the class. They might volunteer to take the whole class so that the mainstream teacher can work with the deaf pupil in a small group of pupils thus enabling the mainstream teacher to get to know the deaf pupil better.

Being exposed to another teacher can have its drawbacks (Thomas 1992) but, according to the research studies, 'working together' was generally welcomed by mainstream teachers as an opportunity to share ideas and problems. A common difficulty was the absence of a dedicated liaison slot in the timetable for collaboration between teacher of the deaf and mainstream teacher. But it was interesting to observe the lengths that teachers would go to find the time to plan together, giving up lunch-times, meeting before/after school.

Encouraging peer support

Learning to respect differences in others, learning to normalise support for a fellow being with a disability is an important ingredient of inclusive education and it is a feature of good teacher of the deaf practice to encourage and facilitate such support among the deaf pupil's peer group. There were many instances in the practices observed of teachers of the deaf taking the opportunity to take the whole class or school for one or more sessions of 'deaf awareness'. Such practice gives scope for creating positive attitudes towards the child who is different because of deafness and for propagandising the idea that *dis*ability does not mean *in*ability. This kind of intervention taps the usually very great potential for peer support and can make the difference between support which is sensitive and useful and help which, though well intentioned, may detract from good communication (for example, mouthing words with exaggerated lip movements and without voice). Invaluable support was observed from pupils who, for example, made a point of speaking slowly and clearly, face-on to the deaf pupil; offered a nudge when the teacher expected attention; repeated the teacher's instructions and explained points that might not have been fully grasped – 'they seem to know by intuition how to explain things to E. . .', to cite a mainstream teacher featuring in one of the studies (Powers *et al.* 1999). Where deaf children were being educated through sign language there was no shortage of enthusiasm on the part of pupils to learn signs and, in some schools, join the signing club to know more of this 'exciting' new form of communication.

Inclusion – a shared achievement

So, to reiterate. The 'ideal-type inclusive school' for the deaf child, with evidences of deaf-friendly practices all round, was triggered in the first place, according to the research findings, by a specialist professional seeking to extract out of each school, its teachers and its pupils, the best possible learning environment for the special pupil. Once set in motion, ownership of the education of the deaf pupil and changes in practice were developed by mainstream teachers and specialist teachers working together, and together reflecting on practice. In the example of the mainstream education of deaf pupils, there can be no doubting the value of mainstream and teacher of the deaf collaboration in order to cross-fertilise ideas and arrive at solutions.

Direct and indirect support

The ways of working of the specialist teachers of the deaf so far described can perhaps be characterised as 'indirect' support. No mention has been made of these teachers directly teaching the deaf child. However, concern for participation and inclusion did not prevent *any* of the teachers of the deaf observed working individually with the deaf pupil, often in a withdrawal situation. They did not, therefore, relinquish the entire education of the deaf pupil to the 'reconstructed' learning environment of the mainstream class.

Every teacher of the deaf who featured in the investigations had concern for the special needs of deaf children to bridge the gap between the demands of the curriculum and their language and literacy levels. Withdrawing the deaf pupil for specialised work in language, literacy, auditory training, sign language development, speech discrimination, has many advantages: the deaf learner is in quiet listening conditions; there is relative freedom from distraction and the levels of on-task engagement are generally high; in the withdrawal situation the deaf child has many more opportunities for participation in conversation (Hopwood 2000), and this can be crucial to the deaf child's language development. In the typical mainstream classroom, pupils are not given a great deal of opportunity for linguistic expression nor for engaging in conversational interaction with an adult (Geekie and Raban 1994; Hopwood 2000). If deaf children are eventually to achieve independence in learning and the goal of full inclusion, the development of listening skills, language and literacy is essential.

One strategy used by teachers of the deaf in withdrawal time was what they called 'pre-tutoring'. Pre-tutoring involves preparing a deaf child *in advance* of a lesson, focusing on ideas/vocabulary of the subject to be taught in the mainstream class. A knowledge of the pupil combined with a knowledge of the work to be covered enables effective pre-tutoring. Pre-tutoring can be very morale-boosting for the deaf child who can, because of advance preparation, be the first one in class to put her/his hand up in answer to a question.

So, I am arguing that withdrawal from the class should not be scorned as segregating and excluding: it can serve a well-defined purpose and can be an effective means-to-the-end of inclusion. One might wish that the service of one-to-one tuition, offered by a person who has good understanding of a pupil's strengths and weaknesses, were extended to many more pupils during the course of their education.

Can practices in deaf education have wider applicability?

I am not arguing that the principles underpinning the successful inclusion of deaf pupils can *easily* be applied to all children labelled as 'special needs'. Deafness, as Gains (1999) suggests, is an 'acceptable disability' and 'likely to generate an appropriate level of empathy and resource allocation'. Deaf children have a clearly identified impairment and, assuming no additional disability, their intellectual capacity 'beneath' the hearing loss is intact. It may be that an important difference between deaf children and many other 'special needs' children is that goals in the education of deaf children are broadly similar to those for children who are not deaf. These goals, it must be said, may be unrealistic and inappropriate for some children who come to be defined as having 'learning difficulties'. Furthermore, the adaptations to the classroom and teaching style that are made for a pupil who is deaf will, generally speaking, be perceived as beneficial to other pupils. But the accommodations felt necessary for some learners, for example 'disruptive' pupils, will not of necessity be advantageous to other pupils in the class. However, what I hope I have demonstrated using the example of teachers of the deaf in mainstream education, is that segregation need not arise when special educators and ordinary schools come together. Despite current statementing procedures, which are generally seen as encouraging support that attaches itself to the individual special needs pupil, teachers of the deaf were observed to work in a variety of ways and were by no means permanently affixed to the individual deaf pupil.

Inclusion – the potential role for specialist teachers

I am certainly not arguing against the idea of schools reconstructing themselves from within in order to create more supportive learning communities (Booth *et al.* 2000). That all schools should aim towards an inclusive ethos seems all the more pressing a goal in the light of a decade or more of government initiatives that place emphasis on 'standards' defined narrowly in terms of academic achievements. This emphasis on standards does not create an educational climate that is conducive to including children who find it difficult or impossible to achieve those standards. However, is it not reasonable to think that specialist teachers, with their special concern for children who struggle, can contribute to an inclusive ethos? Specialist teachers may be a crucial ingredient in challenging the more destructive, and for many pupils, psychologically undermining, effects of a narrow, achievement-orientated curriculum.

The following aspects of observed teacher of the deaf good practice might also serve to demonstrate how any specialist teacher might behave in ways that contribute to inclusive goals:

- teachers of the deaf *shared* their skills and knowledge – they did not keep their specialisms to themselves;
- teachers of the deaf were *supportive* and *encouraging* to mainstream colleagues – they did not undermine them;
- teachers of the deaf expected to *learn from their mainstream colleagues* and work with them to arrive at solutions to problems;
- teachers of the deaf preferred to be perceived as *collaborators* rather than external consultants;
- teachers of the deaf maintained a *proactive* stance: they did not simply complain when things were not right – *they made things happen*;
- teachers of the deaf's primary goal for their pupil was *independence in learning* – they did not want their deaf pupils in the long term to 'need' them.

Conclusion

I have tried to respond to those 'inclusionists' who are wary of a powerful 'specialist' presence in the mainstream school. The teachers of the deaf who featured in the three research investigations did not set out with 'school improvement' as their primary goal. Nonetheless these teachers of the deaf added a new ingredient to the schools they worked in which changed those schools, almost certainly, for the better. The principle that emerged was that a strong concern on the part of teachers of the deaf for the well-being of the individual 'special' pupil led immediately to a focus on the learning environment of the school. This in turn led to a collaborative way of working with mainstream teachers which resulted in a 'reconstruction' of that learning environment from the 'bottom-up', as it were. Practices moved forward to the creation of a more 'inclusive' school and I offer support for my conclusion with a comment from a mainstream head teacher who featured in one of the research investigations:

'A good teacher of the deaf benefits all children and the school.'

(Powers *et al.* 1999)

References

Ainscow, M. (1997) 'Towards inclusive schooling'. *British Journal of Special Education* 24(1), 3–6.

Ainscow, M. (1999) *Understanding the Development of Inclusive Schools*. London: Falmer Press.

Booth, T., Ainscow, M., Black-Hawkins, K., Vaughan, M. and Shaw, L. (2000) *Index for Inclusion*. London: Centre for Studies on Inclusive Education.

Dale, D. (1984) *Individualised Integration*. London: Hodder and Stoughton.

Dyson, A. (1991) 'Rethinking roles, rethinking concepts: special needs teachers in mainstream schools', *Support for Learning* 6(2), 51–60.

Gains, C. (1999) 'Editorial', *Support for Learning* 14(3), 98.

Geekie, P. and Raban, B. (1994) 'Language learning at home and school', in C. Gallaway and B. Richards (eds), *Input and Interaction in Language Acquisition*. Cambridge: Cambridge University Press.

Harrison, D. (1993) 'Promoting the educational and personal development of deaf children in an integrated setting', *Journal of the British Association of Teachers of the Deaf* 17(2), 29–35.

Hopwood, V. (2000) 'The effect of teaching context on language interaction with deaf pupils in mainstream schools'. Unpublished PhD thesis, University of Manchester.

Hopwood, V. and Lynas, W. (2000) *Supporting the Education of Deaf Pupils in Mainstream Schools: A Typology of Practice* (in press). University of Manchester. Research supported by Teacher Training Agency.

Lynas, W. (1999) 'Supporting the deaf child in the mainstream school: Is there a best way?' *Support for Learning* 14(3), 113–21.

McCracken, W. (1999) 'Good practice in deaf education'. Paper presented at the Royal National Institute for the Deaf (RNID) Conference *Learning from Success*. December. London.

Powers, S., Gregory, S., Lynas, W. *et al.* (1999) *A Review of Good Practice in Deaf Education* London: RNID.

Slee, R. (1996) 'Inclusive schooling in Australia? Not yet', *Cambridge Journal of Education* **26**(1), 9–32.

Thomas, G. (1992) *Effective Classroom Teamwork: Support or Intrusion?* London: Routledge.

Webster, V. and Webster, A. (1997) *Raising Achievement in Hearing-Impaired Pupils.* Bristol: Avec Designs.

CHAPTER 14

The inclusion of children with visual impairment in the mainstream primary school classroom

Pauline Davis and Vicky Hopwood

Background

This chapter is based on the findings of a research project, funded by the Economic and Social Research Council (ESRC R000223108), on the inclusion of children with visual impairment in the mainstream primary school classroom. More than 60 per cent of primary school-aged children with a visual impairment (blind and low vision) are now educated in the mainstream (Clunies-Ross and Franklin 1997). Given the impetus for inclusive education, this trend seems set to continue. For instance, the revised *Code of Practice on the Identification and Assessment of Special Educational Needs* (DfES 2001) states that:

> There is a clear expectation within the Education Act 1996, that pupils with special educational needs will be included in mainstream schools . . . the Government believes that when parents want a mainstream place for their child the education service should do everything possible to try to provide it. (p. 4)

> Admissions authorities for mainstream schools may not refuse to admit a child because they feel unable to cater for their special educational needs. (p. 4)

Research studies have shown consistently the benefits of increasing the child's access to opportunities for wider social interaction and learning (e.g. Webster and Roe 1999). Since policies for the inclusion of children with visual impairment have been in place for a considerable number of years it seemed timely to examine the inclusion of children with visual impairment in the mainstream education system. Given that the main place where learning takes place in a school can be reasonably expected to be the classroom, it seemed that the key indicator of the success of inclusive policies should be the quality of the learning environment created for the child in school. This research project on the inclusion of children with visual impairment in the mainstream primary school classroom set out to:

- understand the circumstances of the teaching and learning in mainstream primary schools for children with visual impairment;
- examine teaching practices and classroom organisation so that children with visual impairment can be more effectively supported;
- consider how such teaching practices can be encouraged within school with the support of outside service organisations.

In summary, the focus of our research was on how policies for educating children with visual impairment in the mainstream primary classroom translate into practice.

At the time of writing this chapter, no other major research that focuses on teaching and learning with respect to children with visual impairment in the primary phase of education had been conducted in Britain. Indeed, research in the field of inclusive education, in line with the philosophy of education for all children, has tended to focus on all the children in a classroom or in a school, rather than on a particular group of children (Farrell 2000). In this respect our approach was somewhat unusual as, in the schools we visited, we focused on a particular child, rather than on all the children in the class. We would argue that through studying the inclusion of particular groups of children the gap between policy-rhetoric and practice-reality can be lessened, as cognitively it becomes easier to understand the complexities of the special need under examination, while still maintaining a mainstream focus. We believe this to be especially so for children classed as having low incidence special educational needs such as visual impairment. As McCall (1998) has argued, because of their low frequency, disabilities like visual impairment *have a tendency to be overlooked in grand designs.* Furthermore, there are specific issues relating to the nature of every specific special educational need or relating to the type of provision already in place that require attention. In the case of the education of children with visual impairment, issues of particular relevance are that:

- 'Visual impairment' is an umbrella term for a wide variety of conditions, with the detailed practicalities for inclusion depending very much on the particular condition of a child. Specialist diagnosis and expert advice is essential to ensure that the specific visual needs of a child can be met.
- Children with visual impairment often have complex needs, which call for accommodation by the class teacher to ensure that they are afforded their full entitlement to the curriculum (Arter, Mason, McCall, McClinden and Stone 1999). For instance, children with visual impairment can quickly become visually fatigued when concentrating on schoolwork for sustained periods of time and so may require regular periods to rest their eyes. Current research also

indicates that reading through Braille imposes significant cognitive demands for blind children compared with their sighted age-peers who read through print (Greaney, Tobin and Hill 1999). Furthermore, a child with severe visual impairment is likely to require additional support in developing social and life skills. For instance, Webster and Roe (1998) have highlighted the importance of social encounters to promote visually impaired children's cognitive and linguistic as well as social development:

- Policies and practices for educating children with visual impairment are known to vary widely across local education authorities (LEAs).
- Visual impairment is a low incidence need, which has particular implications regarding the capacity building of mainstream class teachers and teaching assistants (TAs).

The research project comprised case studies of 17 mainstream primary schools selected in conjunction with the services responsible for visual impairment in six LEAs in the North-West of England. In each school, interviews were conducted with all staff who had a stake in the education of the child with a visual impairment in the school. We, therefore, interviewed the head teacher, the Special Needs Co-ordinator (SENCO), visiting teacher (peripatetic teacher), TA and class teacher. Over 80 interviews were conducted in total. In addition, we observed the class teacher, TA and visiting teacher working with the child with visual impairment. Whenever possible, the observation sessions were followed by informal discussions with the teachers, which concentrated on their understandings and interpretations of the classroom situation.

There is considerable variation in policies and practices regarding inclusion between LEAs (Ainscow, Farrell and Tweddle 1999). Hence, in this inquiry the LEAs were selected to reflect a variety of policies for the provision of children with visual impairment. Access to the schools was made in conjunction with the service responsible for visual impairment in each LEA and schools were selected to provide access to children with a wide range of visual impairments, ages and abilities. Thirteen of the 17 schools were mainstream schools without an additional attached unit or resource base for the visually impaired. Of the remaining four schools, one housed the area resource base for children with visual impairment, one was resourced specifically for pupils with a visual impairment and two schools were resourced for children with different special educational needs; for example, one had a moderate learning difficulties (MLD) unit.

We focused on 23 children for the research, 12 boys and 11 girls. The children ranged in age from 4 to 12 years of age. Five of the children were Braille users. Three of the children had documented additional difficulties. Most of the children we visited attended their *local* mainstream primary.

During the process of conducting the research several themes emerged, which led to further lines of questioning; however, in this chapter we will draw attention to the following areas or themes, which promise to be useful for those people concerned with overcoming potential barriers to the development of effective policy and practice for inclusion:

- There appeared to be a lack of consistency in the definition and understanding of the term 'inclusion' among those people who participated in the research.
- There was a need for features or characteristics of inclusive teaching practice to be clearly defined;
- There are features of provision that seem to lead to inclusive teaching practices taking place.

These themes are used to structure the remainder of this chapter and incorporate a discussion of some of the potential barriers to inclusion along with suggestions as to how they might be overcome. The latter part of the chapter suggests a possible way forward in the organisation of the provision for children with visual impairment that may best facilitate an effective road to inclusion.

The term 'inclusion'

Examination of the LEA school and service policy documentation, and analysis of the interview data showed that there is inconsistency in the meaning placed on the term 'inclusion'. As indicated by the definitions provided by some of the participants, inclusion, it seems, is a multifaceted concept with varying interpretation and definition:

> 'Enabling access to the curriculum to the same level as the others by adapting resources or teaching methods for him to do that, take part as fully as possible . . .'

> '. . . To some extent it depends just what inclusion is . . . inclusion, I think probably within the special school context is about making sure that they can make the best of the curriculum that the school is offering, which I suppose is exactly what is happening in the mainstream too.'

> 'Inclusion should be preparing for lifelong learning. If inclusion is only just in the school environment . . . then it is not going to work . . . We have to change the culture within schools and we have to change society.'

We found that for many teachers, the term *inclusion* was used synonymously with *integration*, the implication being that once the child is in the school then inclusion has taken place. Sometimes inclusion meant *good practice*. For some participants, *inclusion* meant special schools for some children, at least some of the time. For others, *inclusion* referred to inclusion in the community as a whole, not just in the school. The main uses of the word inclusion that we identified were:

- inclusion as social inclusion
- inclusion as integration
- inclusion as something more than integration
- inclusion meaning 'full participation in'
- inclusion meaning 'not withdrawal'
- inclusion meaning 'limited withdrawal from the main classroom'
- inclusive education meaning 'the development of unitary provision for all children'
- inclusive education meaning 'being taught in a mainstream setting some of the time'
- inclusive practice used to mean effective practice or good teaching or simply what is best for the child.

The lack of precision in the use of the term 'inclusion' emerged as a key barrier to the development of inclusive practices, for this indicates a lack of common purpose among staff in schools and is a potential source of confusion. For instance, it was noticeable that some teachers and teaching assistants had reservations about fully embracing inclusion. Their reservations were not unrelated to a perceived need for periodically withdrawing the child from the mainstream classroom. Withdrawal from the classroom in certain circumstances was believed to be an appropriate measure to meet the needs of the child. For example, pupils may need to learn various skills such as listening and tactile awareness, braille, life skills (such as how to make a cup of tea or how to dress themselves), and skills of mobility and orientation which require a specialist trainer.

> 'I think you have got to get the right balance . . . I think that if you do too much in the classroom you miss out on the specific skills that the children need. For example, mobility, you know, you've got to withdraw for that and you've got to plan that you do that at a time when there are not a lot of children moving around. Braille skills . . ., I feel that children need to be somewhere where it is quiet and where they can really concentrate to pick that up.'

However, withdrawal from the classroom was viewed by many teachers as contrary to the aims of inclusion. There was a tension, therefore, between notions of 'what is right for the child' and the concept of inclusion. Indeed, finding that inclusion is not automatically embraced by the teaching profession is not new (Ward, Center and Bocher 1994; Clark, Dyson and Millward 1999; Fieler and Gibson 1999); however, staff having a positive attitude towards inclusion and 'can achieve' attitude towards the child are most important if inclusive teaching practices are to be developed. We therefore point to the need for the provision of staff development and training related to understanding and interpreting the concept of inclusion.

Inclusive teaching practice

Indeed, as our investigation progressed we used the classroom observation sessions to examine our own conception of effective (or inclusive) teaching for a child with visual impairment. Consider the following classroom encounters:

During one of our visits to schools we observed the class engaged on different activities in groups. Most of the pupils were working independently while the class teacher worked with one particular table on group reading. Present in the classroom was Samuel who is blind. He was working on written activity alongside the children on his table and made use of an electric brailler. There was much discussion among the children about the writing. This included the sighted pupils telling Samuel certain jargon and slang expressions. This activity provided an important opportunity for peer interaction, which on this occasion was facilitated by the fact that the TA, knowing the child was capable, had left him to get on independently.

During the Literacy Hour Sanjay, a boy in Year 1 who has low vision, was seated at a table next to the carpet where the rest of the class were sitting during a Literacy Hour session. The class teacher conducted the shared reading activity from the front. The class were reading a poem which was placed on a flip chart by the side of the teacher. Sanjay had his own enlarged copy of the text, which was placed on a work stand on his desk. The TA sat next to Sanjay, but at the far side of the room, so as not to separate the child from his peer group. The class teacher used a pointer to highlight the words in the text as the class read together. The TA had an identical pointer which she used in the same way to highlight the words of the text on Sanjay's own copy. The class teacher took full responsibility for Sanjay and checked he was following and keeping up. During class discussion, the class teacher allowed plenty of time before seeking answers to questions. In this way Sanjay, with the help of his TA, when needed, was able to access the lesson and to provide answers equally alongside his peers.

We consider this to be inclusive practice because:

- Sanjay was part of the main lesson;
- the TA provided supplementary but not the sole input;
- other children might also benefit from 'extra' time to assimilate information;
- the class teacher and TA were working in partnership.

Of particular benefit was the way in which the class teacher allowed Sanjay time to formulate responses to questions and to follow and access the text. This meant that the TA did not have to reinforce work at the same time as the class teacher was addressing the rest of the class.

Alternatively, Joanne is in Year 6 and is blind. She is supported full-time in her local school by a team of teaching assistants and visiting teachers from the sensory impaired service. Joanne was part of a group working with the class teacher. A copy of the book was provided for her in Braille and during the session there was little direct involvement from the assistant. The children in the group were selected to read aloud sections of text. Joanne followed the text and read a section out loud when it was her allotted turn. All the pupils seemed fully engaged by the class teacher and participated well. Having finished reading the text the pupils were then asked to find the meaning of particular words using a dictionary. Joanne took part in the task alongside the other pupils and used a talking dictionary to locate the meaning of the words.

As we examined these encounters alongside many others we began to describe teaching as inclusive when all (or nearly all) of the following features could be identified:

- The class teacher takes responsibility for the child.
- The child participates to the same degree as or better than the average of the other children in the class;
- The child sits so as to be part of the main activity in the lesson.
- Access to the curriculum is facilitated through the use of adapted resources and equipment.
- The teaching assistant (if there is one) works actively to facilitate the child's independence and development.
- There is evidence of prior planning and discussion of the lesson.

Central to our conception of inclusive teaching is that the child is fully engaged in the learning and social aspects of the classroom as would be expected to be the case of the other children in the room. Importantly, the child should not work in isolation with a TA for sustained periods of time.

Features of provision leading to the development of inclusive teaching practices

The following is a list of measures that we suggest can lead to the development of inclusive practices for visual impairment. However, many of the features identified will also be applicable to children with other special educational needs and other features are likely to prove of general benefit to all children in the classroom:

- Fostering positive 'can do' attitudes towards inclusion and the child among all staff.
- The class teacher, TA and visiting teacher working together as a team (so that inclusion for children with visual impairment is not considered easy by the school because 'the service does all that is required').
- Class teachers, TAs and visiting teachers having a common conception of the notion of inclusive teaching practice.
- A priority role of the visiting teacher being to disseminate specialist knowledge to class teachers and TAs.
- Establishing formal time for communication between the visiting teacher, class teacher and TA.
- Quality training for TAs to enable an increase in knowledge and a diversification of skills. (Of particular concern was the low level of training available for some TAs. We found that sometimes TAs were not paid for the time they were absent from school in order to attend training courses; that training courses were often over-subscribed or involved the TA travelling a great distance at his or her own expense in order to attend; and that sometimes the range of training short-courses available was very limited).
- The TA being viewed as belonging to both the school community and the community of the service.

Finding a way forward

The view is emerging in the field that to further develop the inclusion of children with special educational needs in the mainstream, we need to develop mechanisms to enable capacity building for mainstream and support staff. Indeed, as the focus on inclusion moves towards mainstream classroom practice, it is clear that capacity building of mainstream teachers and support staff should become a central concern. A key to achieving this is providing time for staff to share knowledge and expertise.

In order to ensure that the educational and sight needs of a child are met, it is crucial that guidance to teachers and parents is of the highest standard. This requires the translation of a full medical diagnosis into guidance on the educational needs of a child. For example, a child may need to have his or her desk raised and for it to be at an angle of 20 degrees; alternatively, for some children, enlarging a worksheet is ineffective in helping a child with low vision to see better. Mainstream teachers and support staff need to receive accurate and ongoing advice as there is a spectrum of conditions associated with visual impairment and the nature of a particular child's condition and needs are very likely to change over time. Providing this type of advice to the school and class teacher is an important role, and many would argue a role that requires a qualified teacher of the visually impaired. Similarly, the main input in teaching a child braille requires the expertise of a qualified teacher for the visually impaired and the main input on mobility training must, legally, be provided by a trained mobility officer.

Furthermore, because visual impairment is a low incidence special educational need many teachers will have never taught a child with this disability. For others this might be a one-off experience or an experience that happens every few years. It would be impractical then for mainstream class teachers to acquire the same level of expertise in visual impairment as a visiting teacher or a specialist teaching assistant. However, there is still very much that can be achieved by mainstream class teachers taking an active interest in facilitating the practice of specific skills. For instance, there are many opportunities within a mainstream classroom that allow mobility skills to be developed. The mainstream teacher, therefore, requires knowledge specific to the needs of the child in his or her class, as well as support in developing a wider repertoire of more inclusive teaching methods.

In our research, we found that, in some services, the relationship between the support service and mainstream class was such that this type of capacity building flourished. This was due to the cooperation and good will that existed between the particular mainstream and service staff concerned. Not only were the support staff highly skilled but they were responsible for a small enough geographical area to allow visits to schools to take place on a regular basis. However, we also found that such good practice does not occur routinely in all schools or LEAs. When one of the factors identified above was missing, professional development between service staff and mainstream teachers was less likely to prove as effective.

'The challenge for HI and VI services is . . . how to provide support which is empowering and capacity building . . .' (service head participant). In particular, if the trend towards forming large generic services for special educational needs, rather than the more established and smaller services specifically for the visually or sensory impaired, continues, we also add that the challenge is how to provide support, which is empowering and capacity building regarding the education of children with special educational needs, without low incidence disabilities such as visual impairment becoming overlooked in this 'grand design'.

In summary, we recommend that:

- measures are put in place to enable services to capacity build in mainstream schools;
- schools taking a child with visual impairment also agree to actively encourage a cooperative and learning partnership with the service;
- the quality visual impairment specific training is provided to all learning support staff;
- more work is done to define and develop inclusive teaching practices in schools.

There remains a need for further research to be conducted regarding the inclusion of children with visual impairment. In particular, we need to monitor and evaluate initiatives designed to develop the capacity building of teachers in the mainstream; we need to evaluate the provision for children with visual impairment in secondary schools, and we need to understand and improve the organisation and management of the process of transition that takes place as a child moves from primary to secondary school.

Acknowledgements

We would like to thank the services responsible for the education provision of children with visual impairment in: Bury, Cheshire, East Lancashire, Manchester, Oldham and Trafford for their participation in this inquiry. We also wish to thank all the pupils, their parents and school staff; particularly, we thank all those who gave up their time to be interviewed and those who permitted us to observe and discuss their working practices. We would also like to thank the Economic and Social Research Council for their generous support in funding this research.

References

Ainscow, M., Farrell, P. and Tweddle, D. (1999) 'The role of LEAs in developing inclusive policies and practices', *British Journal of Special Education* 26(3), 136–40.

Arter, C., Mason, H. L., McCall, S., McClinden, M. and Stone, J. (1999) *Children with Visual Impairment in Mainstream Settings.* London: David Fulton Publishers.

Clark, C., Dyson, A. and Millward, A. (eds) (1995) *Towards Inclusive Schooling.* London: David Fulton Publishers.

Clunies-Ross, L. and Franklin, M. (1997) 'Where have all the children gone? An analysis of new statistical data on visual impairment amongst children in England, Scotland and Wales', *British Journal of Visual Impairment* 15(2), 48–53.

Department for Educational and Skills (DfES) (2001) *Code of Practice on the Identification and Assessment of Special Educational Needs (Revised).* London: DfES.

Farrell, P. (2000) 'The impact of research on developments in inclusive education', *International Journal of Inclusive Education* 4(2), 153–62.

Feiler, A. and Gibson, H. (1999) 'Threats to the inclusive movement', *British Journal of Special Education* 26(3), 147–52.

Greaney, J., Tobin, M. and Hill, E. (1999)' Learning to read through touch: findings from a study of 317 Braille readers', *Journal of Visual Impairment and Blindness.* London: RNIB.

McCall, S. (1998) 'The future is green: an overview of the 1997 Green Paper on children with special needs, Excellence for All Children', *The British Journal of Visual Impairment* 16, 5–10.

Ward, J., Center, Y. and Bocher, S. (1994) 'A question of attitudes: integrating children with disabilities into regular classrooms', *British Journal of Special Education* 21(1), 34–9.

Webster, A. and Roe, J. (1998) *Children with Visual Impairments.* London: Routledge.

CHAPTER 15

Interdisciplinary support for children with epilepsy in mainstream schools

Gill Parkinson

Introduction

Epilepsy is one of the most common neurological conditions to affect children and adolescents in the UK. It is estimated that at some point in their lives one in 150 people will be given this diagnosis, 75 per cent of them before 20 years of age. The epilepsy does not always have a clear origin or cause (Hanscomb and Hughes 1999). Indeed, some children will 'grow out' of it. Nevertheless, teachers and allied professions working in schools are likely to encounter a number of such children during their working lives.

Until comparatively recently, children with epilepsy were either excluded from mainstream education or were permitted to attend only with highly elaborate, medically orientated support systems in place. Even now, children with epilepsy often have restricted curriculum and social access to facilities in mainstream schools. Head teachers are naturally anxious about increasing levels of accountability and the need, perceived or otherwise, to have specialised staff provision on hand to meet the mixed demands associated with such children. To whom should the teacher turn for advice on learning, academic progression, behaviour and levels of performance in subjects where the child with epilepsy might be perceived to be 'at risk'?

It is important to remember when working with such children that the condition, and the seizures (or fits) which are part of its manifestation, is a symptom not an illness. It is also a condition that can be easily misunderstood. It can generate fear and mistrust among the child's peers and the professionals who come into contact with that person. It is not the intention of this chapter to go into the nature of epilepsy, its causes and classification, and methods of treatment. All these issues certainly have implications for both management and interdisciplinary working in the school environment and beyond. Nevertheless, those involved in teaching, assessing and supporting need to be aware of the significance of such conditions, what to expect realistically from a child with epilepsy and how they can expect it to manifest itself within the school setting.

In 1896 the Education Department in London established a Committee on Defective and Epileptic Children chaired by the Chief Inspector of Schools. The Committee decided that if a child did not have more than one seizure a month, he or she could then attend an 'ordinary' school. Children who did not meet this criteria should either, they said, be placed in an institution run by a charity or another similar voluntary agency, or attend a residential special school.

However, these plans were not taken up by the School Board who in 1899 supported the passing of the Elementary Education (Defective and Epileptic Children) Act. This was a much less stringent piece of legislation where 'provision' was much more loosely defined than previously recommended by the Committee on Defective and Epileptic Children. Epilepsy then became amalgamated with other 'handicapping conditions'. Increasingly, as subsequent Acts were revised or rewritten, the model of education for such children became more medically orientated, with the children becoming increasingly more disconnected from their mainstream peers. Children were labelled as 'epileptics' and indeed in the 1944 Act regulations stated that as a group they were 'severely disabled' and must be educated in special schools.

The turning point came in 1953 when the 'Health and Handicapped Pupils' Regulations permitted children whose epilepsy was felt to be well controlled, into mainstream education. Present-day legislation in health and education now firmly lay the emphasis on inclusion of all children with SEN in mainstream settings whenever possible. This was demonstrated in the recent government White Paper 'Excellence in Schools' and the Green Paper *Excellence for All Children: Meeting Special Educational Needs* (DfEE 1998). The latter outlines how the government aims to improve the achievements of children with SEN in England over the next few years, with target setting to be met initially in 2002. In February 2001 the Secretary of State for Health announced the first ever government health inequalities targets for England which includes a new 'National Services Framework for Long-Term Health Conditions'. Their first stated target is:

> to reduce health inequality amongst children. Health at the beginning of life is the foundation of health throughout life.

(DoH 2001)

This legislation will have particular relevance to the support of children with epilepsy in schools, where meeting their medical needs is often a stumbling block to access to a satisfactory level and quality of inclusion within mainstream environments.

In what ways does such legislation have relevance for the service planner, head teacher, support worker or the child with epilepsy, who may have additional difficulties? The Green Paper *Excellence for All Children* stressed the need for early identification and intervention as being paramount to successful education of these children. This, together with the provision of appropriate, informed support is important if the child is not going to experience academic and social stumbling blocks by the time he or she reaches secondary school. In addition, lack of recognition of additional problems such as language disorder can inhibit access to the National Curriculum, impede progress and result in the child developing other emotional and behavioural difficulties. In order to meet these complex challenges it is important to implement various strategies, policies and procedures all of which should be governed by key principles. Such principles include:

- a clear understanding of each other's roles and responsibilities;
- active involvement with parent partnerships;
- practical support, within the Framework for SEN provision and via external agencies (Health, Social Services and the voluntary sector).

In the remainder of this chapter each of these important and interconnecting principles is discussed in more detail in relation to improving inclusive services for children with epilepsy.

Roles and responsibilities

In their *Teachers' Guide* (BEA Information sheet 2001), the pivotal role of the teacher in early diagnosis is emphasised:

> The teacher can be a great help in the diagnosis of the type of epilepsy a child may have, through an accurate written description of the seizures. Communication between teachers, parents and doctors cannot be stressed strongly enough. This . . . also prevents the child from becoming inhibited or withdrawn, or experiencing unnecessary learning problems.
>
> (British Epilepsy Association 2001)

To have a declared intention in the school's or LEA's policy documentation to 'work together' is not specific enough. Dyson, Lin and Millward (1998) in a national study of inter-agency cooperation for children with SEN in the light of the Code of Practice (DFE 1994) restated the need for close and informed cooperation. However, despite widespread consensus 'joint-working' has proved difficult to sustain in practice and there is a long history of difficulties in this area (Dyson *et al.* 1998). One area of difficulty highlighted related to problems with information access, exchange and avoidance of unnecessary duplication. The potential for this to happen can be seen when looking at the possible number of people involved in the education, care and support of children with epilepsy within a mainstream school environment (see Figure 15.1).

This list does not include contact with other more specialised services such as paediatric neurology, or the liaison required with statutory LEA officers, voluntary agencies or transport providers. All need to be clear about their roles and responsibilities; with whom to liaise (named person); and when to inform others of changes in circumstances, either child-centred or in terms of service delivery. Systems and structures will need to adjust as the child's health and academic needs change and as he or she moves through the educational system from primary to secondary education.

The way to achieve clarity of definition of roles and responsibilities, so avoiding unnecessary duplication of assessment and support, seems to be to build into the system a regular review procedure (already in place in schools but not in all LEAs). This review system should actively set out to monitor the 'cooperative activities in which they are engaged' (Dyson *et al.* 1998), paying particular heed to the balance and emphasis on take-up of service provision and the range of approaches and tasks such services are asked to support.

At local authority level such systems would be useful to ensure:

- greater information exchange between education, social care and health services. Some of the common barriers to this were identified by Law, Lindsay, Peacey, Gascoigne, Soloff, Radford and Band (2000) as being:
  a) lack of common boundaries between agencies;
  b) lack of common shared record keeping on children;
  c) difficulties in definitions of posts with consequent recruitment and retention problems (in relation to Speech and Language Therapists (SLTs) in this instance);
- greater recognition of the needs of people with epilepsy and therefore a need for
- a coordinated programme of awareness-raising and training for teaching and allied staffs; plus
- production of clear policy guidelines (jointly devised) for schools in support of students with epilepsy and their families.

At school level the needs were similar with the emphasis on additional training for designated members of staff being required.

In some schools it is generally recognised that there are difficulties and time delays in inter-agency information dissemination and exchange. Mainstream schools are, with the increasing knowledge base and roles of SENCOs, now more likely to know how and what services to access to assist the range of needs they are asked to support when associated with the child with epilepsy. Examples of such service 'definitions' are named contacts in their local Social Services Department (SSD) or Speech and Language Therapy Service (SLT Service). 'Border' disputes

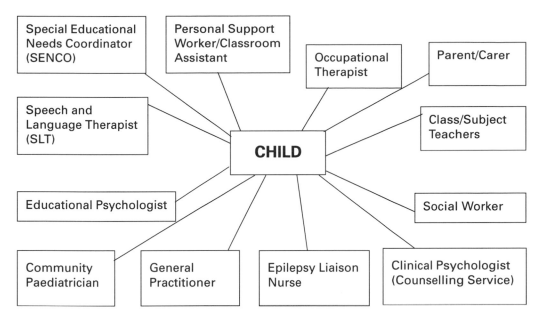

Figure 15.1 Support system for a child with epilepsy

over who will pay for SLT Services are particularly common in mainstream schools, where historically health services have only had to provide overtly medical supervision to meet local health needs. Therefore, the concept of using 'defined' service access is a particularly useful one in such circumstances. The framework for statutory assessment and review has helped to improve the somewhat fragmented network of service need with their differing organisational frameworks, definitions of need and priorities regarding service delivery.

However, examples of good practice in lines of support are being set up. Clear lines of communication are being created as people become involved and, indeed, the agencies themselves become more informed about the nature of epilepsy, its management, treatment and implications for increased inclusion in schools. One can see from Figure 15.2 how good lines of contact have been established between the SENCO or designated support worker, parents, head of year/head teacher and other agencies.

At a strategic level, an increased number of LEAs, Primary Care Groups (PCGs) and SSDs have improved their lines of communication with the advent of statutory assessments which consider the educational as well as the health needs of children with epilepsy. Gradually service delivery is striving towards the ideal of seamless support and provision. While this is far from a reality in many parts of the UK, the introduction of person-centred or joint action planning for individuals is becoming more evident within local authority and school provision. Descriptions of models of cooperation which are found to be working are in a DfEE report entitled

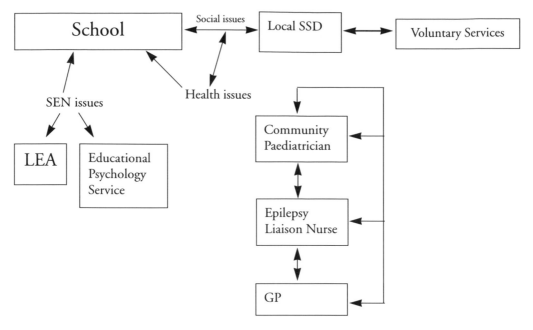

Figure 15.2 Good lines of contact

'Effective Communication between Schools, LEAs and Health and Social Services in the Field of Special Educational Needs' (Dyson *et al.* 1998).

Involvement with parent partnerships

If a plan of support is to be drawn up to enable the child with epilepsy to be maintained in a mainstream school, then the parents of the child need to be involved from the outset, since it is they who are gatekeepers and coordinators of the information required to make the plan work. This 'key' role can be shared with a person from one of the statutory agencies, who ideally should be a 'named person'. Whether one adopts a trans-disciplinary, interdisciplinary or multi-disciplinary model of dissemination (Lacey and Lomas 1994), one needs to ascertain that the following are included in such a plan:

- an unambiguous statement of the child's educational, medical and social needs;
- a plan of support which includes human, material and time resource provision;
- linked to the above, the training needed to put these in place;
- the method (and timescale) of implementation;
- the procedures adopted to monitor and review outcomes.

This may necessitate a review of existing policies and procedures relating to:

- administration of emergency drugs
- first aid in the classroom
- record keeping of seizures
- risk assessment procedures
- school outings
- PE
- swimming
- laboratory-based study
- access to community facilities in school hours.

Policies may need redrafting or changing. It is wise to involve parents and those with relevant knowledge and expertise from the outset. This engenders and enhances a spirit of cooperation from the outset, reducing the risk of confrontation at later stages because everyone has assured a joint responsibility for the policies agreed. Even with all aspects of the policies' implementation agreed, it is still advisable to ensure an evaluation system is in place with dates set to review and monitor outcomes. In all instances the policy should reflect three key principles:

- an inclusive philosophy;
- reflection of a whole-school approach;
- effective communication between all parties involved in the decision-making and implementation stages.

In the interests of safety and support for staff and students and peace of mind for parents, the school may wish to set up individual health *and* educational plans. They may also wish to review their insurance/indemnity cover for 'at risk' activities. A record should also be kept of the named people included in inter-agency liaison, pertinent to a particular child or group of children with a common need. Parents can be invaluable sources of help in this type of information gathering since they are more likely to be familiar with local epilepsy services.

Support within the Framework for SEN Provision

The intention of the revised *SEN Code of Practice* aims to preserve the principles and safeguards of the present Code, while simplifying procedures and keeping paperwork down to a minimum.

(DfES 2001)

The intended emphasis is to lessen the burden of paperwork and document collation required as part of the current system of SEN procedures, and so focus more on the practicalities of SEN support. This gradual change in emphasis from paper to people has begun, but movement to support children with epilepsy and additional needs in mainstream schools remains slow. This is not surprising since services such as Speech and Language Therapy struggle to cope with an average of 4,257 child population to therapist in England and Wales (Law *et al.* 2000). Over two-thirds of SLT departments now provide a service to mainstream schools and 60 per cent of the children receiving such a service at primary and secondary level have an SEN. According to LEA figures about 10 per cent of children with statements have speech and language difficulties as their primary need while 40 per cent overall have it mentioned in their SEN.

However, in children with epilepsy without generalised learning disability, Parkinson (1999; Parkinson and Martland 2000) found that up to 40 per cent of children in a research study carried out at a national children's epilepsy assessment unit had undiagnosed language impairments. Such language disabilities were by their nature and severity, enough to affect their access to learning. The presence of such communication difficulties is generally recognised in the literature to inhibit social and emotional development, restrict friendships and decrease the child's acceptance on equal terms among his or her peers. Combined with epilepsy, the situation can become serious if such problems are not recognised by the child's teacher, psychologist or others responsible for their care and education. In such instances staff training not only in the nature of epilepsy but its causes and implications for other problems which might be present, should be built into the school's Development Plan and management systems.

The research study commissioned by the DfEE into the needs of children with speech and language difficulties (DfEE 2000) drew out 13 key themes which the researchers felt highlighted current tensions regarding the roles and responsibilities of the present systems, and ways in which further improvements might be made to support such children. It is not the intention to list all 13 themes here. However, many are worthy of mention since they could easily be applied to children with epilepsy in terms of implications for improved interdisciplinary working in mainstream school settings.

- **Funding:** The joint concepts of equity and inclusion espoused puts a real demand on existing services for children. Too few professional groups (including SLTs) were available to provide a satisfactory raft of support for meeting the needs of such individuals.

  The researchers felt that there was an overwhelming necessity to clarify funding roles and sources. It was felt that LEAs should take the role of lead commissioners but *not* necessarily providers of SLT and allied health-based services.
- **Requirement for common records and data sets:** Such record keeping would engender 'agreed parameters as a baseline for service organisation'.
- **Identification process:** More use should be made of the baseline assessment now required at school entry.

- **Common boundaries between LEAs and Health Trusts (HTs):** Only 14 per cent of the authorities sampled had common boundaries and this can be an important issue in terms of the equity of provision. Joint strategic planning and the application of common audit measures are likely to lessen the potential negative impact. This approach has implications for joint planning when budgets are devolved down from LEAs to head teachers and HTs to Primary Care Groups or trusts.

- **Joint collaboration between LEAs and HTs:** The benefits and difficulties in such arrangements are well documented elsewhere. Such partnerships work better at strategic and practitioner levels when there is clear understanding of roles, where each appreciates the context in which the other is working, e.g. where teachers understand the importance of language in the whole curriculum and therapists' involvement is supported by the whole-school system. Shared vision was also felt to be a central issue here.

- **Increasing demand for SLT Services:** This is increasing, as is the demand for other services, as more children are included within mainstream education.

- **Prioritisation systems:** This is a feature of health and SEN systems, but not yet in mainstream education. Where they do exist they do not always concur, which is likely to result in a confusing message being sent to parents.

- **Problems in workforce planning:** Problems with recruitment, retention and funding at posts were felt to hinder increases in staffing, particularly as at present LEAs are not part of the NHS consortia.

- **Education, training and Continuing Professional Development (CPD):** Concern was expressed at all levels about the insufficient knowledge. Such gaps stem from differences in basic training and it was felt that the professional bodies concerned should address this. The researchers highlighted the need for accredited training programmes, which are delivered to and attended by the different professional groups.

- **Expectations of colleagues and parents:** Often complex needs of children with SEN can be perceived in different ways by professionals, e.g. whether the approach should be one of facilitation, rehabilitation or removing obstacles to the child's access to society as a whole. Different approaches need to be acknowledged if inter-professional working is to succeed.

- **Parents and carers:** Parents' and carers' experiences of involvement in the educational system are not always happy ones. They are keen to be actively involved and as such should be looked upon as a valuable resource. Differences between agencies and their lack of communication (perceived or otherwise) increased parental anxieties. Such concerns were working together, collaborating effectively.

The establishment of sound working practices, an awareness of the valuable contribution that can be made by all parties, can help and enhance the lives of children with epilepsy. Parents are needed to assist and influence the nature of and access to education to which their child has a right within a framework that aims to increase an inclusive environment in our schools.

Conclusion

This chapter has considered key interconnecting principles that can help parents, teachers, LEAs and other services to improve their practice in the education of children with epilepsy within inclusive settings. Clearly there are still many hurdles to overcome and many teachers remain uncertain about their skills and competencies in this area. However, through following the guidance suggested in this chapter, it is possible to create the conditions for improving services moving practice forward.

References

British Epilepsy Association (BEA) (2001) *Epilepsy: Teachers' Guide.* Information sheet. London: BEA.

Department for Education (DFE) (1994) *Code of Practice on the Identification and Assessment of Special Educational Needs.* London: DFE.

Department for Education and Employment (DfEE) (1998) *Excellence for All Children: Meeting Special Educational Needs.* London: DfEE.

Department for Education and Employment (DfEE)/Department of Health (DoH)/SEN Excellence for All Working Group (2000) *Provision of Speech and Language Therapy Services to Children with Special Educational Needs (England).* London: DfEE.

Department for Education and Skills (DfES) (2001) *Code of Practice on the Identification and Assessment of Special Educational Needs (Revised).* London: DfES.

Department of Health (DoH) (2001) *National Services Framework for Long-Term Health Conditions.* London: DoH.

Dyson, A., Lin, M. and Milward, A. (1998) 'Effective communication between schools, LEAs and health and social services in the field of special educational needs'. Research Brief No. 60. London: DfEE.

Hanscomb, A. and Hughes, L. (1999) *Epilepsy.* National Society for Epilepsy, in association with UCB, Parma, UK.

Lacey, P. and Lomas, C. (1994) *Support-Services and the Curriculum: A Practical Guide to Collaboration.* London: David Fulton Publishers.

Law, J., Lindsay, G., Peacey, N. *et al.* (2000) 'Provision for children with speech and language needs in England and Wales: facilitating communication between education and health services'. Research Brief No. 239. London: DfEE.

Parkinson, G. (1999) 'Complex epilepsy and childhood language disability'. Unpublished PhD thesis, Manchester Metropolitan University.

Parkinson, G. and Martland, T. (2000) 'The nature of language disability in children with complex epilepsy', *Development Medicine and Child Neurology* 42(85), 16.

CHAPTER 16

The teacher who mistook his pupil for a nuclear incident: environment influences on the learning of people with profound and multiple learning difficulties

Mark Barber

Whether or not the new National Curriculum Guidelines for pupils attaining significantly below age-related expectations, or debates about the future roles of special schools or, indeed, the various types of provision available are likely to promote the inclusion of pupils with profound and multiple learning disabilities (PMLD) is open to question. The question with which most practitioners are confronted on a daily basis is, however, 'How might I include this particular student in the events of the day or indeed in a social encounter that is both recognisable and meaningful to them?'

Including a pupil in a meaningful encounter is not a question of geography, it relies on the learner recognising that they have been included (Ouvrey 1997; Ouvrey and Saunders 1996). This can only be achieved if the learner is familiar with the situation, and if they have opportunities to assert their preferences, exert some level of control or be able to get involved in successful transactions with their environment.

This chapter presents a novel perspective of learning disability which is informed by an information processing perspective of the cognitive processes involved in acquiring knowledge and skill. The logic of the perspective leads the reader to consider a style of intervention or teaching based on the promotion of social cognition (e.g. Rogoff 1990; Ware and Healey 1994; Nind and Hewett 1994; Ouvrey and Saunders 1996; Grove, Bunning, Porter and Olssen 1999).

We live in a hugely complex environment of fluidly changing events that 'continuously and simultaneously compete for attention' (Rovee-Collier 1987). Any strategy that a learner attempts causes changes to the arrangement or 'configuration' of the opportunities around them. This requires the learner to monitor not only what their actions have changed, but also how they must adapt subsequent actions to accommodate these changes. Typically, we acquire expert behaviours or skills that enable us to take advantage of events, and if we encounter a novel situation, we can usually borrow what we know from other arenas of our experience to remain involved with the flow of events (Bates, Benigni, Bretherton, Camaioni and Volterra 1979). But for learners for whom the environment changes too quickly and in too complex a manner, the complexity of the environment must be managed if inclusion in the flow of events is to be maintained. This chapter looks at how this fundamental level of inclusion, that of inclusion in the learning process, might best be achieved.

Background

Can we learn about the experience of consciousness of a person with PMLD by looking at catastrophic incidents in nuclear power stations? It seems a ridiculous idea, but it is not.

The Generic Error Modelling System (Reason 1990) or GEMS was developed following a decade of research into human error, and analysis of operator actions during catastrophic incidents in the power generation industry. It examines the interface between operators and the complex environments in which they work. GEMS leads to a perspective of consciousness and problem solving that appears to be very relevant to practitioners working with clients experiencing PMLD.

GEMS (Reason 1990) is a rationale accounting for how we interact with our surroundings. It is based on three levels of cognitive involvement:

1. The lowest or *'Skill Based'* level of cognitive resources, represents the level at which the least amount of cognitive supervision is involved. While habitual or routinised actions involve the least amount of cognitive involvement, they also represent our most skilled patterns of behaviour, i.e. when we take very little notice of what we are actually doing (e.g. walking or riding a bike).
2. The next *'Rule Based'* level is also known as the 'level of flexible action patterns' (Zapf, Maier, Rappensperger and Irmer 1994). 'The activity at the Rule Based level is to coordinate and control a sequence of skilled acts' or schemes (Rasmussen and Lind 1982). Decisions are taken on an '*If* (situation) *then* (action)' basis, for example:

   If (the sink is overflowing) *then* (turn the tap off).

or

   If (a possible communicative partner is close by) *then* (attract their attention).

3. The third or highest *'Knowledge Based'* level can be conceptualised as a theoretical knowledge resource. It is at this computationally powerful but

effortful level of cognitive involvement that active and conscious consideration of the problem 'as a whole' is attempted.

Central to this approach is the principle that it is the environment that is hugely complex, and not our actions in it, and that humans can manipulate some types of information more easily than others. The fact that we can intuitively process the enormous amounts of perceptual data that allows us to drive our cars at 70 mph on a road that is hugely congested with other vehicles, but have trouble dividing 197 by 3.9 would seem to confirm this. Rather than presenting a model of how learning is acquired, GEMS is concerned with how we use our knowledge and 'know-how' to stay synchronised and involved with the events that constantly occur around us (for more detailed accounts of GEMS see Barber 2000; Barber and Goldbart 1998). The approach is based on the notion that interactive strategies and recovery plans are arrived at through the learner monitoring what problems look like and using strategies that 'work best most of the time'. GEMS also accounts for the occasional difficulties that occur when the strategy or 'rule' that has been intuitively chosen is incorrect, or when a dominant feature of the learner's surroundings 'captures' their attention, or indeed when the execution of a strategy is waylaid by its similarity to another frequently used repertoire of behaviour.

These problems account for the experience many of us have been through, when we set off to the shops on a Saturday morning, only to find ourselves in the car park outside our place of work, or when we go to the kitchen to check the oven, but find ourselves making a cup of coffee: GEMS predicts that whenever a periodic attentional check (at Skill Base level) is omitted, the most active (i.e. recently or successfully used) 'scheme' in the cognitive resource will govern subsequent activity. The control of routine or habitual action might be compared to a 'rather curious railway system where all the points are set by default to follow the most popular routes' (Reason 1987b).

How GEMS informs us about PMLD

All very interesting, you may say, but how does this account relate to learners who experience PMLD?

Reason's account of human interaction in complex environments relies on a massively interconnected cognitive resource. Problem-solving and recovery strategies are arrived at through referencing problem configurations to previous experiences in similar conditions. Our choice of strategy, problem solution or recovery is influenced by what we used most successfully (and therefore memorably) on most other occasions that looked like this. 'Feature led' searches are made within the cognitive resource, of similar situations with the same significant 'calling conditions' that are also discriminated in the current 'problem' and previous successfully used strategies, so that the best available match is identified.

Successful interaction in this model relies on good information – the 'agent' must be able to discriminate the significant features of the 'problem configuration' so that a good match between problem and probable solutions may be made.

But when information gathering channels are compromised, or when the storage (or recall) of memories or schemes is incomplete, the whole system that allows the rapid management of the vast amounts of data that we intuitively manipulate, becomes 'data limited'. Inadequate information about the environment and profoundly compromised resources of interactive repertoires lead to the 'best available match' becoming the 'least worst match'.

PMLD and data limitation

Profound and multiple learning disability (PMLD) or profound intellectual and multiple disability (PIMD) can be defined as the combination of two or more severe impairments, one of which is a profound learning disability (Ware and Healey 1994). Being among the most 'difficult to teach' of students (Keogh and Reichle 1985), people with this level of intellectual disability have been characterised as functioning at the 'extreme lower levels of cognitive attainment and adaptive behaviour' (Kaufman 1981). This description reflects the fact that 'such children typically acquire few self-care, communication, social or leisure skills. In short they are children with extremely limited behavioural repertoires' (Remington 1996). In addition to PMLD, many of these children experience secondary sensory and physical impairments or medically debilitating conditions' (Rainforth 1982). Indeed individuals with learning disabilities are up to 100 times more likely to have a visual impairment than those without (Ware and Healey 1994) and the incidence of hearing impairments in this population may well approach 70 per cent (Bunning 2001) depending on the method of audiological assessment used.

The combination of hearing and visual impairment is a potent one, as the two senses interact with and supplement each other, providing information about important events occurring around the individual. Hearing also extends our vision allowing us to better detect significant signals that important events are about to happen – hearing a knock on a door, or the sound of the dog barking are both auditory indications that someone is about to arrive. Auditory detail could also be said to augment the visual information we discriminate, enabling us to attribute additional detail to what we simply see (e.g. whether an object is hollow or solid). Combined hearing loss and vision impairment then, appears to be a synergetic coupling, where the effect of the combination produces a greater loss, in terms of sensory information, to the individual than that which would result from a simple addition of the two individual impairments. It is uncontroversial then, to propose that individuals who experience PMLD from birth onwards, frequently 'miss out' on much of the crucial environmental information that learners need to make sense of the environment and the different types of events in which they become involved (Barber 1994). In addition to the impoverished levels of information that they can discriminate and the frequent combinations of multiple sensory and motor disabilities that limit the ability to learn and acquire skilled behavioural repertoires, these people also experience profoundly compromised cognitive capacities which limits the processing, storage and recall of the information that they do perceive (Barber and Goldbart 1998).

How GEMS relates to PMLD

The extended experience of the combination of immobility, deprivation from environmental information and limited cognitive processing can be seen to place obvious limits on the levels of acquisition of the invaluable experience of physical interaction with events. Compounding the poor levels of successful experience of physical encounters, the role of people with PIMD in social encounters has been frequently documented as developing quickly into one of 'recipient' of events, rather than one of equal partnership (Brinker and Lewis 1982; Golden and Reese 1996; Ware and Healey 1994), where partners negotiate the direction and meaning of an encounter 'in order to bring events to their preferred conclusion' (Barber 2000; see also Grove *et al.* 1999).

By definition, individuals who experience PMLD have at their disposal extremely few behavioural responses with which to engage what is a very complex and fluidly changing environment. Our perceptually driven cognitive system typically ensures that we can engage fluid events and synchronise our movements with other occurrences within the frame of elapsing time, but it requires rapid information and diverse experience to work effectively. The interconnected operation of memory and recall ensures that approaching events can be 'read', related to intellectually stored previous experience and anticipated, so that we can join in what can be conceptualised as a 'flow' of events. Reason (1987c) expresses the ability to scan elapsing events as they approach, in order to decide which part of our surroundings to engage, as 'placing one's head in the data flow (i.e. monitored ongoing events) and waiting for a recognisable pattern to occur'.

To someone with only a hammer, every problem looks like a nail (Reason 1990)

One could conceptualise the experience of conciousness of a person with PMLD as being similar to the experience of going to meet a distant or unfamiliar relative from a crowded, rush-hour train. Standing at the platform gate, the train disgorges its passengers, who approach you as a heaving myriad; your task is to identify the familiar individual from the rest. Similarly, an individual with PMLD is faced with the task of recognising situations among the host of events around them, in which they can apply their successful behavioural repertoires. Frequently, by the time a promising opportunity to engage, for instance, an approaching staff member has been identified, the opportunity has passed and the disabled individual must again scan for interactive opportunities.

Once a familiar opportunity is recognised, further difficulties occur. The logic of GEMS suggests that for someone with few interactive repertoires, the primary problem is to identify situations that their limited range of interactive repertoires may be applied to. To someone with only a hammer, every problem looks like a nail; for people who have very little experience of engagement in successful encounters, the problem of identifying a strategy or interactive scheme to match the current calling conditions of their surroundings becomes insurmountable. The few schemes they can successfully 'deploy' to meet an opportunity may not correspond to the calling conditions of the current situation. A pupil who can eye-point or smile but not reach or produce controlled vocal sounds cannot effectively attract the attention of a teacher who is not looking at them (Barber, Goldbart and Munley 1995). Thus, the critical issue is not the repertoires of the disabled individual, or 'what they can do', but whether these schemes are appropriate to the opportunity at hand. 'It is not the flexibility of the learner's skills that enables interaction to occur, but the flexibility of the situation that allows the inclusion of the learner' (Barber 2000).

For the majority of their day, clients and pupils with PMLD do not experience either a controllable or responsive environment (Ware 1996; Barber 1994). This is not improved by the types of interactions in which they *are* involved. The 'social' interactions that individuals with PMLD do appear to encounter frequently have little about them that distinguishes them from the background presence of other elapsing events that occasionally include the individual with PMLD, and distract them from internal 'state' awareness. The isolation from controllable events that many learners with PMLD experience for much of their waking hours has already been identified as leading to learned helplessness (Seligman 1975; Berger and Cunningham 1983). It is understandable therefore that in the face of what must appear to be a frequently chaotic and largely unpredictable physical and social environment, many people with PMLD orient progressively more to the sensory experiences that they can generate for themselves.

It is proposed that the distress that many individuals show when they are included in social encounters derives from the fact that teachers and therapists are frequently disturbing their clients from their controllable, predictable and pleasurable sensory experiences. Indeed, the arrival of a staff member can easily be seen to be an experience of mixed emotions for the client, who cannot be sure if the approach signals that they are about to be moved into a different position, fed, changed, placed in some therapeutic equipment, or to be involved in an activity in a different part of the room or indeed building. From the perspective of the individual with PMLD, the agendas of staff and therapists are usually unannounced. The clients' experience may be more akin to monitoring and accepting elapsing events and waiting until they present a configuration which allows them to engage them.

The increasing requirements of the environment

When pupils do become involved with social interactions, there is evidence that the transactional requirements frequently become too great for them to successfully stay involved unless richly interpreted meaning is routinely assigned to their actions by their communicative partner (Barber 2000).

Research has periodically focused (Carpenter, Mastergeorge and Coggins 1983; Cirren and Rowland 1985; Park 1997; Wetherby and Prizant 1992) on the characteristics of profoundly intellectually disabled learners' use of the hierarchy of communicative functions described by Bruner (1981) as initiation to regulate the behaviour of others (IRB), initiation to achieve joint attention (IJA) and initiation to achieve social interaction (ISI). A number of these studies, reflecting the progression through these communicative hierarchies, note that severely and profoundly learning disabled individuals appear to have difficulties in acquiring the apparent 'critical mass' (Barber 2000) of experience that enables protodeclarative or joint attention functions to emerge (Cirren and Rowland 1985; Park 1997; Wetherby and Prizant 1992). Viewing the environment in terms of data flow could shed some light on this issue.

When an individual communicates in order to regulate the behaviour of a communicative partner, the dialogue is frequently motivated by the urge to satisfy an emerging need. This communicative function can be viewed as the use of another person to achieve a task outside of the physical ability of the communicator. An eye-point to a full cup might be interpreted as a request for a drink, or interpreted by the viewer as a request for a drink. The typical response to this action results in the delivery of the drink. Following this, the communicator has ample evidence that his or her attempt to control another person was successful. The skilled partner approaches, the thirst is quenched, and the cup is empty.

But when the communicator attempts to attract the attention of the skilled partner to something of interest to them (IJI), e.g. a sparkling piece of jewellery that catches their attention, evidence that the initiation has been successful is more subtle: the partner may approach and acknowledge the attention-getting behaviour of the communicator, but realistically, because of limited signalling or difficulties that the communicator has in directing their partner's attention, the partner may well be unsure of the focus of the communicator's attention. In the absence of anything obvious (e.g. a drink or nearby object, etc.) the partner will frequently assume that the communicator is drawing their attention to some other need. We do not look for what we do not expect, but repeatedly anticipate our client's needs, based on our knowledge of them. Whether attention is successfully directed or not, the evidence for the communicator that their attempt was successful is less obvious and therefore more complex.

To successfully discriminate that social interaction has been successfully initiated is even more difficult for someone with PMLD, as within this function there is no necessity for any physical joint focus for attention. As with the previous function, it is likely that in many cases the meaning of the communicative attempt is not clear to the partner (see also Grove *et al.* 1999).

Following the GEMS perspective, we do most what we do best. The selection and use of a repertoire depends on how 'active' (Reason 1990) or prominent it is in the cognitive resource. Its position, relative to other schemes, depends on how successfully it has been used in previous, similar circumstances. If there is good evidence of the success of the use of IBR, but the discernible evidence from IJI or ISI is vague or ambiguous, the style of engagement most likely to be used in the presence of an available partner will be the more successfully discriminated IBR.

To assure its reuse, it is vital that the learner can discriminate that a rule or scheme was successful, otherwise reselection is unlikely. Placed in the context of a diverse cognitive resource, this process typically establishes the most efficient and successful schemes to enable us to engage our fluid environment, but in the context of limited cognitive and physical resources, it further narrows interactive possibilities.

Implications

Accepting this approach, one is led to identify that the central problems for individuals with PMLD and multisensory impairments (MSI) include:

- recognising available interactive opportunities that correspond to their behavioural repertoires;
- acquiring successful interactive experience;
- maintaining and extending interactions once they have been initiated.

In the face of an unfamiliar problem, the 'data limited' (Reason 1990) problem solver is likely to compare current conditions to past encounters and pick the 'least worst strategy' (*ibid.*) or action scheme that is identified in the cognitive resource. If the fit between strategy and configuration works and involvement is achieved, the increasing complexity of the encounter either leads the learner to repeat the successful strategy to achieve a recognisable event rather than varying, or trying to refine it and risk losing the anticipated environmental response. Alternatively, the social response to their attempt at interaction demands further involvement, requiring responses that are not active among the learner's resource of repertoires.

To enable the learner to remain involved, the environment and social targets need to be immensely flexibile, responsive and availabile. Events need to be signalled so that the learner recognises them, i.e. the 'features' of the encounter correspond to easily recognised features of previous successful interactions. Rather than simply *responding*, learners need the experience of *establishing* the topic of the interaction. This would allow them to perceive that events can respond to their actions in a controllable manner, rather than becoming more complex or unpredictable, or more subtle and thus indistinguishable from the rest of the data flow. Vygotsky's (1962) notion of the skilled partner 'intermentally' supporting the learner to success by 'scaffolding' the difference between what the learner can do and what success in a situation requires can be seen to have great relevance to this perspective.

Small islands in the chaos

This approach requires teachers and therapists to consider a number of important issues. When engaging their clients, are these more interesting than the events clients can generate for themselves? When they respond to their pupil's behaviours or encourage them to interact with objects, are they increasing the requirements of the engagement more than the pupil would prefer? When we introduce new or different toys to a familiar game, are teachers just becoming unpredictable and therefore less accessible? Accepting that a large proportion of our student's day is beyond their control, therapists and educators should ensure that their time spent together with learners should at least be predictable, recognisable and responsive. The increasing complexity of the transactional environment presents huge problems not only to the disabled learner, but also to the 'skilled' partner. How, practically, does one limit the complexity of an encounter, but maintain the client's focus and motivation to interact?

A style of interaction that responds to many of the issues raised in this chapter can be used by teachers and therapists working with people who have extremely compromised cognitive and physical resources. By involving pupils in frequent, recognisable and guided social encounters, the communicative significance of their own behaviours can be highlighted to them: physical or vocal turn-taking dialogues can be guided into imitation, where the skilled partner's actions will respond to the behaviours of the learner, so that they perceive events that respond and vary contingently with their own contribution.

The level of social responsiveness and flexibility involved in this style of interaction has been noted to increase signs of positive affect (Nind 1993) in 'hard to reach' clients and is being increasingly recognised as, when compared to many other approaches, a 'least worst' style of providing rich experience of successful social interaction.

To separate our attempts at communicating with clients from the rest of the frequently unpredictable data flow that they experience, it seems logical to identify them by sign-posting or signalling the encounter. This can be seen as carving out an 'island in the chaos' so that the client will recognise that for this part of the day, the encounters in which they are involved will respond to their contribution and can therefore be engaged successfully. Greetings or initiations at the beginning of encounters might involve appropriate touch, proximity or responses that are consistent and recognisable to the client. Thus, their 'feature led searches' are provided with clear information to activate more accurate anticipation. Although responding to the client's contributions, the skilled partner can usually guide encounters so that over time, repertoires or interactive routes can be developed, negotiated and later anticipated or initiated.

Constructing encounters so that they occur in response to the client's repertoires rather than in response to practitioners, effectively places a ceiling on the complexity of the interaction. Teachers can provide social encounters that respond to the actions and perceived intentions of the client, so that in effect, their repertoires and signals correspond to the requirements of the environment. The practitioner therefore accepts the learner's repertoires, and rather than attempting to increase their complexity, constructs interactions around them.

The skill of the teacher, then, is to ensure that all of the problems that the learner will encounter during a social encounter can be solved, or at least can be engaged, with just a hammer.

Acknowledgement

I would like to thank Dr Juliet Goldbart (Manchester Metropolitan University) for her advice during the writing of this chapter.

References

Barber, M. (1994) 'Profound and multiple learning difficulties: contingency awareness: putting research into the classroom', in J. Coupe O'Kane and B. Smith (eds), *Taking Control*. London: David Fulton Publishers.

Barber, M. (2000) *Skills, Rules, Knowledge and Three Mile Island. Accounting for Failure to Learn among Individuals with Profound and Multiple Learning Disabilities*. Unpublished PhD thesis, Manchester Metropolitan University.

Barber, M. and Goldbart, J. (1998) 'Accounting for failure to learn in people with profound and multiple learning disabilities', in P. Lacey, and C. Ouvrey (eds), *People with Profound and Multiple Learning Disabilities*. London: David Fulton Publishers.

Barber, M., Goldbart, J. and Munley G. (1995) 'Student initiations and staff responses: identifying optimal contexts for pupils with profound intellectual disabilities'. Paper presented to BILD Conference, Oxford, 17 September.

Bates, E., Benigni, L., Bretherton, I., Camaioni, L. and Volterra, V. (1979) *The Emergence of Symbols: Cognition and Communication in Infancy*. New York: Academic Press.

Berger, J. and Cunningham, C. (1983) 'Development of early vocal behaviours and interactions in Down's Syndrome and non-handicapped infant-mother pairs', *Developmental Psychology* 19, 322–31.

Brinker, R. P. and Lewis, M. (1982) 'Discovering the competent handicapped infant: a process approach to assessment and intervention', *Topics in Early Childhood Special Education* 2(2),1–16.

Bruner, J. S. (1981) 'Social context of language acquisition', *Language and Communication* 1, 155–78.

Bunning, C. (2001) Personal communication.

Carpenter, R. L., Mastergeorge, A. M. and Coggins, T. E. (1983) 'The acquisition of communicative intentions in infants eight to fifteen months of age', *Language and Speech* 26(2), 101–15.

Cirren, F. M. and Rowland, C. M. (1985) 'Communicative assessment of non-verbal youths with severe/profound mental retardation', *Mental Retardation* 23(2), 52–62.

Golden, J. and Reese, M. (1996) 'Focus on communication: improving interaction between staff and residents who have severe or profound mental retardation', *Research in Developmental Disabilities* 17(5), 363–82.

Grove, N., Bunning, K., Porter, J. and Olssen, C. (1999) 'See what I mean: interpreting the meaning of communication by people with severe and profound intellectual disabilities', *Journal of Applied Research in Intellectual Disabilities* 12(3), 190–203.

Kaufman, J. M., (1981) 'Are all children educable?' *(Special issue) Analysis and Intervention in Developmental Disabilities* 1(1).

Keogh, W. and Reichle, J. (1985) 'Communication intervention for the difficult to teach severely handicapped', in S. F. Warren and A. K. Rogers Warren (eds), *Teaching Functional Language* Austin, TX: Pro-Ed, 157–94.

Nind, M. (1993) *Access to Communication: Efficacy of Intensive Interaction Teaching for People with Severe Developmental Disabilities Who Demonstrate Ritualistic Behaviours*. Unpublished PhD thesis, Cambridge Institute of Education.

Nind, M. and Hewett, D. (1994) *Access to Communication*. London: David Fulton Publishers.

Ouvrey, C. (1997) *Educating Children with Profound Handicaps*. Birmingham: BIMH Publications.

Ouvrey, C. and Saunders, S. (1996) 'Pupils with profound and multiple learning difficulties', in B., Carpenter, R. Ashdown and K. Bovair (eds), *Enabling Access: Effective Teaching and Learning for Pupils with Learning Difficulties*. London: David Fulton Publishers.

Park, K. (1997) 'Early theory of mind and the emergence of early communication'. Paper presented to BILD Conference, Oxford, 17 September.

Rainforth, B. (1982) 'Biobehavioural state and orienting: implications for educating profoundly retarded students', *Journal of the Association for the Severely Handicapped* 6(4), 33–7.

Rasmussen, J. and Lind, M. (1982) *A Model of Human Decision-making in Complex Systems and its Use for the Design of System Control Strategies.* Denmark: Riso National Laboratory DK4000.

Reason, J. (1987a) 'A preliminary classification of mistakes', in J. Rasmussen, K. Duncan and J. Leplat (eds), *New Technology and Human Error.* Chichester: Wiley, 15–23.

Reason, J. (1987b) 'The psychology of mistakes: a brief view of planning failures'. in J. Rasmussen, K. Duncan and J. Leplat (eds), *New Technology and Human Error.* Chichester: Wiley, 45–53.

Reason, J. (1987c) 'Generic error modelling system (GEMS): A cognitive framework for locating common human error forms', in J. Rasmussen, K. Duncan and J. Leplat (eds). *New Technology and Human Error* Chichester: Wileys, 63–87.

Reason, J. (1990) *Human Error.* Cambridge: Cambridge University Press.

Remington, R. E. (1996) 'Assessing the occurrence of learning in children with profound intellectual disability: a conditioning approach', *International Journal of Disability, Development and Education* 43(2), 101–18.

Rogoff, B. (1990) *Apprenticeship in Thinking: Cognitive Development in Social Context.* Oxford: Oxford: University Press.

Rovee-Collier, C., (1987) 'Learning and memory in infancy', in J. Osofsky (ed.), *Handbook of Infant Development.* New York: Wiley.

Seligman, M. (1975) *Helplessness: On Depression, Development and Death.* San Francisco, CA: Freeman.

Vygotsky, L. S. (1962) *Thought and Language.* Cambridge, MA: MIT Press.

Ware, J. and Healey, I. (1994) 'Conceptualising progress in children with profound and multiple learning difficulties: creating contingency sensitive environments', in J. Ware (ed.), *Educating Children with Profound and Multiple Learning Difficulties.* London: David Fulton Publishers.

Ware, J. (1996) *Creating a Responsive Environment for People with Profound and Multiple Learning Difficulties.* London: David Fulton Publishers.

Wetherby, A. M. and Prizant, B. M. (1992) 'Profiling young children's communicative competence', in S. Warren and J. Reichle (eds), *Causes and Effects in Communication and Language Intervention.* Baltimore: PH Brokes.

Zapf, D., Maier, G. W., Rappensperger, G. and Irmer, C. (1994) 'Error detection, task characteristics and some consequences for software design', *Applied Pyschology: An International Review* 43(4), 499–520.

Section 5

CHAPTER 17

Building tomorrow together: effective transition planning for pupils with special needs

Filiz Polat, Afroditi Kalambouka and Bill Boyle

Introduction

For many years issues concerned with planning effective transition into adult life for pupils with special educational needs (SEN) have occupied the minds of governments, researchers, practitioners, parents and the young people themselves. It is generally recognised that transition represents a difficult time in the lives of these young people and their parents/carers. Many of them have been in special schools since they were five years old. Services provided by the school and other LEA support staff to school-aged pupils are, on the whole, relatively easy to comprehend and government-led initiatives, for example SEN legislation and Ofsted inspections, suggest that the whole process of education is well planned and managed. However, things do not look so simple as students move into transition. Parents and young people are confronted with what may seem like a bewildering array of choices or lack of them. Other services, in particular Social and Careers Services, may have a new role to play in their lives; there may be prospects in the further education sector or possibly opportunities for employment. In addition, a whole new raft of benefits may become available.

As educational provision at school for young people with SEN becomes more inclusive, it is important to assess the impact that this might have on transition and on the extent to which these young people become fully inclusive members of society. The aim of this chapter, therefore, is to review some of the literature on transition and to relate this to key findings from a national longitudinal transition study funded by the DfES.

Research evidence on transition outcomes of young people

Although transition has been a focus of debate among professionals, policy makers and major stakeholders in the field of special education over the last three decades, research suggests that the outcomes for young people with SEN are far from positive (see, for example, OECD 1996; Ward, Dyer, Riddell and Thomson 1992; Florian, Dee, Byers and Maudslay 2000a; Florian, Maudslay, Dee and Byers 2000b; Cohen, Khan and O'Sullivan 1999).

There appear to be a wide range of school-related factors that have an impact on this process. These include type of school (special or mainstream), the provision of Careers Education and Guidance Services (CEG), the organisation and support provided by the transition planning services, and the encouragement and involvement of parents in transition planning (Wagner, Blackorby and Hebbeler 1993).

School type

Discussions on the impact of school type on transition outcomes are inevitably intertwined with the students' types and degrees of disability. It is self-evident that special schools tend to cater for pupils with more severe and complex disabilities and that pupils with SEN in mainstream schools tend to be more able. Therefore transition outcomes may be more related to the 'category' of SEN rather than to the school type. In this context it is interesting that Ward *et al.* (1992) and Hirst and Baldwin (1994) found poorer post-school outcomes for those young people who were educated in segregated settings. Hirst and Baldwin (1994) attributed the poor quality of transition of people with SEN to the segregated educational settings and to the inadequacy of support services during the post-school period. They also found that young people who attended special schools had nowhere to go after leaving school and were at greater risk of perceiving themselves as being worthless and helpless. Ward *et al.* (1992) also suggested that there were better post-school outcomes for pupils with SEN who were educated in inclusive settings and that this was probably due to the nature of special needs of this group. Therefore it appears that pupils with SEN who are more able and educated in mainstream schools tend to experience more satisfactory transition outcomes.

Careers Education and Guidance

One aim of Careers Education and Guidance (CEG) offered as a subject in secondary schools is that it is expected to have a positive impact on post-school outcomes related to employment, education or training (see DfEE 2000d; 1999; Gill and Edgar 1990; Scuccimarra and Speece 1990; Doren, Bullis and Benz 1996). The most important indicators of good CEG are that it should be well planned and include sufficient investment in skill training up until the students are successfully employed. Ward *et al.* (1992), however, concluded that for many young people, further education courses and work training schemes lacked direction and planning. They found that many of the young people experienced long periods of training and yet still had poor employment prospects. Other studies have demonstrated that young people with SEN had received insufficient careers education and advice while at school and concluded that there was a deficit in service provision for young people with SEN during their transition from school to work (Anderson and Clark 1982; Walker 1980; Hirst 1985).

Parental involvement and input in transition planning

Successful transition planning should also motivate both the pupils and their families to make a contribution to their transition plan. Parental involvement has consistently been found to be positively related to successful schooling and transition for young people with and without SEN (e.g. Danek and Busby 1999; Wagner *et al.* 1993; Heumann 1993; Young 1993; Sinclair and Christenson 1992; Rumberger, Ghatak, Poulous, Dornbusch and Ritter 1988; Bennett 1988). Furthermore, other factors are thought to have an impact on the quality of parental involvement in transition planning such as family expectations and resources, their history of relationships with schools and other agencies, and other factors within the family (Danek and Busby 1999). The literature suggests that many young people with SEN, particularly those with moderate learning difficulties and behavioural problems, tend to come from lower social classes (Hirst and Baldwin 1994; Marder and Cox 1991) and this has the potential to have a further negative effect on their transition experiences (e.g. Kaufman and Bradby 1992; Fairweather and Shaver 1991; Heal and Rusch 1995).

Impact of individual characteristics on transition outcomes

The individual characteristics of young people with SEN (e.g. SEN type, gender and ethnicity) play an important part both in transition planning and in the post-school outcomes of these young people. As stated above, the extent and type of a young person's disability is clearly related to transition outcomes as many recent studies have shown (e.g. Cohen *et al.* 1999; Florian *et al.* 2000a; 2000b; Polat and Farrell 2000). The American National Longitudinal Transition Study (NLTS) data and other surveys have documented a wide variation of experiences and post-school outcomes according to the main SEN/disability category (Gregory, Shanahan and Walberg 1989; Ward *et al.* 1992; Wagner *et al.* 1993). The common theme from these studies suggests that those who have complex and profound difficulties and emotional and behavioural difficulties (EBD) have poorer transition experiences and, as a result, poorer post-school outcomes.

The literature reveals contradictory results of post-school outcomes according to gender; while some studies found no significant gender differences (e.g. Levine and Edgar 1995), others concluded with the opposite finding (e.g. Hasazi, Gordon and Roe 1985; May and Hughes 1986; Wagner, Newman, D'Amico, Jay, Butler-Nalin, Marder and Cox 1991). Ethnicity also seems to have a negative impact on the post-school outcomes of all young people with or without SEN (e.g. DfEE 1999; 2000d; Marder and Cox 1991).

To conclude, it must be noted that the majority of research evidence presented in this section pre-dates the two Codes of Practice (DFE 1994; DfES 2001). In addition, several other key reports have been published recently each of which addresses key aspects of transition policy and planning (e.g. the Green Paper, DfEE 1997; the Department of Health White Paper, DoH 2001; the Connexions Service, DfEE 2000c; the DfES Green Paper on extending opportunities and raising standards for pupils aged 14–19, DfES 2002). Therefore there is a pressing need for further research to be carried out that can begin to explore the impact of recent developments in this important area.

Scope of the study

This chapter discusses some of the key findings from Wave 1 of a national longitudinal study on the transition of young people with SEN from school to adult life. This investigation included 617 schools (362 mainstream and 255 special schools) which provided background information on 3,204 pupils (1,837 of whom attended mainstream and 1,367 attended special schools) and interviews with 2,364 parents and 2,313 pupils who were in Year 11.

The overall aim of the study was to obtain information about the transition process for this large sample of young people with SEN from the young people themselves, their parents and SENCOs/senior teachers. There is insufficient space in this chapter to discuss the findings in detail. Readers wanting further information should consult the final report (Polat, Kalambouka, Boyle and Nelson 2001). However, some of the important aspects of the study are referred to below.

Transition planning

Despite recent moves to improve transition experiences for young people with SEN, only 51 per cent of the schools in the sample reported having a post-16 transition policy that was part of their SEN policy. Furthermore, although the vast majority (92 per cent) included transition planning in the Year 11 annual review, for a small minority (172 pupils) no such plan seemed to be in place. In general, pupils with mild, severe to profound learning difficulties and EBD/Attention Deficit Hyperactivity Disorder (ADHD) seemed less likely to have their first annual review with a transition plan in Year 10 or before. This finding is consistent with previous findings (e.g. Ward *et al.* 1992; Wagner *et al.* 1993) that revealed poorer transitional outcomes for pupils with severe/profound learning difficulties (SLD/PMLD) and EBD.

There were also differences across SEN types as to whether the first annual review with a transition plan had been held. According to reports from parents, the groups that were most likely to have an annual review with a transition plan were young people with autistic spectrum disorders and sensory difficulties. Those with SLD/PMLD, speech/language difficulties and EBD were least likely to have had such an annual review.

The Code of Practice (DFE 1994) states the pupil's right to be involved in decision making during transition and to make a contribution by expressing a view. However, approximately a quarter of the pupils (24 per cent) did not actually attend their meeting according to schools' reports. There were significant differences between pupils, across SEN type, as to whether they attended their review or not. For example, it was reported by schools that more than half of pupils with SLD/PMLD and just less than half of the pupils with autism did not attend the reviews. Similarly, according to the parents' reports, of those who did not attend the reviews, the majority of these had severe/profound learning difficulties, autism and EBD.

Overall, the data revealed that there was a consistency between what was reported by parents and by schools in relation to their participation in transition planning. The consistency between the school's and parents' reports was also evident in relation to SEN types. The impact of SEN type on transition experience and outcomes of young people is well established in the literature (e.g. Wagner *et al.* 1993; Ward *et al.* 1992). The data in the present study revealed poorer transitional experiences for those with SLD/PMLD and EBD. This finding is consistent with previous national studies (e.g. Florian *et al.* 2000a; 2000b; Cohen *et al.* 1999).

In general, the data with reference to transition planning of young people with SEN suggest that special school pupils with statements and their parents seem to benefit from the system much better when compared to their peers in mainstream schools and without statements. However, those pupils with EBD and their parents seem to benefit less from the system and were less involved in the whole transition process.

Information and services provided to parents

In order to participate fully in transition planning, parents need to be extensively informed about the process by the school. The data in the current study revealed differences between what schools reported on the transition planning process and what pupils and their parents/carers stated. The vast majority of schools claimed that they always provided information related to post-16 transition planning. The data suggest that more parents of pupils in special schools and of pupils with statements were provided with information compared to parents of pupils in mainstream schools and without a statement. Similarly, differences were observed according to SEN type; only a quarter of parents of pupils with EBD/ADHD said that they received information while almost half (46 per cent) of parents of pupils with sensory difficulties received this type of information. Based on this finding, parents of pupils with EBD appeared to get the least information and were found to be the least satisfied in comparison to parents of pupils with other SEN types. The services offered to parents varied across type of school. Overall, special schools provided parents with information related to post-16 transition more often than mainstream schools did. The lack of information provided by agencies and schools to parents/carers was found to be a major issue in other studies (e.g. Cohen *et al.* 1999). This discrepancy between parents and schools may be due to various reasons and it is almost impossible to make any interpretations based on the type of data gathered in this study. However, similar discrepancies between schools, parents and other agencies were revealed in previous studies (e.g. Bowers, Dee, West and Wilkinson 1998).

More than three-quarters of parents said that school was preparing their child for transition to adult life either 'quite well' or 'very well', just under a quarter (23 per cent) said that schools prepared young people 'poorly', while less than one in five (18 per cent) thought that it was just 'adequate'. Overall, parents of pupils in special schools and of those with statements were satisfied with the schools' preparation of young people for transition from school to adult life. Parents of pupils with EBD/ADHD were the least satisfied group while parents of pupils with sensory difficulties were the most satisfied group.

Young people's experiences in and outside of school

The majority of young people, especially those in special schools, appeared to enjoy the academic and social life at school. Out of school social life seemed to vary across type of school and severity of SEN. Overall, pupils in special schools appeared to be more socially isolated and to participate in leisure activities less. One may speculate that the protective environment of segregated education does not really prepare young people for the mainstream of life where they may need some social skills to interact with others. However, this finding may also be due to the fact that the outside school environment may not be inclusive and welcoming and be irrelevant to the readiness of young people to integrate in society.

Pupils in special schools, overall, had lower aspirations and expectations with reference to future career, place of residence and having a family. Few special school pupils wanted to study at another school or college or look for a job although most of them wanted to live independently and have a family.

Summary and implications

The transition from childhood to adult life can be difficult for many young people but most eventually adapt and take on a variety of adult roles. For those on the margins of society the problems often have a longer and lasting impact and their transition to adult life and social inclusion may be prolonged. The ability of young people with SEN to attain adult status (Clark and Hirst 1989) and to be included socially could therefore be regarded as a measure of the adequacy of service provision during the transition years in overcoming the adverse consequences of disablement. It also could be regarded as a measure of success of an inclusion philosophy that extends beyond schooling.

To date available research evidence in Britain has revealed that opportunities offered to young people with SEN on leaving school are rather restricted. These findings are similar to those reported in international studies. However, the main body of research in this field in the UK derives from studies that have been carried out some time ago since when there have been substantial changes in legislation and practice. The most recent research evidence in England comes from Florian *et al.*'s (2000a; 2000b), Cohen *et al.*'s (1999), and Polat and Farrell's (2000) studies on the transition of young people with SLD/PMLD and EBD. Overall these studies confirm findings from past British studies that there is a need to improve service provision for young people with SEN, both while they are at school and afterwards. Nevertheless, although these studies have provided valuable information, they do not cover the whole range of special needs found in mainstream and special schools in England. Considerable evidence on the post-16 transition of young people with SEN within the boundaries of the UK comes from a similar Scottish study (Ward *et al.* 1992), where education legislation and related policies often differ from those in England and Wales. Routlege (2000) argues that despite the implementation of the SEN Code of Practice (DFE 1994; DfES 2001), with its important transition-related elements, many people are still not benefiting from effectively coordinated transition support. This suggests that well-defined, explicit legislation is only a first step in improving transition planning. In a sense the quality of positive/successful transition outcomes are not individually based per se, rather they can be regarded as a measure of adequacy and continuity of inclusive service provision during the transition years in overcoming the adverse consequences of disablement.

However, there are some promising movements in the field of general and special education that focus on improving services for those who are at risk of being at the margins of society. In particular the revised Code of Practice and the Connexions Service aim to tackle the problems of implementation of the legislation systematically in cooperation with the other main stakeholders, e.g. schools, LEAs, Health Authorities, Social Services, Learning and Skills Council, parents and pupils. However, it will be some years before the impact of these initiatives can be judged.

Acknowledgements

The research reported in this chapter was undertaken by the Centre of Formative Assessment Studies (CFAS) at the University of Manchester in cooperation with National Opinion Poll and was funded by the Department for Education and Skills (DfES). The views expressed in this chapter are those of the authors and not necessarily those of the DfES or University of Manchester. We would like to thank all SENCOs/teachers, parents/caregivers and pupils who participated in this study.

References

Anderson, E. M. and Clark, L. (1982) *Disability in Adolescence*. London: Methuen.

Bennett, W. (1988) 'Parents' key to educating handicapped children', *Education Daily*, 31 March.

Bowers, T., Dee, L., West, M. and Wilkinson, D. (1998) *Evaluation of the User-Friendliness of the Special Educational Needs Code of Practice*. London: DfEE.

Clark, A. and Hirst, M. (1989) 'Disability in adulthood: ten-year follow-up of young people with disabilities', *Disability, Handicap and Society* 4(3), 271–83.

Cohen, R., Khan, J. and O'Sullivan, P. (1999) *Young Adults Transition Project – Working Paper 3: Views and Experiences of Young People and Carers*. Project funded by Optimum Health Services: NHS.

Danek, M. M. and Busby, H. (1999) *Transition Planning and Programming: Empowerment through Partnership*. Gallaudet University Pre-College National Mission Programs. Washington, DC: Gallaudet University.

Department for Education (DFE) (1994) *Code of Practice on the Identification and Assessment of Special Educational Needs*. London: DFE.

Department for Education and Employment (DfEE) (1997) *Excellence for All Children: Meeting Special Educational Needs*. London: DFEE.

Department for Education and Employment (DfEE) (1999) *Youth Cohort Study: The activities and experiences of 16 year olds: England and Wales 1998*. London: HMSO Statistical Bulletin.

Department for Education and Employment (DfEE) (2000a) *Youth Cohort Study: Education, Training and Employment of 16–18 year olds in England and Wales and the factors associated with non-participation*. London: HMSO Statistical Bulletin, May 2000.

Department for Education (DFE) (2000b) *The draft SEN Code of Practice on the Identification and Assessment of Pupils with Special Educational Needs and SEN Thresholds: Good practice on identification and provision for pupils with special educational needs*. London: HMSO.

Department for Education and Employment (DfEE) (2000c) *The Connexions Service: prospectus and specifications*. London: HMSO.

Department for Education and Employment (DfEE) (2000d) *Outcomes from Careers Education and Guidance (Phase II) – A Tracking Study*. London: DfEE Research Brief RBX 9/00.

Department for Education and Employment (DfEE) (2000e) *Connexions: The Best Start in Life for Every Young Person*. London: HMSO.

Department for Education and Skills (DfES) (2001) *Special Educational Needs Code of Practice*. London: DfES.

Department for Education and Skills (DfES) (2002) *14–19: Extending Opportunities, Raising Standards*. London: HMSO.

Department of Health (DoH) (2001) *Valuing People: A New Strategy for Learning Disabilities for the 21st Century*. London: HMSO.

Doren, B., Bullis, M. and Benz, M. R. (1996) 'Predictors of victimisation experiences of adolescents with disabilities in transition', *Exceptional Children* 63(1), 7–18.

Fairweather, J. S. and Shaver, D. (1991) 'Making transition to post-secondary education and training', *Exceptional Children* 57, 264–70.

Farrell, P. (2001) 'Special education in the last twenty years: have things really got better?' *British Journal of Special Education* 28(1), 3–9.

Florian, L., Dee, L., Byers, R. and Maudslay, L. (2000a) 'What happens after the age of 14? Mapping transitions for pupils with profound and complex learning difficulties', *British Journal of Special Education* 27(3), 124–8.

Florian, L., Maudslay, L., Dee, L. and Byers, R. (2000b) 'What happens when schooling ends? Further education opportunities for pupils with profound and complex learning difficulties', *Skill Journal* 67, 16–23.

Gill, D. and Edgar, E. (1990) 'Outcome of vocational programme designed for pupils with mild disabilities: The Pierce county vocational/special education co-operative', *The Journal for Vocational Special Needs Education* 12(3), 17–22.

Gregory, J. F., Shanahan, T. and Walberg, H. (1989) 'High school seniors with special needs: an analysis of characteristics pertinent to school-to-work transition', *International Journal of Educational Research* 13(5), 489–99.

Hasazi, S. B., Gordon, L. R. and Roe, C. A. (1985) 'Factors associated with the employment status of handicapped youth exiting high school from 1979–1983', *Exceptional Children* 51, 455–69.

Heal, L.W. and Rusch, F. R. (1995) 'Predicting employment for pupils who leave special education high school programs', *Exceptional Children* 61(5), 472–87.

Heumann, J. (1993) 'The Heumann touch', *Counterpoint* 14(1), 10–14. Horsham, PA: National Association of State Directors of Special Education.

Hirst, M. (1985) 'Could schools do more for leavers?' *British Journal of Special Education* 12(4), 143–6.

Hirst, M. and Baldwin, S. (1994) *Unequal Opportunities: Growing Up Disabled*. London: HMSO.

Kaufman, P. and Bradby, D. (1992) *Characteristics of at-risk pupils in NELS: 88*. Washington DC: US Department of Education.

Levine, P. and Edgar, E. (1995) 'An analysis by gender of long-term post-school outcomes for youth with and without disabilities', *Exceptional Children* 61(3), 282–300.

Marder, C. and Cox, R. (1991) 'More than a label: Characteristics of youth with disabilities', in M. Wagner *et al. Youth with Disabilities: How Are They Doing? A Comprehensive Report from Wave 1 of the National Longitudinal Transition Study of Special Education Pupils*. Menlo Park, CA: SRI International.

May, D. and Hughes, D. (1986) *An Uncertain Future: The Adolescent Mentally Handicapped and the Transition from School to Adulthood*. Dundee: Department of Psychiatry, University of Dundee.

Organisation for Economic Cooperation and Development (OECD) (1996) *Education at a Glance/* France: Organisation for Economist Cooperation and Development

Polat, F. and Farrell, P. (2000) *Long-Term Impact of Residential Provision for Pupils who Attend Nugent House School.* A Research conducted by Centre for Educational Needs, University of Manchester on behalf of Nugent Care Society.

Polat, F., Kalambouka, A., Boyle, W. and Nelson, N. (2001) *Post-16 Transitions of Pupils with Special Educational Needs.* London: DfES.

Robertson, J., Emerson, E., Letchford, S., Fowler, S. and Jones, M. (1995) *Where Are They Now? A Follow-up of Children who have Attended Beech Tree School.* A Research conducted by HARC on behalf of the Mental Health Foundation.

Routlege, M. (2000) 'Collective responsibilities, fragmented systems: Transition to adulthood for young people with learning disabilities', *Tizard Learning Disability Review* 5(4), 17–26.

Rumberger, R., Ghatak, R., Poulous, G., Dornbusch, S. and Ritter, P. (1988) *Family Influences on Dropout Behaviour: An Exploratory Study of a Single High School.* Presented to the American Educational Research Association Annual Meeting, New Orleans.

Scuccimarra, D. and Speece, D. (1990) 'Employment Outcomes and Social Integration of Pupils with Mild Handicaps: The Quality of Life Two Years After School', *Journal of Learning Disabilities* 23, 213–19.

Sinclair, M. F. and Christenson, S. L. (1992) 'Home-school collaboration: A building block of empowerment', *IMPACT-Feature Issue on Family Empowerment* 5 (2), 12–13.

Wagner, M., Blackorby, J. and Hebbeler, K. (1993) *Beyond the report card: The multiple dimensions of secondary school performance for pupils with disabilities. A report from the National Longitudinal Transition Study of Special Education Pupils.* Menlo Park, CA: SRI International.

Wagner, M., Newman, L., D'Amico, R., Jay, E. D., Butler-Nalin, P., Marder, C. and Cox, R. (1991) *Youth with Disabilities: How Are They Doing? A Comprehensive Report from Wave 1 of the National Longitudinal Transition Study of Special Education Pupils.* Menlo Park, CA: SRI International.

Walker, A. (1980) 'The Handicapped School Leaver and the Transition to Work', *British Journal of Guidance and Counselling* 8(2), 212–23.

Walker, A. (1982) *Unqualified and Underemployed: Handicapped Young People and the Labour Market.* London: Macmillan.

Ward, K., Dyer, M., Riddell, S. and Thomson, G. O. B. (1992) *Transition from School to Adulthood of Young People with Recorded Special Educational Needs.* Scottish Council for Research in Education for the Scottish Office Education Department.

Young, R. A. (1993) *Parental influence in the career and educational development of children and adolescents: An action perspective.* Presentation to the Fifth Annual International Roundtable on Family, Community and Social Partnerships. Atlanta, GA.

CHAPTER 18

An inclusive society? One young man with learning difficulties doesn't think so!

Iain Carson

While the focus of this chapter is based upon small-scale research, the purpose is not primarily to disseminate the findings, but to provide a voice for a young gay man with learning difficulties who, as a result of an unsatisfactory 'inclusive' educational experience, felt unprepared for the discrimination that he encountered within the wider society. In order to protect his anonymity, a pseudonym ('Simon') has been adopted and the names of his schools, teachers and other members of staff have been changed. Additionally, in an attempt to understand the nature of the discrimination that young gay men with learning difficulties can encounter, extracts from an interview with a non-disabled young gay man ('Stuart') have been included.

Historically, men (and women) with learning difficulties were actively discouraged from developing close relationships, mainly because of a fear that they may lead to sexual relationships and thus procreation. Present-day attitudes often allude to the view that encouraging or supporting people with learning difficulties to develop relationships might lead to sexual abuse and thus, should be avoided. It is acknowledged that vulnerability and sexual abuse are issues of concern, and some of these will be discussed later in this chapter. However, to deny someone a basic human right on the grounds that problems *might* result is unacceptable.

The use of special schools for children with learning difficulties versus inclusion within the mainstream sector has been a controversial issue for many years and there are arguments for and against both options (Kaufman and Hallahan 1995: Oliver 1996; Hornby, Atkinson and Howard 1997). While some of the issues will be discussed, this forum will not be used to debate the educational pros and cons of the system, but to examine some of the discriminatory social experiences resulting from it.

Simon is a 19-year-old young man with learning difficulties who perceives himself to be gay. He started his education in a special school at the age of five but transferred to a mainstream school at the age of 11.

Simon's story

I went to Bank Street School when I was five and stayed there until I was 11. I had a special friend called Michael and lots of other friends too. Michael and I started school on the same day but when I moved to a new school he didn't come with me. All of the other children were like me, they were disabled; the teachers said that we were handicapped but my mum said I wasn't, she said I was special. Some of the other children were more disabled than me, they couldn't even talk and some of them were in wheelchairs. I liked Bank Street, we did lots of painting and drawing and sometimes we did reading and writing, we played lots of games too. Sometimes I used to wish that I could go to the same school as my brother because he did lots of things at that school, he even played football with his friends.

When I was 11 my wish came true, my mum told me that I was going to Woodhill High School, which is where my brother was. My teacher at Bank Street said that it would be very hard but my mum said that I would be the same as all the other boys and girls. Woodhill was very big and there were lots of people there; we had to go to different classes with different teachers and I didn't know anyone there except my brother, and he was in a different class. I tried to make friends with some of the other boys but they didn't like me, they laughed at me and called me names, one boy said I was a 'looney' and another one called me a 'mental retard'. Some of the girls were nice to me but they didn't want to be my friend. I didn't like school anymore and wished I was back at Bank Street. There was a woman called Miss Smith, I think she was a sort of teacher. She used to sit next to me in all of the classes and help me with things that I didn't understand. She told me not to talk to the boys who called me names and that she would be my friend, she was nice but she was old, so I didn't want her to be my friend. I wanted to be like my mum said, the same as the other boys and girls.

I can remember wondering if I was gay when I was about 13, though I didn't know what gay meant then, but I used to like boys more than girls, especially boys in my big brother's class. Some of the boys who used to call me names sometimes called another boy 'gay' or 'poofter', they said it was because he was a sissy and behaved like a girl. So then I thought maybe I wasn't gay, because I didn't behave like a girl, I just liked boys! I used to want to talk to one of the teachers about it because he once said that it was ok to be gay in one of his lessons, but the teachers always told me that I had to talk to Miss Smith, not them. Miss Smith was nice but I didn't want to talk to her about being gay because she was a woman, a bit like my mum. So, I didn't talk to anyone because I didn't have any friends and I wasn't allowed to talk to the teachers. Maybe if I'd still been at Bank Street I could have talked to Michael or one of my other friends. Once I thought that I might talk to my mum and dad about it, but then I heard them talking about gay people on a television programme, they said it was dirty to be gay so I decided not to talk to them.

When I was about 16 and a half I still didn't have any friends at school and people still called me names, even the younger boys were horrible to me. Miss Smith had left and a new woman called Mrs Hewitt came to help me in the classroom. One day a woman came to talk to all of us about HIV, which is something to do with AIDS. I know about AIDS now but I didn't when I was at school. She said that condoms were very important especially if you were gay, because you could die if you didn't have condoms. When the woman went, Mr Bentley, the teacher, said if we didn't understand anything we could talk to him because it was important. I went to see him because I was gay and I didn't know about condoms: he told me that I had to talk to Mrs Hewitt. I didn't want to talk to Mrs Hewitt about being gay but I wasn't allowed to talk to anyone else, so I did. She said that I didn't need to know about condoms because I didn't need them, only the other boys in the class would need them, and she said that I couldn't be gay either because it wasn't nice!

When I was 18, just after I left school, I saw a programme on television called 'Queer as Folk'; I had to watch it in my bedroom because my mum and dad said it was a bad programme. It was about gay people in Manchester who went to bars and had lots of friends and lots of fun. I thought that if I went to some of these bars I could have some friends too. So, one night when my mum and dad thought I was going to the Gateway Club (which I hated), I went into Manchester to look for the bars I had seen on the television. There were lots of them, all full of men, and some women too; they all seemed to be friends with each other. I felt a bit scared and nervous so I went into this bar that didn't have too many people in it: I bought a drink and stood in the corner. I stayed there for quite a long time but nobody spoke to me, they didn't even say hello, so I went home. Maybe nobody spoke to me because I didn't speak to them, so a few weeks later I went back to the same bar. There was a group of people about the same age as me so I went over and said hello. Some of them turned their back on me and one of them laughed at me: I told them that I was gay and just wanted to be their friend. The one who laughed said that 'spastics' shouldn't be in gay bars, they should be in mental hospitals. It was the same as being at Woodhill, nobody wanted me to be there and they didn't want to be my friend.

From the age of five, Simon was discriminated against by being sent to a special school. He was denied the opportunity to participate in mainstream education with the rest of his peers; he was segregated from society. However, during his six years of enforced segregation he made many friends, including a special friend. His mother rightly believed that her son should not have to spend his entire education being excluded, fought for two years with her local education authority (LEA) to have him included within the local mainstream school, and was successful. Many LEAs believe that moving children with learning difficulties from special to mainstream schools tends to imply that they are 'included' once they are there (Ainscow, Farrell, Tweddle and Malki 1999). Yes, Simon was taught in an integrated setting, and yes, he followed the same curriculum as his peers: a learning support assistant was employed to enable him to achieve this. However, integration does not mean inclusion: clearly, Simon was integrated into a mainstream setting, but he was by no means included in the culture of the school. It is important to point out that some LEAs have adopted a more considered approach towards inclusion. Ainscow *et al.* (1999) cite the policy of one such establishment:

> . . . remove the boundaries between special and mainstream schools and to promote our commitment to inclusion by enhancing the capacity of the latter to respond to diverse abilities, backgrounds, interests and needs. Inclusion in education may be seen as the process of increasing the participation of children in, and reducing their exclusion from, the community, curriculum and culture of the local school thereby raising education standards for all.

In order to successfully implement such a policy it is necessary to involve the entire school, i.e. all of the teachers, all of the pupils, all of the support staff and all of the parents. Some schools have successfully demonstrated that this is achievable; sadly, they are a minority. Had Woodhill High School been more committed to inclusive education, Simon would have had some friends, he would have been able to discuss his uncertainties about his sexual orientation (though not necessarily satisfactorily) and issues related to HIV and, of particular importance, he would probably have been better prepared to participate in society. Education is about preparation for life, and within contemporary society, HIV education is a very important component of that process. Simon left school believing that, regardless of what the media and health educators were saying about HIV and condoms, he did not need them, because Mrs Hewitt said so. This is tantamount to a preparation for death! He also left school believing that he should not, or even could not, be gay, because Mrs Hewitt said, 'that it wasn't nice'. Not only did he leave school friendless and very seriously misinformed, but also with an imposed negative status and stigma in relation to how he perceived himself.

We all know from our own experience of school that homophobic abuse and ridicule is not an uncommon experience for boys who experience same-sex attraction. Frankham (2001) provides us with a comprehensive catalogue of the recent memories of some young men's experience of such oppression. There are clearly some similarities between Simon's experience and the young men involved in Frankham's research, e.g. Michael thinking that because he wasn't effeminate he couldn't be gay, and the general 'need to tell' someone that you thought you were gay. However, the similarities end there. The uniqueness of Simon's situation can be summarised through the following points:

- He had no friends at all, and therefore, no one to 'come out' to.
- It was made clear to him throughout his mainstream school experience that he could not, and in fact should not, approach the teachers over any issue.
- He was a member of two oppressed groups, i.e. he was gay and he had learning difficulties, and thus, exposed to double discrimination.
- He was seriously misinformed by a person in authority in relation to both HIV and his right to a sexuality.

While the participants in Frankham's research clearly had some very unsatisfactory experiences, they did have friends, and indeed, eventually felt able to 'come out' to some of these friends. They may not have considered their teachers very approachable in relation to discussing their self-perceived sexual orientation, but they were certainly not barred from approaching them. In relation to HIV education, it is likely, as Frankham suggests, that they got very little; however, it is very unlikely that they were informed that they did not need to worry about using condoms. Basically, just because Simon happened to have learning difficulties, it was automatically assumed that, not only would he not have an active sexual life, but also that he was not entitled to one. Where comparisons cannot be made is in relation to the post-school experience in terms of how prepared individuals were to cope with society at large and the discrimination they might encounter within it.

It is likely that, once they had left school, most of the young men involved in Frankham's research would have the opportunity to access their local gay community if they chose to, or at least, make friends with other young gay men living in their area, thus giving them a sense of identity and the possibility of developing networks with like-minded people. As he described in his story earlier in this chapter, Simon attempted to do this but he was told very clearly and somewhat cruelly, that even though he was gay, he did not belong: he did not belong because he had learning difficulties.

This is just one of the possible scenarios that young men like Simon will encounter. In order to provide some insight into how some non-disabled gay men perceive people like Simon, extracts from an interview with Stuart (pseudonym) have been produced below. Stuart is a young gay man in his early twenties who admits to frequenting his local gay scene and a number of public places for the purpose of sex. He states that he would only ever have sex with a man who was younger than himself, preferably between the ages of 16 and 21. It is by no means suggested that this is representative of all non-disabled gay men, the purpose is purely to provide the reader with an indication of the issues that need to be considered when planning an HIV/sex education strategy for young (particularly gay) men with learning difficulties as part of the National Curriculum. It needs to be said, however, that the inclusion of 'Stuart's story' is with much reservation: his attitude and behaviour (towards people with learning difficulties) are the epitome of the oppressive and discriminatory structures within our society that so many of us are striving to eradicate. However, people like Stuart are a reality that confronts people with learning difficulties on a daily basis: it is hoped that by reading his story a greater understanding of some of the issues that people with learning difficulties face will be generated.

Stuart's story

In relation to the vast majority of people with learning difficulties, I don't think that it is an ideal situation for them to be living in the community, I had no idea that this was something that was actually encouraged. I suppose that it depends on the degree of their disability, if they only had mild learning difficulties, then maybe that would be alright, maybe they could cope. I would only ever consider developing a friendship with a person who had learning difficulties if they were associated with someone I already had a friendship with. I would try to avoid such a development as much as possible. I don't think that they should be encouraged to develop friendships because this might lead to an emotional relationship and they wouldn't be able to cope with that. It could also result in them having children and that wouldn't be a good idea. Emotional relationships are difficult enough for non-disabled 'intelligent' people. In relation to the gay scene, I don't think that this is a good place for people with learning difficulties because there is a lot of pressure to look attractive and be regarded as attractive. There are also a lot of short-term relationships on the gay scene and I think that would cause them difficulties in determining where things were going. I also think that they may be open to abuse.

On two or three occasions I have been attracted to young men with learning difficulties because they met the criteria I look for in a young man. On two occasions I had sex with them in a public place, it was purely a physical thing, I certainly wasn't emotionally attracted to them. I would never consider developing a long-term relationship with a man with learning difficulties, partly because of their mental capacity, they wouldn't stimulate me, but also because I'd be embarrassed to be seen with them in public. I don't think that they have anything to offer but a quick sexual encounter, which would be quickly forgotten. I wouldn't even consider having regular sex with a man with learning difficulties. I did consider that I might be breaking the law by having sex with men who have learning difficulties but it didn't stop me from doing it.

Friendships

As children grow, and go first to preschool groups and then to school, they develop friendships of their own choosing with some children from the many they meet (Widdows 1997). The development of friendships is an important part of any child's life and a key component in their learning process. Simon made many friends during his early years at a special school, and his story implies that this was important to him. Clearly, this did not happen when he transferred to a mainstream school, he spent seven years without a single friend. All of us value our friends because they make us feel valued, without them our life would be rather lonely and isolated. It is no different for children; friendships are a vital part of their social and emotional development, a vital part of their life. In relation to teenagers who are starting to perceive themselves as gay, such friendships are even more important. Knowledge of parental attitudes (such as in Simon's case) towards homosexuality, and thus, fear of rejection by parents is often given by gay teenagers as the main reason for non-disclosure (Walker 2001). Evidence suggests that having no one to talk to about such issues leads to isolation and disproportionately high rates of suicide and attempted suicide (*ibid.*). A statement from Nathan, one of the participants in Walker's research, identifies the torment and anguish that many of these young people experience:

I'm not sure whether I thought I was the only person. No, I never thought I was the only person that was gay. I just, I felt that, I felt very, very, isolated, um, very alone and rather unloved . . . and so I just, I just took an overdose.

Nathan does not have learning difficulties; he is now at university and is a member of gay-identified social networks. It is therefore very likely that he has gay friends, a sense of identity and, of much importance, a feeling of being included in a section of society that he feels comfortable with. Simon on the other hand has no friends, the result of spending seven years in a mainstream school; not only was he rejected by his gay peers, but ridiculed and discriminated against: he has no sense of identity and feels totally excluded from the society in which he lives.

Evidence suggests (Davies 1997) that Simon may decide to start attempting to meet people like Stuart for the purpose of sex in public places. Not necessarily because he wants to engage in such activities, but because he may feel that this is the only way he can make 'friends' and develop 'relationships'. Davies (*ibid.*) describes such a scenario:

Apart from staff, Sonny had no friendships or relationships with people who did not have a learning disability. It became clear that however abusive some of these contacts may have been, Sonny valued them as something of importance

to him at this time in his life.

Like Simon, Sonny was excluded from society for several years: unlike Simon, Sonny's exclusion was a result of being incarcerated in an institution. While their experience of exclusion was very different, some of the outcomes were very similar, i.e. neither of them was given the opportunity or the support to develop friendships and relationships. Should Simon decide to follow in Sonny's footsteps, the potential for abusive encounters is significant. The research conducted by Thompson (1997) indicates that gay men with learning difficulties will simply comply with the demands of the men that they meet, and often this is neither their choice nor preference. Many engage in such activities simply to make contact with men who do not have learning difficulties, regardless of the fact that some of these men may abuse them.

Conclusion

Simon's experience is not unique. Ainscow *et al.* (1999) indicate 'the evidence suggests that when such students come into the mainstream from special schools they often remain relatively isolated'. There are many reasons why this happens, mostly related to policy design and implementation, but also associated with the attitude and commitment of LEAs and teachers. As stated at the beginning of this chapter, there are wide-ranging arguments for and against the inclusion of children with learning difficulties in mainstream schools. For example, many parents of such children firmly believe that special schools provide a better education for their children simply because they appear to be better resourced. However, these arguments aside, it is every child's right to be educated alongside their peers within the mainstream, and thus, the only way forward is to work towards inclusion for all. Indeed, at the time of writing, the Disability Rights Commission have published a proposed Code of Practice relating to the Special Educational Needs and Disability Act (2001); the proposed Code indicates that current legislation strengthens the duty of LEAs to provide a mainstream place for children classified as having special educational needs. However, unless LEAs produce adequate policies that can realistically be implemented in practice, progress in this area will be slow.

Inclusive education is about many things and this chapter has focused on a very small part of the whole process, i.e. to be included in the culture of the school. All children have the right to develop friendships and relationships; some of them require support to enable them to achieve this. Likewise, all children have the right to access their teachers when they feel the need to, not to be directed to someone who has not been trained to do the job. The fact that Simon was gay and lacked understanding about the transmission of HIV is an important point. The National Curriculum Guidance relating to Key Stage 4 clearly states that all 14- to 16-year-old children should not only understand that HIV can be sexually transmitted, but be able to discuss issues surrounding it also; it is a compulsory part of the sex education curriculum in secondary schools. Simon's teacher recognised the importance of this, he invited any member of the class who did not understand to approach him – except Simon, who was directed to a learning support assistant! Why Simon was treated in such a way is not clear. It may be because his teacher felt unable to work with a young person with learning difficulties, or he may have wrongly believed that Simon was entirely the responsibility of the learning support assistant.

A further issue to consider is the fact that many teachers believe that Section 28 of the Local Government Act (1988) prohibits them from providing information about lesbian and gay issues and thus, try to avoid this territory altogether. This is not the case. As the National Children's Bureau (1994) points out, the Department for Education Circular 5/94 (Annex A) clearly states that this law 'applies to the activities of local authorities themselves, as distinct from the activities of governing bodies and staff of schools on their own behalf'. It is very possible that both Simon's teacher and his learning support assistant were misinformed in this area, hence their avoidance of gay-related issues.

Clearly, the issues raised in this chapter require further and much more in-depth research. It is important that this is conducted within an emancipatory paradigm, and thus fully involves young people with learning difficulties themselves in determining how we can best support them in relation to the issues identified.

References

Ainscow, M., Farrell, P., Tweddle, D. and Malki, G. (1999) *Effective Practice in Inclusion and in Special and Mainstream Schools Working Together.* London: HMSO.

Davies, S. (1997) 'A Provider Perspective', in P. Cambridge and H. Brown (eds), *HIV and Learning Disability.* Kidderminster: British Institute for Learning Disabilities.

Frankham, J. (2001) 'The "open secret": limitations on the expression of same-sex desire', *Qualitative Studies in Education* 14(4), 457–69.

Hornby, G., Atkinson, M. and Howard, J. (1997) *Controversial Issues in Special Education.* London: David Fulton Publishers.

Kaufman, J. M. and Hallahan, D. P. (1995) *The Illusion of Full Inclusion: A Comprehensive Critique of a Current Special Education Bandwagon.* Austin, TX: Pro-Ed.

National Children's Bureau (1994) *Developing and Reviewing a School Sex Education Policy: A Positive Strategy.* London: National Children's Bureau.

Oliver, M. (1996) *Understanding Disability: From Theory to Practice.* Basingstoke: Macmillan.

Thompson, D. (1997) 'Safer Sex: Work with Men with Learning Disabilities who Have Sex with Men', in P. Cambridge and H. Brown (eds) *HIV and Learning Disability.* Kidderminster: BILD.

Walker, P. H. (2001) 'Sexual identity, psychological well-being and suicide risk among lesbian and gay young people', *Educational and Child Psychology* 18(1), 47–61.

Widdows, J. (1997) *A Special Need for Inclusion: Children with Disabilities, Their Families and Everyday Life.* London: The Children's Society.

Index